I SAID WHAT I SAID:

Observations, Declarations, Rants, Missives and Musings of a Black, Semi-Successful Bass Player from the Projects, Living in a Mostly White Right World

KENERY KENT SMITH

Copyright © 2023 Kenery Kent Smith

All rights reserved. Printed and bound in the United States of America.
No part of this book may be used or reproduced, stored in a retrieval system, or transmitted in any form or by any means, electronic, mechanical, photocopying, recording, or otherwise, without the prior written permission of Kenery Kent Smith, except for brief quotations included in a review of the book or embodied in articles.

The scanning, uploading, and distribution of this book via the Internet or via any other means without the permission of the publisher is illegal and punishable by law.
Please purchase only authorized electronic editions and do not participate in or encourage electronic piracy of copyrighted materials. Your support for the author's rights is sincerely appreciated.

Cover Design: Bryant Smith
Interior Design: Janie Lott
Published by: K2S Productions

I Said What I Said: Observations, Declarations, Rants, Missives, and Musings of a Black, Semi-Successful Bass Player from the Projects, Living in a Mostly White-Right World. Kenery Kent Smith. First Edition.
ISBN: 978-1-6664-0430-2
1. Non- Fiction. 2.Memoirs 3. Opinions

Contents

FOREWORDS BY JAIME A. GILL AND NATALIE MURPHY	4
CHAPTER 1: N'TRODUCTION, PT.1	10
CHAPTER 2: N'TRODUCTION, PT. 2	21
CHAPTER 3: THE PRE(R)AMBLE	35
CHAPTER 4: WHO YOU IS?	43
CHAPTER 5: LOVE IS A MANY SPLINTERED THING	69
CHAPTER 6: BACK ON THE BLOCK: THE DATING GAME	121
CHAPTER 7: THE CREATIVE SOUL LAID BARE	140
CHAPTER 8: THE GREAT ESCAPE	150
CHAPTER 9: TRUST	167
CHAPTER 10: YOU IS SMART. YOU IS KIND. YOU IS BOOTIFUL.	174
CHAPTER 11: I'M BLACKETY BLACK AND I'M BLACK, Y'ALL	191
CHAPTER 12: WORDS FOR THE LEVITES	218
CHAPTER 13: OH, THE (IN)HUMANITY!	234
CHAPTER 14: WHITE LIGHT	251
CHAPTER 15: IT WAS THE BEST OF TIMES; IT WAS THE WORST OF TIMES...	278
CHAPTER 16: STOOPID GOOD-LOOKINGS	288
CHAPTER 17: BETTER GIT IT IN YOUR SOUL	295
CHAPTER 18: BLACK LIKE ME (AND SWEETPEA 'N NEM)	309
CHAPTER 19: CLOSING ARGUMENTS	321
CHAPTER 20: RHYMES AND REASONINGS	325
CHAPTER 21: MY WRITE FOOT	356

Foreword Pt. 1
HE SAID WHAT HE SAID... FOR A REASON!

I didn't grow up collecting comic books, but I have always been amazed of the stories of superheroes. If I ever had the opportunity to create a superhero, or better yet to BE A SUPERHERO, my superpower would be to read people's minds. I would love to be able to hear the thoughts before a person says them, or moreover, know the thoughts that people will never share. That would definitely be intriguing.

This book is the world's opportunity to have that superpower. *I Said What I Said: Observations, Declarations, Rants, Missives, and Musings of a Black, Semi-Successful Bass Player from the Projects, Living in a Mostly White-Right World* — is our opportunity to read the mind (literally) of Kenery Kent Smith. The journey through each page is not just a page through a book, it is a glimpse into the mind of a man, a black man, an American, a musician, an author, an artist, a gift. His words give us an unique perspective into his world.

Not only does Kenery provide a muse — HE IS A MUSE! His bravery to share his experiences, his perspective, his pain, and his passions is remarkable. Remarkable because it is raw, honest, engaging, and entertaining.

In this book, you will not only "see" Kenery, but I believe it also serves as a mirror. The sharing of his story serves as an amazing opportunity for you to reflect on your life, your experiences and how they shape your mood, your responses, your relationships, and your movements through your life's journey.

Kenery and I met on social media through mutual friends and supporting friends on their video podcast. We often agreed in the "virtual audience" on various topics. Then one day, I saw a post that he compared building a guitar to life, and I was completely blown away. It was immediately obvious to me that this man had so much to offer the world. His ability to see the world through such an artistic lens is refreshing and very much needed in our world today.

I invite you to read each page with an open mind and fully engage with all that is being shared.

Be aware of what you are thinking and feeling as you are reading, and then examine why. Why do you feel what you feel? Why are you thinking what you are thinking? And then, what provoked those thoughts and emotions? May these observations, declarations, rants, missives, and musings remind us all that we don't have to think the same, or have the same experiences, to be able to co-exist and create beautiful harmony BECAUSE OF OUR DIFFERENCES.

Thank you Kenery for being our superhero and creating the space that we can feel safe in not having all the answers, not being perfect, but still being fully equipped to offer something to this world. This is Kenery's story…but it is reflective of so many of our stories. May you be engaged. May you be inspired.

— Jaime A. Gill

Award-winning Author, *Lessons for the Little Girl*

Foreword Pt. 2

It is with great pleasure that I introduce you to author Kenery Kent Smith, who I fondly refer to as Big Brother. Kenery and I met in high school, attending Hyde Park Career Academy on Chicago's south side. We clicked instantly, not knowing that we'd be forever connected. I'm grateful that he and his big smile are still a part of my life. I'm even more honored that he has asked me to write this foreword for him.

If you've never met Kenery, prepare yourself for a unique experience as you read, *I Said What I Said*. Kenery has always been a deep thinker, gently and sometimes not so gently opinionated, and a man who stands on what he believes. A kid from the projects, he is a passionately creative through and through. He's a writer, a musician, and he builds guitars. All you have to do to see and feel the passion he carries is watch him play his bass guitar.

After his music, Kenery's next love is words. This book will transport you through the world in which we live, according to Kenery. His knowledge of social, political, and historical issues is mind-blowing and will make you laugh, rethink some things, and hit you square between the eyes. Page after page you will be introduced to, and challenged by, new and different ideas, feelings, and questions about the goings on in and around us.

I Said, What I Said, is a testament to Kenery's exceptional writing ability and his passion for storytelling and life. You will be captivated by his use of the English language combined with well-placed Kenery-isms. I love a good Kenery-ism. What is a Kenery-isms? Those are words created by the Worderer himself. Yes, he created the word "Worderer". No explanation is required, but just in case, it's someone who skillfully uses a lot of words. Believe me when I say Kenery is a Worderer (a modern-day Wordsmith).

Kenery has poured his heart and soul into this book. With every phone call, text message or face to face we've shared, I could hear his enthusiasm to share what was on his heart with world. You will experience his unique ability to craft his observations, thoughts and feelings that are not only relatable, but also memorable. His writing style is engaging and will keep you turning the pages.

So, sit down with your favorite beverage and a dictionary (laughing but very serious), as you embark on this literary journey. I encourage you to open your mind and let *I Said What I Said* take hold. I have no doubt that by the end of it, you will be left with a sense of wonder and awe.

— Natalie R. Murphy

Award-winning Author, *Then Came You*

One

N'TRODUCTION, PT. 1
TELL ME A BEDTIME STORY

Maybe saying "yes" wasn't the best idea.

I mean, if I'm being totally real, then yeah—I really wanted to sleep with her. And even while under the subtle influence of alcohol, going to the far Northside house of a fine woman whom I didn't know at all; a woman who didn't look or act like a drug addict or a hooker, and who wanted to have sex with me? Sure, why not? I didn't have my own car at the time; mine had been rear ended a few weeks prior while I was sitting at a stop sign on my way to a long night of playing music, by a rich, drunken, entitled White kid with a sports car. So, when that woman in the club did her "voulez-vous coucher avec moi ce soir" move on me, my not having my own ride seemed like it had no downsides whatsoever. I mean, c'mon. Fine horny woman: check. Virile, young, attractive yet unattached musician: check. Duh. So I rode with "Voulez-Vous" to her potential Temple of Pleasures.

N'TRODUCTION, PT. 1

Have you ever had the feeling that you've just entered the Twilight Zone, and nobody on the trip had announced the stop ahead of time?

I have.

When we arrived at Voulez's house, it wasn't so much the creepy, dimly lit living room. It wasn't the cramped space and the musty sofa I had to sit on while waiting for Voulez to change into something more revealing, more comfortable. It wasn't even the nonchalant attitude she seemed to have about a 3:00 AM hookup at a music club with a stranger; after all, I was there and consenting to it all too, wasn't I?

But maaaaaaybe…maybe it was the fact that it was revealed en route to her Thunderdome, that Voulez had a theretofore unmentioned seven-year-old daughter. Whom we had to pick up—from her ex's house, which was apparently along the way. So Voulez had her daughter. And she had her there—right there. In the house. With me—a total stranger of a man. Aaaaaaaannd… on top of that, Voulez left her seven-year-old daughter. With me. A man she'd just met. In the living room.

In the middle of her candle factory.

QUWHAAAT?

Yep. I said candle factory. Voulez apparently made candles as a side hustle. Scented, colored, and occasion-specific candles of all shapes and sizes. And they were on display, in all their glory, all across the living room as far as the eye could see. On tables. In boxes. On the floor. In chairs. And there were wax drippings everywhere; it looked as if an angry, frustrated, unhinged painter had flung his palette full of colors and hues across the room in a fit of raging insanity.

And so Voulez left me. In the candle factory. With her seven-year-old daughter. So that said child could keep me company. At 3 AM. While Voulez changed into something more revealing, more comfortable. More comfortable. For late night booty call stranger-sex. All while her seven-year-old daughter was in the house. Right. There. In. The. House.

Have you ever felt THEE most convicted and uncomfortable that you have ever felt in your whole damn life right before you were supposed to have crazy hot sex?

I have.

I have also had to talk my way out of that selfsame hot sex, using excuses, flowery words, and lies about having an estranged girlfriend whom I neglected to mention and would feel guilty about betraying in that way.

I have slept/not slept in a beautiful woman's bed, fully clothed, staring into the darkness at the angry, blinking red light of conviction emanating from the digital display of a bedside clock, all the while simply holding that beautiful yet misguided woman in my arms…eagerly waiting for the sun to reappear. And desperately waiting for the hour when that very first morning Green Line "L" headed south would rescue me from a potentially life-altering mistake of my own making.

In the many years since walking out of that club with Voulez, I have learned so much more about who I truly am. I have learned that I am indeed capable of foul acts for selfish reasons. That my pride in viewing myself as a "good person" can cause me to ignore my own warning signs, or to make self-justified decisions that may not come with positive outcomes. I have grown. I have become wiser in my decision-making, more thoughtful of the possible consequences of my actions.

Listen, I have never been a bad person as far as I'm concerned; I've never been the stereotypical musician who is just "out there" as most people like to believe we are. I've always known God, thanks to my mother. I have always had a very healthy conscience, so doing wrong to others, specifically to women, has never been my M.O. As a younger, single man, I was simply lonely, horny, and slightly less thoughtful of the consequences of my actions.

But again, let's be clear: even though I do strive on the daily to be right with God—I was neither then or now, a total saint. Yet I am also a heterosexual Black male, who has a pretty healthy sexual appetite and who enjoys the company and companionship of women. Typically one at a time—ha! Because trying to be a "playa" just looks like way too much mental work, and far too much of an investment of time and energy for the diminishing return of simply stroking your ego and your…well…you know. This is especially true when you are by nature a terrible liar and have a very active conscience like I do. Don't get me wrong: variety in women is…intriguing. The Chase™© is fun indeed. Flirting is fun. Meeting beautiful, intelligent, and fun-loving women is FUN. I love the challenge AND the reward. But the notion of sleeping around, it just ain't really my thing; it never was.

Besides the obvious detriments such as unexpected pregnancies, STDs, and a trail of heartache waiting somewhere down the line for myself or someone else, I'm simply not built that way. I cannot connect sexually with a woman without also, on some meaningful level, connecting with her emotionally as well. Because sex—lovemaking, if you prefer—is not simply a physical coupling; it's a SPIRITUAL experience. It goes far beyond bodily stimuli and carnal satisfaction. It is an exchange of energy and a surrendering of self that is much more than that coveted orgasm(s) or that high score-worthy ejaculation.

Beyond the sensitivities that accompany my spirit because of my Christian upbringing and beliefs, I've always felt that sex is something to be shared with someone who can be trusted with your spirit, your very essence. Because the fact is, that is exactly what you are giving over to another person when you copulate; you are sharing a part of your soul, your very being. This is especially true for women, since women are physiologically, and more often than not emotionally, the receiving partner during the act of lovemaking.

Sure, there are condoms and diaphragms and sponges and trick quick pullouts, etc. But as a woman, she is ultimately the person on the receiving end of what that male is sending to her, physically, emotionally, and spiritually. These are facts. And yeah, many women consider themselves to be the dominant or the more sexually driven partner in any relationship they may find themselves in. But that's a whole 'nother topic which definitely requires its own book! Also, just to be clear, in case it came up in anyone's mind while reading this book—as open minded and inclusive as I try to be in life, I can only speak with ANY type of authority on heterosexual relationships. So, if you are reading this and are not of the hetero persuasion, don't feel ignored. I simply have no firsthand wisdom, outside of love in general, to offer up to you.

But to get back on topic: these things are the reasons why it is imperative for men to be accountable and for women to be responsible. That late night with Voulez-Vous was obviously an irresponsible choice that she had made; whether it was due to nothing more than a straightforward physical attraction and my convenient availability, or done out of loneliness, and a desire to be intimate with a man who seemed to be someone who would not take advantage of or destroy her, physically, mentally, or emotionally. But even more so, it was, of course, also a choice which I had to be even more accountable for. If I had allowed myself to push past my discomfort with the circumstances of that evening—the daughter, the environment, the very nature of our hook up—Voulez-Vous could've been left with a situation to deal with, which could have had any number of negative repercussions for herself and, especially, her daughter. Yet for me, it was a situation that, as a single man, I could have easily walked away from its consequences. V-V was obviously in a very vulnerable space, which of course, taking into account her level of emotional immaturity, could potentially put both Voulez and her daughter in an even more vulnerable and dangerous position someday.

So, I had to be the one who made the decision that, while it most certainly deprived us both of some really—really—REALLY great immediate gratification, helped Voulez avoid, at least for that one night, the pitfalls of being a lonely single woman and parent, in the aftermath of a drunken hookup with a stranger, dealing with the possibility of having to explain it all to her daughter and the impact that situation could possibly have on the child long term.

I had to look at the situation not only as a man, but as a friend. A brother. A father. And it would not be the last time I had to make the hard (pun not intended but fully recognized) choice to be the decision maker in a situation that required a clear-headed assessment. I essentially had to tamp down Carnal Kenery and enlist the services of Conscientious Kenery. Much to my own chagrin. And by the way, I haven't always succeeded in my efforts or good intentions. But, hey, no one is perfect.

If you really pay close attention, there is always that moment, no matter how fleeting, where most people experience a tiny window of clarity: where we hear that still, small voice; that "danger Will Robinson" warning, just before doing something that we should not be doing. Sadly, it seems that most people are not in tune enough with who they are to even hear it, let alone recognize, acknowledge, and act according to its advice. Soul-searching and self-assessment seem to be in very short supply these days. It's too much work for some. Too revelatory for others. And far too self-convicting for most. Better to beg for forgiveness than to ask for permission; that is the formula for today's human being. We often make decisions with an eye on kicking the can of responsibility for those decisions down the road. All too often, our awareness of the different levels of consequence for just a single action—the immediate, the short term, and the long term—are realizations which are far too heady, work-intensive, and involved for us to contemplate.

And so we pay it forward. To our future selves, and to the future selves of anyone else involved in our actions who will be affected by those decisions. Sadly, within the Black Diaspora, we tend to live by that flawed creed. Party today because tomorrow ain't promised. Get it in now. Live your life to the fullest each day, damn the consequences. We sometimes even try our best to invoke Biblical scripture in order to justify our actions:

Take therefore no thought for the morrow: for the morrow shall take thought for the things of itself. Sufficient unto the day is the evil thereof. (Matthew 6:25-34)

Yeah, uh, Black Folks. Stop taking Scripture out of context in order to fit your selfish needs.

This Biblical passage doesn't apply here. At all.

: The point here is this: we as both individuals and a as a Diaspora—have lost the plot of being a village that holds one another accountable. We have strayed far from the course of being responsible for the wellbeing of ourselves and each other and have instead morphed into an unrecognizable roving swarm of culturally compromised locusts, devouring everything we can, as fast as we can. Not planning for our collective and individual futures. Not helping one another out. Not calling one another out in love. Not extending grace or kindness or empathy or understanding. Not collectively or individually providing wisdom, guidance, mentorship, or apprenticeship to our future generations. Not embracing the wisdom, guidance, mentorship, apprenticeship, or lessons of those generations that came before us. And certainly not making those hard decisions when it comes to being responsible for one another, even when the other person is being irresponsible. What do you imagine Huey P. Newton, Eldridge Cleaver, Malcolm X, MLK, Harriet Tubman, William Still, etc., etc. would think of where we have landed in our efforts to uplift our own?

We have fallen for the okey doke of believing that we can live the very same "American Dream" that our White counterparts live.

We cannot. At least, not most of us. Not quite yet. And not free and clear of great mental, emotional, and spiritual sacrifice.

Because this American Life was not built for us—not the way it is currently formatted. Yes, WE built it for THEM with our blood, sweat, and tears. Yes, we can enjoy a relatively wonderful life with hard work and a little good fortune. We can connect with those who connect with us; we can meet, love, marry, and build together. But we will always have to work at LEAST twice as hard to build, achieve, and maintain that life. Let alone be able to pass it along as generational wealth and prosperity. We don't live in that seemingly passive White world where opportunity, hard work, and bootstrap-pulling equal success.

We instead exist within an active war zone—an active crime scene, really. Where diligence, double the effort, twice the sacrifice, and twofold the commitment to ourselves and each other are a prerequisite. We cannot afford selfishness. We cannot afford those within the Diaspora who are out here preying on their own—many of whom already have nothing. We cannot afford those within the Diaspora who give no thought to the repercussions of their actions (or inactions) toward one another. Or those within the Diaspora who simply pretend that there is no melanin within them; or who pretend that they have "arrived," and thus believe that they do not have to look back and pull others forward. Maybe they believe that, like Lot's wife, they will turn to salt and lose everything they've gained if they do. And we cannot afford those within the Diaspora, who take love for granted and deal with one another through broken, loopholed contracts instead of solid and solemn covenants; through an honest handshake, a promised word of honor and good faith, or a sacred vow spoken in front of God and Human.

We do not have the luxury of living a temporary, disposable life. Not with things. Not with thoughts. Not with actions. And certainly not with people.

And so, when it was apparent that Voulez-Vous had made an irresponsible decision—and that I had committed an irresponsible action—it was incumbent upon my soul, and the soul of the Diaspora, to then take a stance of accountability. To take ownership of both the possible outcomes of my actions, and the prospect of how said actions could diminish the person I aspired to truly be; a man who loves honestly, selflessly, and passionately. A man who, in spite of the ease and temptation of taking the wider path—would more often than not take the narrow, more difficult path towards the purpose of my own destiny.

And before I walked out of that club with her, I most certainly already knew deep down in my Shondo that Voulez-Vous was not part of that destiny.

Two

N'TRODUCTION, PT. 2
SUBTITLE NOT INCLUDED

Write a book, huh?
But—why? How? And about what?
Hell, I don't know.
Lissen...

I am a person who has LOTS of thoughts, LOTS of ideas, LOTS of opinions. And LOTS of words. A damn cornucopia of words. They continuously and contiguously reverberate inside my mind throughout my waking hours; my sleeping hours are not immune to this ravaging, either. Feelings and emotions. Figurin' and fussin.' Questions and quandaries. On and frickin' on, nonstop. It's like being Charles Xavier, you know, Professor X of the X-Men—always hearing voices and thoughts coming from other people because he has the mutant psychic ability to read minds. Except that all the voices in my head are from one point of origin.

Me.

Sometimes, I WISH I could make the constant live-streaming of thoughts and words stop. Because it causes my life to haunt itself. It creates unwanted instant replays at the most awkward moments. My own personal Zoom call with myself often manifests as constant and unwanted self-evaluation. It causes me to second-guess my actions. It sometimes makes me doubt the truths of some of my life choices.

Not actually having the benefit of Professor X's mutant powers, I don't know if these challenges are things that everyone else deals with, too. I'm fairly certain that to some degree or another, they do. But many folks choose to tamp down on the idea of taking a tour and account of their inner selves; either because they don't want to be bothered, or because they can't handle knowing who they truly are. We are seeing a whole shitload of this behavior ta-now, ta-day. We are seeing liars, deniers, and seat-of-the-pants-flyers come out of the beautifully varnished woodwork.

At this time in history, we are clearly and more abundantly seeing people who are unapologetically and freely revealing the worst of who they are. We are witnessing the ugliest aspects of humanity come to light. The true hate and loathing that has resided within the hearts of people who you may have believed were "good people" is seeping out like the infected puss that it is. We are suffering fools in a way that is poison to those of us who are not fools. It's not as though I didn't already know that all of this bile existed in the world; of course it's not the first time for this bladder release of humanity's immoral and amoral waste. Daddy and Momma Smith didn't raise no fool, so I was already more than aware of the darkness lurking in the hearts of men and women.

Being BIM (Black In 'Murica) makes awareness of the real world a prerequisite for survival. But the unveiling has reached epic proportions. The dysfunction has reached literal cult-like status not seen since WWII—at least, not as flagrantly and as mainstream as it has today. And the struggle to process it all is real, y'all. It's overwhelming. It's consuming. It's depressing. It's disheartening. At times it can be maddening. And it's a particularly heavy load to bear when it attacks as you are healing from what already seemed like the worst betrayal in the history of betrayals; a "Condition of the Heart," if you will.

Everything I just said is fact, and not just my Personal Truth. Yet, even as it all saddens me, even as the chaos of the world threatens to engulf my soul, it also strangely inspires me. It demands of me to do something that will fulfill me in a positive way and counteract the impending doom that has been forecast by current events, both personal and global. The turmoil around me presses me to do something that will curb the negativity that tries to invade my mind and spirit. And it requires that I do something that, hopefully, will connect with someone else who is wading neck-deep in the bullshit of Alternative Facts, the bile of the hate-filled people who are fueling those lies and that rhetoric, and the sad revelations of the fractured characters of those close to them who claim to love them.

So, hello.

My name is Kenery Kent Smith; pleased to meet you.

And I am writing a damned book.

I am baring my soul for your entertainment, mockery, and reading pleasure. And I am starting with an open letter that, even though it was written in 2016, sadly has as much, if not more, relevance today than it did then.

DEAREST AMERICA
An Ode to Her Four-Year Love Affair with a Narcissistic Pseudo-Dictator

Dearest America,

I don't know who you are anymore.

Sure, I know that you've never truly liked me. At least, not in the way that I truly wanted and needed you to like me.

From the very beginning, our relationship has been tumultuous at best. We rarely agree on anything. We have had some really terrible fights and said some things to each other that were cruel and unforgivable, even though many things spoken were our personal truths concerning one another.

But from my perspective, I've fought long and hard to be treated better by you. I've allowed you to hurt me time and time again—because the promise of who you could potentially become seemed to be just "one more" fight away from realization.

See—I know you have the potential to be great. You possess so many wonderful qualities. You have been a great leader. You have been kind to many. And you seem to have unselfishly given up a part of yourself when others were in need.

You never cease to amaze me with the great ideas you come up with to better yourself. Always thinking of new ways to do more—to be more. I like that in you. I've always said that your potential knows no limits—except those that you impose on yourself.

For instance, I've always thought that it was a bad idea for you to outsource your work to others just to save a little money. Sure, it made sense to you at first. Our finances and budget were not as well-managed as they should have been. But we made it work. And we got by without giving up too much of our dignity or pride.

But then one day it seemed as though you went out of your way to hurt me. I had given you the best of who I was—of who I could become. And you treated me with so much disrespect and apathy that I was truly taken aback. Here I was, thinking that we had come to an understanding about what we meant to each other. We had fought together against many common enemies. We swore together that we would eradicate ideologies and principles that we watched slowly destroy other couples. Couples like the Nazi Party and Germany. Communism and

Japan. Communism and Russia. Communism and China. Communism and Cuba. Muslim extremism and Iran—or Iraq—I get the two of them confused sometimes. You DO remember them, don't you? I know that it's hard for you to see the consequential similarities you and I share with some of those poor, doomed lovers. But the similarities are there, nonetheless. And so is the potential to make some of their awful mistakes.

And, yes, I knew that our just being cordial to each other was only going to last a little while. But I thought that when you saw what I'd done for you in a better, more enlightened light, when you saw and recognized the years and the invaluable contributions that I've made to you—that revelation would help you better to understand me. And to understand all the things I have given up just to be with you.

Hell, just the achievements I've worked hard to realize and the goals I've achieved to help save your butt in the last eight years alone should have endeared me to you. Let alone the hundreds of years before that that I've endured your often cruel treatment of me. I kept telling myself "It's not me, it's them; it's just that they're still young and angry about their own problem-filled childhood." How foolish of me for trying to psychoanalyze you without looking at my own issues. Because we do both have some serious issues.

Like—you did physically and verbally abuse me for a long time. You did devalue me, and you tried to erase my identity. You told me I was ugly. That I would never amount to anything. You stole my innocence. You used me. And you did just pretty much come into my home and forcibly take me from my mother. So, there's that.

But now, now even in light of all I've endured being with you—you truly have me afraid for you.

You seem bent on self-destruction. You are willing to hurt yourself in order to hurt me. And it seems that your sadism knows no bounds. Can't you see that the decisions you are moving toward making won't just affect me? They will end up destroying you, too! Because they are decisions based on the truly worst aspects of your nature.

Your hate. Your lies. Your self-indulgence. Your hypocrisy. Your self-loathing. Intolerance. Shortsightedness. Greed. Envy. Corruption. Your need to dominate and control others. Narcissism. Pridefulness. Double mindedness. I could go on and on.

Don't get me wrong. I know I have things I need to work on, too. Self-hate. My habit of being my own worst enemy. Slowly killing myself through my own inner turmoil. My lack of self-awareness or of having a true sense of identity. My failings with inner unity and harmony. How I allow myself to listen to anybody who tries to tell me who I am—who I should be.

I know I can be lazy too. I always want to be entertained. And I rarely plan ahead—rarely plan for the future. I spend most of my time and money living in the moment. I'm always looking outside of myself—looking to find a "leader": someone to save me or fix me or solve problems that I could surely solve myself. If only I cared enough to do so.

And, yes, I know I'm easily distracted. Shiny Objects and all. And many things I say—actions that I take—are to my own detriment.

Sure, much of what I do is to self-soothe. Because you have hurt me. A lot.

But even though right now we're not officially together, I know you've been courting someone else. Someone who reflects the darkest parts of your soul. And you seem to be hanging out together more and more. It looks like you're trying to have a dangerous liaison with someone who will surely destroy you and everything you've worked so hard for. And you're apparently willing to go over the edge of a dangerous cliff just to hurt me with this potential new relationship.

Let me be clear, America—I am not jealous in any way. I would say that they can have you—lock, stock, and barrel. Except for the fact that we are inextricably tied together. We have children together. We have birthed some awesome ideas together and accomplished many seemingly impossible goals. Some of our children are very much grown and successful, doing quite well, despite us. I'm very proud of what they have become. But many are still babies.

And the potential detriment of your new beau's bad influence coupled with your own issues, well, it's a recipe for the utter and complete destruction of our children's futures.

But you don't seem to care about that. All you want to do is keep me down, steal from me, and have me under your tenuous control at best. And, at worst, to completely wipe me from existence. Even though both scenarios will not just destroy both our potential futures. What you don't see is that both paths lead to our mutually assured destruction right now. Wake up.

I know that your hatred of me stems from fear and your own self-hatred and insecurities. Because you know that somewhere, deep down inside, I know what my true potential is. And the thought of my imminent realization of total self-awareness frightens you. You also hate that you grudgingly love too many things about me to admit. That's why I sometimes catch you watching me, imitating me. That's why you steal aspects of who I am for your own benefit.

Because even after all your efforts to hide my roots from me, the amazing qualities that are a part of my core—my heritage, my birthright from the beginning of time—those qualities continue to manifest themselves in everything I achieve. There is nothing I cannot do when I'm allowed to flourish unfettered. I don't have to pilfer anyone else's ideas to be great. I am a CREATOR because I am HIS creation. His FIRST on this earth. And I know you hate me for that.

But, hey, I try not to hold that against you.

So, go ahead—you do you. Destroy all we've built together.

Sleep with that idiot you're seeing. Continue to hate me for no good reason. I really am one of the best parts of you. You never would have achieved all the great things that you have achieved without me. Period.

True speak.

Until you admit and accept the simple fact that these are truths you cannot deny; until you embrace my differences as assets, and not as potential threats to who you are; until you make good on your broken promises to me, and until you are truly sorry for all the wrong you've done to me...

Well, you're doomed.

We're doomed.

But hey, don't say I didn't warn you.

Hugs and Kisses,
Black America

WORDERER

Even though I use lots of words on social media—about my life, my experiences, and my truths—I am, by nature, a very private person. But I am also fiercely protective of writing my own narrative. I don't like the results of the speculation, misinformation, and outright lies that I've seen when it comes to other people's life stories—those who didn't have the opportunities, the abilities, or the wherewithal to tell their own stories. Sometimes using too few words can result in a failing to convey the complete context of a sentiment or a statement. Sometimes using too many can muddle the sentiment and intent of self-expression altogether. And dear God, quite often, I use LOTS of words; this book possibly being one blaring example. My overly expressive presence on Social Media being the other.

But that is simply because I am a very passionate and expressive person. And I sincerely always try my level best to not be misunderstood. I try to make sure that I use the right words, in the right combination, in the right context. But "right" is, of course, a relative designation. In light of my constantly...grammatically indulgent musings, I have given myself a descriptive title using a word that I have newly coined:

Worderer.

Now, I'm just a kid from the ghetto; as previously stated; a product of Robert Taylor Homes and two loving parents who grew up alongside two often annoying but always amazing brothers. I'm not famous—or even infamous, as far as I know. Simply a kid who did his best to grow into a man who loves God, family, music, and life. A man who has loved hard and passionately, gives the very best of himself that he knows how, and who can only pray for a legacy that, while it may not be world changing or earth shattering, may be one which has, at the least, positively touched a few lives here and there along the journey. So, I am writing this book, not just for sales (but yeah—make no mistake, I want sales), for fame and attention, for social media likes, or even for empathy or—heaven forbid—some type of misplaced pity. I am writing this book to impart some honest, practical knowledge—and to control MY own story.

Fun random-ass fact: Out of the 1300 or so FB digital friends I have, I truly only know maybe 10% of them outside of the matrix. And of that 10%, I can only claim a true personal relationship with maybe half. And of those, I only know maybe 20 people up close and personal; we have history, interpersonal interactions, deep friendships born of commonalities, shared experiences, intimacy, or a discovery of having like minds. And genuine love for one another.

I intentionally keep my circles very close knit. Because context adds value and meaning. The context of years of interaction, of people knowing and understanding who you truly are, goes a long way—or at least it should. That knowledge of truly knowing (as well as we can know anyone) the content and the character of a person you designate as friend is everything.

So when I don't understand or disagree with someone, especially someone close to my heart, instead of attacking or dismissing the person or the situation, I will attempt to ask questions. Questions challenge people to think and to work through their opinions, their feelings, and their problems. The right set of thoughtful and relevant questions will activate reflection mode, which can allow those opinions and feelings to be more honestly reviewed, and, in turn, allow those posed questions to be insightfully answered. Asking questions gives breathing room in disagreements, knee jerk responses, and extends the reactionary time of all parties involved. Accusations and broad-spectrum assumptions simply trigger more escalated defensiveness, or they shut people down. In being a proud and active Worderer, I attempt to never tell people what they are thinking or feeling. I honestly have no clue and can only assume; how can I know? Because assumption is potentially just as tragic as misrepresentation or misinterpretation—maybe even more so. As you may know, neither of those things promote a good end to any discussion or debate.

And because words can be both misused and misconstrued, even by those who are typically pretty good friends with words, we must be careful in their uses and interpretations—that is, if we really care about what we are attempting to express, what we are striving to interpret, and about who we are communicating with. Especially when emotions are introduced into the mix. Despite my consistent use of reams of words when I express myself or speak my truths, many people seem to understand what I attempt to say. They may not all agree with me, but that is not what I am going for. They more often than not come out understanding both the point and context of my words, my often-awkward use of the not-my-king's language notwithstanding.

Social media murders intent and purpose. That's just a fact of our new normal existence. And to those who may have been offended by anything that I have said over the course of our conversations about any number of hot button topics (its typically the convos about men, women, and dating... surprise...): I truly apologize. I hope and pray that I do better in the context of this book. One—because I want y'all to buy it, not borrow it. And two, I want y'all to get to know the real me. But if I used the wrong language, said the wrong thing, please...assign it to my head and not my heart. I'm trying. I really am. I am growing. My hope is that this should count for something. I will never willfully disrespect anyone, or any group. And I humbly ask for that same consideration in return.

Three
THE PRE(R)AMBLE

Okay.

Let's start this chapter off with a little sumthin' sumthin' I wrote as a small contribution to my talented friend Jaime Gill's amazing book, *Lessons for the Little Boy*. This particular excerpt is being presented just to give you yet another bit of insight about how my mind works, and how this journey you're taking with me, should you decide to accept it, will be going. Then you can continue at your own peril.

LEARN TO PLAY JAZZ

As a Black Man in America, constantly navigating your way through the forces from without that will seek to limit you, and the forces from within that will seek to define you, knowing your mental, spiritual, and emotional latitude and longitude at all times, is tantamount to truly learning and knowing who you are.

Other men will try to quantify you. Women will seek to qualify you. You will be held up, measured, inspected, counted, analyzed, sorted, dismissed, recalled, scrutinized, excluded, blamed, rejected, falsely accused, unfairly uncredited, un-recompensed, stolen from, misinterpreted, misinformed, and mischaracterized. The world will stand you in the town square, put you on display like property, check your teeth, and look up the crack of your ass. It will clutch its collective purse, cross its existential street to avoid walking on the same side as you, and it will constantly tell you that it doesn't see color, that everything isn't about "race."

All of this will be done by measuring sticks being held up against you for things that you either have no control over, such as your melanin count, or the socioeconomic status you were born into. Or they will be characterizations based on antiquated, unrealistic, and frankly non-Black value systems that have been foolishly, blindly adapted into a culture that is constantly being kept from standing on equal footing with the culture from whence said values were derived. There will be "lists" presented to deem your worthiness of a woman's respect, let alone her loyalty or love. There will be numbers you'll need to add up to, and statuses you'll be required to live up to, simply to qualify for her love. And this will all be done in an attempt to put you into a nice, neat little check box on a list of "desirable attributes" to be brought to a fictional "table."

Or it will be on an application for a school or job, or when you buy your first car.

Rent your first apartment.

Buy your first home.

Move into your first nice neighborhood.

In spite of it all though, as a Black Man in 'Murica, you can learn to navigate it all. You can find your way through the miasma; through the macro and micro aggressions; through the rejections, disappointments and the heartbreaks. You can set a course for personal success and fulfillment that is not based on what anyone else believes about you or how they try to define you—if you learn how to flow in foundation. To be, in the wise words of Bruce Lee, "like water." To improvise.

If you learn how to play Jazz.

Like a beautifully flowing improvised melody, the space you occupy today won't be quite the same as the one you inhabit tomorrow. Yes, there will be times when you will hit some bad notes; in this way, life is more akin to Jazz music than it is to Classical. Classical music, while it has its version of passionate expression, is very structured, with no improvisation of the notes as written allowed.

Jazz on the other hand, well, the whole beauty of Jazz is in its ability to evolve; a Classic Jazz song will never be played quite the same way twice, even by the same person. Jazz lives—and it breathes. As with life, jazz is never stagnant unless you allow it to be.

Because living a beautiful life is about so much more than just hitting the right notes as written. It's about phrasing. It's about intent and purpose. It's about taking chances with the notes of our existence that may or may not seem to fit together from a logical, theoretical point of view.

Instead, life is about weaving together a series of notes, a string of events, in order to tell a story. A great and wonderful story--one which has meaning to the teller, as well as to anyone who hears/sees/reads it. Living a beautiful life is akin to managing structured chaos; it's equivalent to that beautiful Jazz melody you would create on your instrument of choice, in order to express to the world who your innermost you is.

Except that every now and then, the band leader will abruptly change the key of the song. Or the tempo. Or the actual musical genre. Or the venue you're playing in. Or the instrument you are playing on.

And sometimes, while you are playing your melody, even the band members will change--old familiar ones will leave, and new unknown ones will suddenly appear. They will come and go as the music dictates. But, as the lyrics to a famous Jazz standard state, the melody--your melody--still lingers on. You may be forced to adjust your notes here and there, because of course you want, above all else, for the music to sound great. For your life to BE great.

But there will be sour notes. It is almost inevitable. However, whether or not those bad notes actually ruin the song is totally dependent upon how you respond to them. The great Miles Davis famously said, "There's **no such thing as a wrong note**. ... It's **not** the **note** you play that's the **wrong note** - it's the **note** you play afterwards that makes it right or **wrong**."

And that, my friend, is also life. When you make mistakes, when unplanned and unwanted things happen to you and AT you, you likely won't have any control over when they occur. But what you will always have control of is the note you play afterwards. Learn to play your life as well as Coltrane played his saxophone. Embrace your life, bad notes and all. You still can make beautiful music, even when the tune seems to be going sour. But when you know who you are, WHOSE you are, then you'll find that the well that you can tap into within yourself and without in the universe is full of unmatched potential and unlimited note choices.

Hey, Black man. Young Brother. Wide eyed little boy in the ghetto. I implore and advise you:

Learn the art of improvisation in your life. Learn about what is deep inside of you, waiting to be birthed and manifested. Learn to play that beautiful note that can come right after the bad one hits.

Learn to play Jazz.[1]

---

1. Jaime A. Gill, *Lessons for the Little Boy*, (220 Publishing, 2021), 46

DANGER, WILL ROBINSON

Now, I told you from the beginning, before you fell prey to my trap and cracked that cover, that I had lots and lots of words. Many of those words are musings and stories, thus the book title. Others are my attempt to impart some sort of pseudo-wisdom or warning about situations I have been in that I feel are universally experienced—especially within the Black Diaspora, in one form or another. Now those words and their usefulness are, of course, subject to your intense scrutiny and possible ridicule and rejection. But I speak those words in order to try my dammy to help someone else avoid falling into some of the same snares and pits, to dodge just a few of the slings and arrows of outrageous fortune I've found myself having fallen prey to—as a human being, as a Black Man, as a musician, as an entrepreneur, and as a fool in love.

But the truth is that a bunch of pretty-ass words cannot keep you or anyone else from making the same mistakes I have made. 'Cause you know that people rarely take other people's advice to heart, anyway. There's always this false sense of "exceptionalism" in our quiver of excuses to dismiss the advice of others.

Pause.

Sidebar.

QUWHAAAT is the weirdness which makes it damn near impossible for some of us to receive advice from those closest to us? I mean, you can say something to a spouse, family member, or friend, and they will poo-poo it away. Then a so-called expert, or even a damn stranger, will say the EXACT same thing to your alleged loved one. And they'll think that it was the best piece of advice since sliced bread when said "expert" says it. And heaven forbid that purveyor of wisdom is a celebrity whom they find attractive or admire. Then whatever that stranger says, even if it's exactly what you said, is now the Gospel truth. I think that too often people have an issue with believing that someone they know or are close to could possibly know something that they don't. They don't believe that wisdom can be imparted to them unless they are receiving it from someone who is beyond their immediate reach. It is a phenomenon that has always baffled me. A lack of respect of even our own choices of friendships and relationships. It is ultimately not a reflection of those around us who attempt to impart pearls of wisdom. It is a reflection of how little we think of our ability to surround ourselves with amazing people and of our own internalized insecurities about our self-worth.

But I digress!!!

Back to what I was stating before the sidetrack.

When someone offers experience-based advice to certain types of people, those recipients of said advice often think to themselves or express out loud, "Well, that's you, that ain't gonna happen to me!" And you know what? They may be right. If I am the advice giver, you as the potential receiver may not endure the very same challenges in life that I have. And even if, by chance, you do happen to trip over every crack in the sidewalk that I tripped over, you are a totally different person than I am. ALSO, also—why the hell should you listen to me anyway? I'm not a celebrity or a social media influencer (although I've gotta say, somma y'all listen to some really broken and whack people on YouTube and TikTok) or someone who is living a well put together, perfectly managed and maintained, problem-free life. As a matter of fact, if I'm being one hundred, my shit is kind of fractured, too. Broken. Flawed. Messy. Unkempt.

But here's the thing about that fact: so what?

There is always wisdom to be gleaned from others, even if it is the straightforward wisdom gained from seeing others' mistakes firsthand and learning what not to do by example of the consequences others have suffered for their actions. We must be careful not to dismiss the advice of people simply because they are familiar to us, or because they are younger or older or less formally educated. Or different culturally. Or gender-wise. Whatever. Of course, judicial use of discernment is always in order. But let's not allow a false sense of exceptionalism to keep us from becoming exceptional through the wise digestion of the sagacity of others.

After all, we really, really don't know what we don't know.

Four

WHO YOU IS?
A Black Man's Guide to Self-Defining Affirmation

As soon as I stepped outside on that bright new day, the sun greeted my Melanated skin with its daily hello and positivity recharge. It washed over me with a waterfall of warmth and opulence and purpose; it was an acknowledgement of its acceptance of my reddish-brown hue. A validation from God and His universe which said, "You are a part of me, as am I of you. You are loved, nourished, and cherished as I created you—a man of color, a man of rich hues and hair like wool. Feet likened unto the color of bronze. Created in my own image. Here you are, Man of Color, here in My presence, and I will kiss your skin with My being, with the light of the sun which I have created just for you. And I will Bless you in this way each and every day of your life."

And with that daily affirmation, there seemed to be nothing that I wasn't capable of achieving. It was as if I had been tagged with one of those "you are here" stickers that you find on shopping mall maps, showing you exactly where you are positioned in the scheme of things at that very moment, pinpointing your purpose, your station in life. And laying out before you all the possibilities and directions you could go in.

CRAZY JOE AND THE NEGLIGENT NATION

I grew up in the Robert Taylor Homes in the late 60s, 70s, and early 80s. 45th and South State Street, to be exact. And anyone who grew up in the "Projects," or in row houses, or any similar type of urban mass internment that passed for a neighborhood during that time, can attest to the fact that there was AT LEAST one "Crazy Joe" or "Crackhead LaWanda" roaming the neighborhood. That's not making light of mental illness. That's just the fact of how it was viewed.

And these poor wretched souls were looked upon by everyone else as simply being staples of the hood. "That one baby that came out wrong" or "just wasn't right in the head." It was accepted, not really questioned, and inadvertently became part of the folklore of kids who were chased by those pitied and maligned beings. Many of those same kids who claimed that the "crazy kid" was bothering them had, in fact, constantly teased, tortured, and otherwise abused those very same mentally challenged children. And sadly, many adults did the same thing to those outcasts of the community. Shamefully, I'm sure that I was one those childhood teasers of the mentally impaired neighborhood children at some point during my childhood. Because I most certainly was one of the kids who had been chased to or from school by "that big crazy boy."

In those days, prenatal care was a rarity for the impoverished, mainly available only to the Rich and the White. And it was even more of a unicorn in poor Black communities. Add to that the nonexistence of preventive health care, little-to-no health insurance, an overabundance of lead poisoning built into our homes and schools, the food deserts that perpetuated our poor diets by limiting what was available for purchase to "foodstuffs" with loads of preservatives and zero nutritional value. And let's not even talk about exposure to vermin and the multitude of diseases they carry; cigarette smoke that children were directly exposed to by constantly puffing, stressed out parents, relatives, and neighbors; and indirectly via pregnant and nursing mothers who didn't know any better to not drink or smoke during and after pregnancy. And again, no access to mental health services that could possibly help to ease the daily non-stop stresses of living while Black in America. Micro AND macro aggressions. Never-ending financial stress. Unidentified health issues. Drug and alcohol use and abuse as a substitute for unattainable mental health therapy and medications.

It's amazing that we didn't all come out like Crazy Joe.

That being said, it's also no wonder that there is still a problem in our communities today when it comes to mental health. Yes, yes, of course it is an issue that also impacts other low (and nowadays, not-so-low) income communities. In no way am I saying we're exclusively disenfranchised from mental health treatment. Ask any Native American on a reservation that you may know. Like someone in Sioux County, ND. Or anyone abiding in Appalachia. Or Pembroke, NC. Benton Harbor, MI. Quitman County, MS. Tampa, FL. Washington, DC (you didn't see that one coming?). Or any such place where the forgotten and the discarded live in this country, in all its "great again-ness."

What I am saying is simply the fact that this is an historically unique and prevalent issue for Black people. And here are three of the main becauses:

a. The racial persecution and discrimination never seem to end. We can pull up as many bootstraps as you can fit on a boot. But each and every time we step out of the door of our homes, our skin color stays the same beautiful variety of melanated hues and tells the world who they THINK we are. In addition to the psychological ailments of which we fall prey to as a people, many of our physiological afflictions are also directly related to the ongoing and relentless stresses of a Melanated Life.

b. We have a Diasporic mistrust, and rightly so, of the healthcare industrial complex. Say "Tuskegee Experiment" with me. Repeat the name Henrietta Lacks. Be aware of the monsters in the O.R. like J. Marion Sims.

And the jury is still out (not really) on organ harvesting, unnecessary medical procedures, unequal and unfair billing, stupid myths like Black people being more immune to pain than Whites—myths that any halfway-smart person shouldn't believe, let alone a trained medical person—and other whispered urban malpractices. It's no surprise that so many of us are refusing the current COVID-19 vaccine, even as thousands of us are dying disproportionately from the actual virus.

c. We have stigmas about psychiatrists, plain and simple. Visiting one is seen as a sign of "weakness," especially by Black males (and by many of our female significant others. But that's a whole 'nother deep topic, though), to have a need to talk about "feelings" to people we know and trust...let alone some high-priced stranger in a doctor's office. Hell, we have a problem admitting even to ourselves of having a need to talk it out. "Just MAN UP! Push through like a 'real' man!"

In retrospect, that was just some real ignorant-ass thinking right there. Cultural norms born out of the fires of necessity and the need to survive can also backfire on you.

What we need is more of us in a field that is woefully, inadequately staffed by our peers. And when I say "us," I mean qualified, skilled, and caring professionals. Not placeholders or Affirmative Action appointees. If and when we decide to go see someone, we need to be able to see a reflection of US when we look up from that confessional sofa, or across the room from that comfy chair. We need better education about OUR health. We need more access to better services and less food deserts. We need our politicians to stop shuttering mental health facilities and defunding not-for-profit organizations that work with and within our Black communities.

We need—and don't shoot the messenger—our Black churches to step up the earthly help to match up with their heavenly prayers. God requires the WORK to be put in along with the prayer petitions to Him. You spiritual leaders who are not attending to your "flocks" properly, yet who are driving around in Lambos and Bentleys or asking for a private jet donation—y'all need to do more than collecting tithes, sangin' songs of Zion, sitting at imaginary tables of opportunity with a would-be American man-child despot, and "fire and brimstone-ing" everyone into the Pearly Gates. Create incentives for your congregation to learn more about their own health. Partner with community health-care providers. Provide health-care seminars. Open a free or low-cost clinic. Provide the means for those who don't have or can't afford health care to become part of some sort of group plan. You got 10,000 bazillion members? That's the makings of a sizable health-care group.

These spiritual leaders should be helping their people to NOT arrive to see St. Peter ahead of their scheduled time.

Wait, you DO know that you can shorten your God appointed days in this earth, right? Look it up.

Let's get better, people. Let's truly be woke. And let's help one another survive the slings and arrows of A Melanated Life by healing and strengthening our minds as well as our bodies and our bank accounts.

But first, let's acknowledge the problem.

<u>COFFEE</u>

That moment when you realize that you are truly your father's son...

This is my routine EVERY morning. Wake. Pray (not as consistently as I should, but I'm a work in progress). Visit the WC.

And then, I do this...

This being enjoying my absolute FAVORITE time of the day. No one else is awake, so the house is still and dark. Only the light of the new day is shining through the kitchen window, heralding the promise of another chance. It's just me, my God, a Bobo Protein Bar when I'm being good, a slice of pie when I'm not—

And. My. COFFEE.

Also present are my thoughts. My hopes. My dreams. And my fears.

It is a time of pure reflection. A time of planning. A time of woosah. A time to truly enjoy being alive, in spite of the vicissitudes of life that try to make you feel otherwise.

As a child, I used to wake up in the mornings and walk into the kitchen, on the hunt for the cereal du jour, only to find my father already sitting at the kitchen table in the early dawn darkness, coffee cup in hand (no Bobo bar), looking peaceful, yet still haunted. Haunted by the life he was handed. It was a life of not having much of a childhood or formal education and many regrets, but one that allowed Daddy to still become one of the most intelligent and hardest working men I've ever known. And Daddy sat at that table, coffee cup and Lucky Strikes in hand, facing each and every day with the sometimes-overwhelming responsibility of raising three little Black boys in the infamous Robert Taylor Homes. Daddy did this in spite of the weight of paying the ever-increasing bills on a never-increasing-enough government salary. He had the responsibility of keeping a family together, keeping a loving wife loving, keeping his children safe, and providing everything his family needed to rise above and beyond our meager surroundings.

To be honest, my dad was a loner. He often lamented the fact that all he ever really wanted/needed was a suitcase and a place to go. It's not that he didn't love his family. He never left us until God called him home. But the trials of his life were such that he never felt that he got the chance to live it totally on his own terms. As I said, Daddy had regrets—and many of them.

Now on the other hand, I have few, if any, regrets. I have been Blessed to have a pretty great life centered around this Blessed gift of music that God saw fit to give me. It has taken me to places I had only dreamed of (THAT is a whole other story about Prophecy, it's wild. More on that later—keep reading…). That gift has allowed me to meet and work with people who I had previously only admired from afar (I don't have idols…not my thing). It has brought me into communion with wonderful new friends and colleagues. The many sacrifices I have made in its service are more than worthwhile.

So, when I sit in the mornings, sipping my coffee and being at peace in my soul…even just for those few moments, I am grateful for life. I am grateful for love. I am grateful for Blessings, and Favor, and Covering, and Mercy. I am grateful for God. For Family. For Music.

I am grateful for my father. For the sacrifices he made to create a life that, while far from perfect, gave me the wisdom and understanding of what God calls a man to be in this world—steadfast. Strong. Honest. Hard working. Loving. And never giving up, even when that is ALL you want to do.

2018 was in the top three worst years of my life. 2019 was just as bad. We won't even mention 2020 and 2021, at least not yet. But at this moment, 2023 and beyond hold the promise, faint as it may seem, of better. Each day we are allowed to wake up holds that promise.

And to top it all off?

I have coffee.

BLAME IT ON THE A-A-A-A-A-ALCOHOL

Speaking of tasty beverages...

Interesting new self-discovery: I think that I like the IDEA of drinking alcohol more than I do the actual act.

Don't get me wrong. Having a cocktail or a glass of wine, in moderation of course, does relax me. I do enjoy the taste of the wines and liquors that I do imbibe. Alcohol does not make me ill or anything...unless, of course, I drink too much of it or fail to feed my body food and water before or during the act of turning up. I also enjoy the social aspect of commiserating with friends, family, or sharing an intimate one-on-one moment with a beautiful, intelligent, and funny woman over a drink or two.

But I just realized, quite abruptly, that it's really the falsely nostalgic idea of what having a drink represents to me that informs my alcohol consumption. Not escapism, although sometimes the initial intent may be just that. But I know well enough that that route for escapism never truly works. And I said "falsely nostalgic" because my dad never really drank. I believe I saw him with a beer in hand maybe three times in my life. He didn't go out and hang with friends. And he didn't care for all that socializing foolishness: what he called "goodtimin'." He was a loner who smoked Lucky Strikes, stayed home with family, and enjoyed watching boxing matches, war movies, and Westerns.

Conversely, I grew up enamored by classic movies: everything from Casablanca to Stormy Weather, from A Raisin in The Sun to Citizen Kane, Black Orpheus to Guess Who's Coming to Dinner. Vertigo. The Thin Man. The Maltese Falcon. Meet John Doe. To Sir with Love. Carmen Jones. Arsenic and Old Lace, etc., etc.

I loved the clothes. I loved the dialogue. I loved the storytelling, lighting, and the absence of the distraction of color (in most cases). And I loved, minus the overt misogyny, racism, and the occasional slap or two of women, how men were portrayed. How we interacted with one another and socialized in a classy manner. I didn't want to be a social butterfly and out on the town either. But I did want to be around the select people I liked being around and to share great experiences with them.

Pause again.

Yes. I know that until men such as Paul Robeson, Harry Belafonte, and Sidney Poitier came along, Black men were not portrayed as men in Hollywood. We were clowns, comic relief, servants, murderous mindless criminals, or escaped slaves. Sure, there were a few directors who insisted on more real world, equality driven portrayals of Black people in general.

For instance, Orson Wells was a director who seemed to value people of all races as real people. And then you had the true, out-and-out Hollywood allies, like Marlon Brando—who were literally on the front lines with the likes of the Black Panther Party.

But beyond the overly exaggerated stereotypical images of us, many of our onscreen portrayals were simply reflections of the times. We did work as servants and porters and custodians. We did often live in slums or congested neighborhoods. But even though you wouldn't hear much about it in the media and in academia, we were also doctors, lawyers, business owners, etc. And every now and again, you'd see that level of Black greatness reflected in those classic movies. And it was always a beautiful thing. But I digress. Back to liquor!

Having a cocktail after a hard day's work, over a business dinner, while on an extended lunch hour. Imbibing while entertaining a social gathering at your home for an evening, or while buying a drink for a beautiful woman at a classy bar: those ideas appealed to my young mind. Well-mannered, well-coiffed men in long single-breasted wool overcoats with raglan shoulders; fashionable outerwear layered over tailored, well-fitted suits; stylish hats; and polished leather dress shoes. I fell in love with the images of a Humphrey Bogart, a Sidney Poitier, or a Cary Grant wooing the women, making the men jealous, and confidently relaxing at a table in a nice restaurant or a hip jazz club, or seated casually at the bar in the lobby at their current hotel address, taking in the room, all the while relaxing with a glass of wine or a classic cocktail (and maybe a nice cigar) in hand.

THAT is the idea that attaches me to the art of drinking. Not the sloppy drunk, wild party end of alcohol consumption. But the stylish, classy, gentlemanly engagement with good friends, an amazing woman, or with only yourself and your thoughts; it can be had as a stand-alone experience, or at the intersection between a fantastic meal and a great bar snack, whatever floats your boat. THAT is what drinking well looks like to me. And THAT is why when I drink, I am not in pursuit of a high or a temporary escape from reality; more so, I am in love with savoring my love of life, love, friendship, and camaraderie. I enjoy that moment of truly taking stock of and appreciating my manhood—and my Blackness. And more than anything, I enjoy that moment of being in my own good company.

Or, if the occasion allows for it, I very much enjoy those moments of being in the company of those whom I cherish while partaking in the always-to-be-savored indulgence and the pure gratification of the art of imbibition.

CASPER THE FRIENDLY SOCIAL MEDIA STALKER
Random.

I'll admit it. I have sometimes sent out random friend requests on social media to people who look to be good and interesting people and who know some of the good and interesting people I already know. It's what I'd do in person real life, meet, and get to know good people who seem to align with who I am.

So, don't be scurred. I'm normal-ish.

The thing is, when you are an ambivert, meeting new people is mostly a function of necessity. And as a musician, it is the thing that happens as a fringe benefit/detriment of being a performer, traveler, and entrepreneurial businessperson. You MUST meet people in order to eat. You MUST be social and sociable in order to get hired, obtain new clients, and solidify relationships necessary for survival and growth in this industry. This is of course true in most any occupation that is forward-facing or service-oriented. But when you are not naturally a social butterfly, it is part of the concerted effort you make in order to fit.

And again, I say this all the time—with my chest:

In general—I don't like people. Well, most people.

Because in my experience, most people are not real. They are are phony. They send their avatars and representatives out into the world to interact with one other. And that avatar shape-shifts and morphs its very essence according to its environment and its goals and needs, showing one face when looking in one direction while displaying yet another when it turns its head to look elsewhere. Understand, there is a HUGE difference between code switching; pulling forth genuine aspects of one's personality to fit the occasion—and the act of creating a totally fabricated persona whose actions and words are disingenuous at best—and deceitful and malevolent at worst.

True ambiverts are the former. We call into play aspects of our personalities that exist, but that are not particularly always on display. And sometimes, it is uncomfortable to call those aspects of our personalities into service. We may not be as adept at expressing any given characteristic as we are the other. But it's all genuine and real. It's just all well-guarded; the glass is only to be broken in case of emergency.

Which brings us back to Social Media. The Fakest Place On Earth™. Social Media adds yet another layer of lie-ability (see what I did there?) to people's displayed personalities. It allows people to reinvent themselves to the degree of unrecognizableness, even to those who actually know them in real life. It buffers people from consequences of misrepresentation, from the immediate repercussions of angry words misspoken and hateful speech spewed out of ignorance and fear. It shields people from presenting their true selves and rewards lies with "likes" and pseudo-popularity.

On the flip side of that coin, Social Media also allows us access to people who, without the benefit of owning a Lear Jet, having lots of money and free time, and sporting a sparkling outgoing personality, we would likely never encounter. Social

Media allows us to sometimes find likeminded people of a positive nature, to "bump into" long lost friends and family. It gives us access to places and events we may have only dreamt of going to or attending. Social Media allows us to share as much, or as little, of ourselves as we are comfortable with. YES, there's way too much oversharing. But that's to be expected, especially in these strange semi-isolated and divisive times.

And Social Media also, if you're careful and discerning, allows us to make real and true soul-level connections with new people. I'm not talkimbout sliding into people's DMs unannounced and uninvited, like Wesley Snipes slid into the castle throne room in Coming to America 2. I'm talking about seeing someone who looks interesting, who looks safe and sane. Someone whom you may not normally cross paths with, but to whom you may have a connection (with more than one or two friends with whom you have twenty degrees of separation, let's be smart here!) through someone you do know. Interesting, vibrant people who are living their lives and doing wonderful things both great and small.

And so, sometimes, I'll see that type of person on Social Media. And I'll randomly reach out. Not for any specific reason. Could be a potential industry connection. And yes, it could be because they are a she and she is fine but also intriguing and living life. But it could also be, through discernment, someone who may NEED to have a connection to you, and vice versa. It could be someone who, in that moment, could benefit from your acquaintance on a personal, professional, or even spiritual level. And again, that may go both ways. That does NOT mean that any of us should accept every friend request we receive. That's asking for trouble, tenuous multi-friend connections or not.

But in many ways, meeting people online is not that much different than when we meet people in the flesh. People have been able to be deceptive of their true natures and intent since the beginning of time. There are people who are good at high levels of misrepresentation, even when you are looking them directly in their eyes. At the end of the day, people are people; they are those beings that I don't particularly care for. They do lie. They do cheat. They do deceive. But some also love. Some laugh. Some help and not just hurt. Some listen and not just spew. Some people learn, and they share. They flourish. They connect, and they grow apart.

And yet as a whole, I still don't like people in general.

Despite this fact, I keep people around. I continue to meet them when I can and interact with them when I choose, or when it's a necessity. Some I will continue to love despite their being people. Because I'm sure some of them do the same with me. So, I will continue to study people, even as I continue to learn and relearn myself. And I will continue, despite my better and pessimistic judgement, to believe that, more often than not, people have the potential for greatness.

So if you get a random friend request from me, don't be

scurred. I'm just being a friendly people.

GIRLS, WOMEN, LEGS

One day, long, long ago, a little boy discovered girls. I cannot say exactly when it happened. But it happened. Big time. Maybe kindergarten.

See, there was this one girl named Jacqueline. She was chocolate. And beautiful. And she was mean as hell—well, at least she was to me. Jacqueline, who seemingly hated my guts all through grade school, from kindergarten clear on through to the eighth grade.

And I loved her for it.

Despite her apparent disdain for me the entire course of my preteen life. I was even a little obsessed with finding her post grade school. Obviously, a pattern was being set for a life filled with many moments of unrequited love, secret crushes, and shy guy missed opportunities with girls. Ah well.

But...

Soon after discovering girls, in my prepubescent, "mannish" little heart and mind, I suddenly and inexplicably discovered...

Women.

Not teenagers. Not newly minted young adult females. I am talking full grown, "I got a job," "where is yo' mamma, little boy," "ain't you cute—I just wanna put you in my back pocket," Go-Go boot-wearing, sundress-having, bell-bottom hip-hugger-styling, stacks and wedge shoe tightrope-like-walking, rough and tough with their afro puff-sporting, cigarette-holding, car-driving—women.

Now, I don't know what made my attention skip over my prepubescent female classmates or the adolescent and the teenaged and the young adult girls I'd see in the higher grades and head straight for the womenses. I just did. Mind you, I had NO libido to speak of that I could identify as such, or any idea of why I actually liked grown women. But there was just SOMETHING about them that caught my fancy. Women were just—beautiful.

I remember like it was yesterday.

I was about five years old sitting in our living room watching television while Momma was cleaning the kitchen after breakfast. WTTW (Channel 11 if you aren't hip) had gone on one of its daytime broadcast breaks during the lunch hour. So, without the colors (the TV was black and white anyway) and sounds and music of Sesame Street to entertain me, I struggle-turned the channel, because those channel selector knobs back then were a beast to turn, even for adults. And I turned the TV to one of those exercise programs they used to have on midday—you know, for housewives who allegedly had nothing else to do during the day but exercise...

Anyway, this particular exercise program wasn't no Jack LaLanne joint. It was instead this beautiful, curvy, hippy woman in her one-piece exercise leotards, bending and stretching and moving every which way. And I was suddenly fascinated by one specific aspect of her being. So, without hesitation, I went into the kitchen where Momma was. And here is how the ensuing conversation went:

"Momma?!"

"Yes, Kenny?" Momma replied.

"There's a lady on TV ecksasizin'."

She responded, "Oh, they do that all the time, Kenny."

I paused, thought for a second, then asked, "Momma, why do ladies have big booties?"

Momma didn't look up from the dishes she was washing, but instead shook her head, softly chuckled to herself, and didn't miss a beat.

"Kenny, ladies have big booties and hips because they have to carry little babies on them. So, they need the extra cushion so the baby can be comfortable."

Well, I was satisfied with that answer. Yup. Made total sense. Yet I was still very much fascinated with my newfound noticing of the differences between girls' and women's bodies.

And so, with the sudden noticing women's bodies came the noticing of—

Legs.

When I tell you that I became obsessed with women's legs from about age six until forever—lissen. I don't even remember what the trigger was. My mom of course had beautiful legs. Because she also gifted me with pretty decent legs, male version. But this obsession of mine with women's legs was not brought on by some weird Oedipal Complex. C'mon, folks. That would just be plain weird.

Instead, this newfound obsession had to have derived from being at church, of all places. Besides my teachers at school, that was the only place I can think of where I was exposed to lots of women—and lots of women's legs.

Or maybe it WAS my kindergarten teacher's fault. Maybe it was the beautiful, smart, friendly, kind Ms. Scudder's fault. Because she was a woman. And she had women's legs. And Ms. Scudder was (prayerfully still is, bless her beautiful soul) one of the most beautiful people I have ever met. You know. As far as a kid can know.

Because Ms. Scudder was a young—maybe early twenties—White teacher at an all-Black school in an all-Black neighborhood. And from everything I can remember, she wasn't there because she had to be, or because she felt obligated to help the poor little Black children. Ms. Scudder seemingly was there at Zenos Colman Elementary School, teaching little Black children and interacting with Black parents, because she LOVED her calling. She loved teaching. And she loved her students.

And Ms. Scudder had some amazing legs.

Also, Ms. Scudder would often take her best students places

(yes, I was one, and so was Jacqueline, for the record) to participate in impromptu field trips and extracurricular activities. She took us to her own home on several occasions for hot dogs, pizza, and ice cream. She took us roller skating. Miss Scudder even came back to our grade school some years after she had left to become a high school teacher, and she took a few of us out to eat and show us around her new school.

Ms. Scudder was one of the first women I can remember who was not related to me to show me such kindness that it left a positive and lasting impression on me. And with that experience, kindness became part of the equation of attraction I grew up having for women. Sure, I started this about women's legs, and Ms. Scudder in particular. And now that I think about it, most of my grade school teachers were women, and most with wonderful gams (hey, what can I say—like I said, I paid close attention to adults as a kid—more on that later). But only a few of those teachers left such an indelible impression on me as Ms. Scudder.

It's funny the things that, as a child, influence the type of people you later become and become attracted to. As both a child and an adult, I have never had a "type." I take every woman I become involved with for who they are as an individual. Of course, we all have certain preferences, some we are aware of and others we aren't. But I strongly believe that my very positive experiences with Ms. Scudder as a child wholly informed and influenced my eventual ability to not characterize women by type, and instead by the content of their individual characters. I learned from her, and the many other encounters I had with female teachers, mentors, and family from all races and backgrounds—to love and appreciate whatever appealed to me in each woman as her own, unique, shining points of beauty.

In Ms. Scudder, I apparently learned that race, differences in skin tone or coarseness of hair, and the infinite variations in facial features shouldn't matter. Of course, I knew that she was different from me. But Ms. Scudder never once made me feel as if those differences were important. And so, I grew up having those type of expectations of people from all walks of life. Until I didn't. Because sooner than I could have imagined, there came a moment when I learned that race, indeed, made a difference.

CRENSHAW GOES GREAT WITH ORANGES

I was by no means a naïve child. But the summer of my amazing year of kindergarten with Ms. Scudder, I sadly learned what racism was, when my five-year-old self had to go to the washroom while traveling with my mom through Mississippi on a trip to visit Gran'momma. it was a moment that has stayed with me my entire adult life.

Somewhere near Crenshaw, Mississippi, I believe, we were told that we'd have to transfer from our lovely modern double decker Super Seven Scenicruiser Greyhound bus over to a dark and decrepit-looking Trailways bus, complete with no air conditioning, a non-functioning clock above the front windshield, and a pet wasp. See, Greyhounds didn't go as deep into the rural areas of the South as we needed to go; they only served the major transportation hubs and maybe a few smaller towns. So, we did what we had to do in order to get to where we needed to go. And as was inevitable when traveling with children, one of her sons—me—it was ME, of course—had to use the restroom at the bus terminal during that layover, because Trailways onboard restrooms always seemed to be out of order. Always.

Now imagine a beautiful, strong young Black woman traveling alone through rural Mississippi in the late 60s, with her two young sons—one eight, the other five. No husband accompanied that young Black Woman, because her husband—my Daddy—had to work. See, Daddy didn't have the luxury of taking vacation days. He had a wife and two (later three) little Black boys to love, feed, and take care of. And Momma wasn't going to wait for him to go visit her mother. She was, and still is, a very fearless and fiercely independent Black woman.

All this transpired during one of the hottest summers we had suffered through in a while. In Mississippi. In the sixties. Maybe a year and a half after MLK's assassination. And the only restroom available at that particular bus terminal was a "White Only" restroom. Or at least that's what I assume it was. Because thinking about when Momma told me to go into that restroom and use it, I can remember several things very clearly. I remember feeling something that I had never felt before in my five short years of life—the heat of hate and anger radiating towards me from adults. I remember seeing the cold, hard stares boring into me, my brother, and Momma.

I also remember the kindly White ticket agent telling folks to leave us alone and to let those little boys go use the restroom. But most vividly, I remember the overpowering smell of orange peels. Sweet, bitter, peeled oranges. Because it seemed like every White man in that bus terminal was eating oranges.

Or maybe that was simply the smell of bigotry and detestation as it registered with my childhood senses.

I cannot tell you whether or not any racial slurs were hurled in our direction. At that age I wouldn't have known one if I had heard one. The word "nigger" had not yet been introduced to my young mind. It wasn't used in my home. And I had a few years left before the very first time that derogatory label was aimed at me (and yet again at my beautiful guardian angel—my mother) as we were walking from Sears to another shop in the Ford City shopping mall. So even though I felt what I later identified as hate being aimed at me, I was not directly impacted by it in a lasting, negative way. Because Momma simply kept her cool, told me to be quick, and directed me to the entrance of that restricted and forbidden restroom.

I'm here to report to you that it was a very uneventful pee.

Despite his insisting that he didn't have to go, Momma made Joseph go into the restroom with me so that we could kill two birds with one stone. And I remember coming out afterwards, physically relieved, unfazed by the vibe in that space, but still curious as to why it had been such a big deal for me to go to the restroom. I was too young to read the room, so I cannot define what the actual vibe was when we walked back into it. But it didn't really matter once the deed was done. Because I was back with Momma, holding her warm, comforting hand. I felt her covering and her protection from whatever it was I was being protected from. I was with my family. We were on our way to see Gran'momma. And I was going to hug her and listen to her stories and run from wasps and play with the dogs and chase the chickens and sit at that big ole barrel to struggle-churn butter and eat Gran'momma's fried chicken, fruit preserves, and hot water cornbread.

Despite the unidentified weirdness of that long ago moment in a Mississippi Trailways bus terminal, and my prior feelings of discomfort and non-understanding, being back in the loving arms of Momma and in route to see Gran'momma meant that everything was now right with the world.

No matter how many orange peels I still smelled.

Five

LOVE IS A MANY SPLINTERED THING

So, let's talk about Love and relationships, specifically within the Black Diaspora. Ideally, loving someone and being loved by them in return should all be quite simple. Yet the reality is that it can be pretty damn complicated. Mainly because WE make it that way. So buckle up, buttercup, and let's get into the "why" of it!

Now let me state up-front that I have not aught with Love. Me and Love, as far as I know, we still kewl. My words and tone sometimes may suggest otherwise. But I assure you, I'm still a dyed-in-the-wool romantic. I know I say "bah, humbug" to friends and family about many things love and relationship-related. Divorce tends to do that to a person when it's relatively fresh. But I really do still believe in Love.

I just don't much believe in the trueness of people.

This is a reoccurring theme for me folks. So, try to get used to it.

See, i don't believe that most people actually know what real Love truly is.

If you're a follower of Christ (don't worry—this won't get too religiousy, ye who are heathens!), and even if you aren't, the Bible tells us quite clearly in 1 Corinthians 13:1-13 what Love truly should look like. Seems fairly straightforward, yes? I didn't say easy. I said straightforward.

That Bible verse is a clear blueprint for Love that even a fallible bunch of creatures such as we can follow. But despite having an owner's manual for the care and feeding of Love, somewhere, somehow, we often frack it up. Because we as humans will take that blueprint, and we will squeeze our square peg ideologies into the round holes of truth about Love. And that is where the mess begins. We often can't even get friendship right, let alone romantic relationships.

Where to start?

Well, we are selfish. We are self-righteous. We are self-centered. Many of us are not as self-aware as we think we are or pretend to be, because self-awareness requires a modicum of self-evaluation and self-assessment. It requires continuously looking inward with a critically honest Third Eye, a humble soul, an open mind, and a contrite heart. Tall orders for a surprisingly vast number of people.

We are creatures made imperfect and flawed. According to God's Word, we were created a little lower than the angels in hierarchy of the universe. And so our execution of Love will always fall short and be imperfect. But remember, even the angels had an issue with executing A Love Supreme. Because, although the angels lived their whole existence in the presence of Love Perfected, a full one-third of them got their heads turned by the lure of another. And they, in turn, turned their backs on God. But it wasn't really that they became enamored with anyone else. It's that they decided that they themselves were more important than the One whom they promised to love unconditionally.

See, just like when taking the sacred vows of marriage, the angels had a covenant with God. Now I may be old, but I wasn't there, so I don't know if they tried to make things work before they bailed on God or not. I don't know if there was any counseling, any high-level closed-door meetings, any dealmaking, or any soul-searching (I'm not sure if angels have souls). But either way, the result was that those wayward angels broke rank, broke covenant, and then just broke. And they broke camp to follow a musician, I might add.

Ouch.

Sometimes familiarity breeds complacency. Sometimes it breeds animosity. If one person looks to be free and enjoying life, even though that person is also seemingly fulfilling their significant other's life, sometimes, it still causes resentments. My being a Creative was seemingly both attractive and frustrating to my ex-wife. I've been this me all my life. She knew that.

We even had conversations about how our different lifestyles together would look and function in practice. But apparently that wasn't enough for her in the end. Understand, with marriage, people don't really know who they will be under that covenant. Oh, we like to believe we do. But we don't. Not really.

The trick is to always be able to recognize yourself when you look in the mirror each and every day of that covenant. The only change you should see is growth, both within self and within the relationship. That absolutely does NOT mean happiness all the time. But happiness is a fleeting state of being. Ideally, though, JOY should always be present. For example, the joy of having and loving one another should be a fixed beacon in marriage—sometimes further away than others, but always visible. And even more importantly the joy of pleasing God under that sacred covenant between the three of you should be continually active.

Fun fact: some people spend so much time in relationships "testing," or trying to change the other person, that they never get around to actually loving them. This is why we must learn to value, appreciate, and love the people in our lives who possess "good bones." You know, like those well-built old houses you see being flipped on HGTV all the time. And like those houses, some people with good bones may require a little remodeling. Some may even require a gut rehab if they, and you, are willing to put in the work. Because as with houses, there is always a need for repair and maintenance in people. But finding people with a solid foundation is a rarity. So you'd better hold onto and cherish those good-boned people while you can.

It is a very sobering moment when you come to the realization that a person whom you thought was a long-term active participant in your life was only a temporary spectator. And I could literally write a whole book on my marriage alone. But I'm not here for the easy points that an exposé type of read, or that path to a tell-all could possibly garner. Hell, I'm not in the least bit famous, so who would really and truly care to read about yet another failed marriage out of millions?

The truth is that, for the most part, my marriage was a wonderful experience. I believe with all my heart and soul that it started out in True Love. My ex and I seemed like a great match; we had two days separating our birthdays, attended the same high school at the same time (only passing friends, never lovers), seemingly possessed the same sense of humor and love of life, and allegedly held the same spiritual beliefs and moral leanings and such.

The problem was that even with all that sameness and familiarity, there were a few important ingredients missing. One was knowledge of self. I will be bold here and say that, in my opinion, the greater lack in that area was not on my part. But of course I would say that. The fact is that there's always three sides to every story: mine, hers, and the truth. Sadly, my not knowing the wholeness of her part of the story is part of missing ingredient number two (which we'll get to in a bit).

But back to missing ingredient number one.

I consider myself to be a very self-aware person. I am that person who is generally perpetually honest with himself to a fault. That awareness comes out of childhood insecurities visited upon me by my father, God rest his soul. Daddy didn't mean any harm; his words and actions were not malevolent in their intent. But they still had similar effects on my psyche as any teardown by someone you love and respect would have. Daddy's often harsh words—calling a sensitive child things like "crybaby," or saying that crying made me look like a "sissy;" or telling me I was too skinny and that I was all eyes, head, and legs (he may have been right about that though—lol) still made me look at myself and over-scrutinize everything about myself, from my looks to my likes. From my thoughts to my actions. And as with any male child, I wanted so badly to please my father, because I looked up to him. I loved him.

Yet as I grew older, I began to learn of the hardships of my father's own difficult childhood, and the subsequent adulthood that was born from it. As stated before, as an adult, my father was very much a loner who had lived less of an actual childhood and more of an early manhood. He had no choice but to grow up fast at a young age, as most Black Men of his generation had to do. Because in those times and places there was very little resemblance to the childhoods of future generations of little Black boys. There was likely only work and loneliness. Now, I never learned any real details of Daddy's childhood from him directly; he was NOT a sharer or big communicator. He didn't talk about his past much, if at all. But as a diligent son eager to please his father, I studied him. When Daddy did speak, I listened. And in listening, I heard the frustration of his words and the bitterness in his heart, born of being ostracized by his siblings because of his darker skin, abuse by adults, racism, and the lack of having had a proper father figure.

At the same time, I was also Blessed through my listening and observation to learn of the great wisdom and intelligence of my father's complex mind. I learned about Daddy's fierce convictions, born out of hard work and pain. I learned that my father had only achieved a fifth-grade education, yet he was still one of the smartest men I've ever known. I learned that Daddy had been stationed aboard one of the most famous aircraft carriers of WWII and the Korean War, the USS Intrepid. I learned that even though he wasn't a religious man, my father read the Bible from cover to cover, and would also literally read the dictionary in that same manner to expand his vocabulary and his mind.

So as I grew and learned that to my childhood mind, seemingly for no reason, Daddy could be unintentionally cruel, I also learned that he also refused to whoop his children; Momma did an excellent job of handling that task. I'm happy to report that I only got a handful of them in my entire childhood—three or four to be exact. What an angel I was! And even with all of Daddy's faults and flaws, his mistakes made with loving his wife (he was ALWAYS faithful) and with raising his children, I learned of the beautiful mind and the innate kindness of his soul—the way he would teach us about what he did know—saving money, getting an education above all else, avoiding foolishness, and taking care of family—that belied his gruff and seemingly bitter exterior.

With all my childhood observation and scrutinization of Daddy, I eventually concluded and decided quite adamantly that, as much as I loved Daddy, I would never allow myself to become as bitter as he had seemed to become. I would never allow myself to have regrets so huge that they would erode the very fabric of my being to the point where I could not find joy again after such sorrow. I was determined to keep a running self-check on the operational status of Kenery's character, mind, and soul, bodily maintenance apparently optional. I was resolute to never be caught off guard about who I was and where I was at in my own journey. My self-motto became "honesty with self, above all else." And in that way, I could always find the strength to be honest with others.

That shit didn't work.

Well, okay—it worked. A little. But only when I allowed it to work. And I'm not talking about that piece involving self-honesty; I damn well knew myself quite thoroughly, top to bottom.

But that piece about being honest with others? Not always so much. That part of my character often failed early on. Not because I was a coward. But it often failed because I also discovered during my regular self-awareness diagnostics that I did not enjoy confrontation or conflict. I detested drama. When honesty was bound to bring great conflict, I opted for the outer white lie. Peace was my state of preference. Goofy happiness was my desired existence, with a touch of natural conflict to grease the wheels. And to be perfectly honest, sometimes I didn't believe that the situation or the person either respected, appreciated, or was even worthy of my honesty.

We all tell ourselves little white lies here and there in order to get through the day. Or the week. Or the Life. And we typically call them either one of two things: self-motivation or self-preservation. The degree of the white lie determines which category it lands in. Telling ourselves little white lies is typically a harmless thing, unless and/or until it dips into the realm of delusion and self-denial. But when it comes to character and self-evaluation as I've stated, I know pretty much who I am. And I'm often brutally honest about myself with myself. Very cerebral, this guy is. But not so much so that it affects my love and enjoyment of the outside world. I love LIFE! And I enjoy living it, with all its experiences, both good and bad.

As far as my past marriage is concerned, I truly don't think its downfall was so much self-deception on her part (or mine, to a degree), but more about self-denial. There's a meaningful difference. The former is about not even knowing the facts about who you are and what you need. The latter is more about knowing those facts but denying their true importance to who you are and what you desire.

Which brings us to missing ingredient number two.

I believe my ex-wife knew what she wanted out of a marriage. But the fault line here was one part my idealized understanding of what it takes to have a successful marriage, one part being the recipient of luggage from her first marriage, and one part of her inadvertently trying to fit me into a mold that I obviously did not neatly fit into. Sure, I believe I ticked most of the boxes on her list; I don't believe she would've said "I Do" if I didn't. I presented myself as is, with no fillers, no filters, and no pretense. It's the only thing I know how to do because I'm an awful liar, so being fake would not have worked out well. But I also believe, as with most people who fall in love, that what she perceived was an idealized version of me. Or maybe it was simply the me circa 2005 that was appealing; the me who felt that after 42 years of life, he was ready for marriage. The younger, more confident, pre-financial crisis, life challenges, pre-attempts at family blending, pre-realization of the great responsibilities of taking care of a large family, pre-clinically depressed for real, real me.

And I believe that those things she felt she needed from me, realistic or not, were truly of vital importance to her sense of self and security. Because when conflict came along and infiltrated our lives and our strength as a couple was tested along the fault lines of both our characters, those specific elements she tried to weld onto my character gave way. And as with any welding that isn't solid, those fault lines came undone when those stress points became stressed. The consistently applied pressure of life only revealed the fractures that already existed in our relationship—fractures which her self-denial and my unpreparedness made seemingly impossible to hold together, much less repair. To say that I never got real closure or answers as to the whys from her point of view is an understatement. And yet I'm slowly, surely, becoming okay with that fact.

Despite all the pain and heartache I've suffered from my divorce-driven condition of the heart, the fact remains that, honestly and truly, I still believe in marriage; I still believe in Real Love.

I have not aught with Love. Me and Love; as far as I know—we're still kewl.

SHINY OBJECTS

Throughout this book, you will undoubtably notice that I will often use the descriptive phrase "Shiny Objects," maybe far too often. But the phrase is quite relevant to my life philosophy and refers to the less important things in life that often distract from the truly important and substantive things we should focus on more.

But Shiny Objects are more than just physical things. "Shiny Objects" also refers to ideologies, traditions, and roles.

We go through life putting so much weight on sizing people up by these less substantive things—the social status, the bank account, what is brought to those imaginary yet oft referenced "tables" we allegedly bring our assets to for comparison and approval—and the meaningless approval of the Jones' (Ole School heads, I KNOW that song just popped into y'all minds when you read that, ha!). We place such import on these things of relative value that we ignore the things which truly matter. Like character. Honesty. Integrity. Truth. Faithfulness. Perseverance. Compassion. Loyalty. Love.

And many of us will throw away or ignore the person who most readily embodies these infinitely more valuable traits, instead opting for the six-figured flashy guy or the bodied-up trophy woman as status-minded Shiny Objects. Don't get it twisted: a well-appointed material life is a fine thing to aspire to and work towards having. In and of itself there is nothing wrong with living a lush life. But, as with the acquisition of anything of real or perceived high value in life, there is a cost beyond hard work and sacrifice in achieving that goal.

Trust and believe when I tell you, I have seen firsthand the woman who was being lavished with every Shiny Object she could desire in the public eye but who cried private tears of loneliness and heartache from a lack of romantic love, emotional support, and fulfillment. The price she paid for living the glamorous life was to be trapped with a narcissistic, unavailable, and non-empathetic personality that gave her little time and capacity for love, support, or offering a sincere and emotionally supportive shoulder to cry on.

Conversely, let's keep it real: lack will murder a marriage just as thoroughly as overabundance. This is fact. Money is in the top five of every list ever made for the reasons why marriages fail. And that's not surprising, due to the emphasis given to the value of money and status in how we are able to live our lives. Money causes disagreements, insecurity, and resentment. And it most certainly is not a guarantee for "happy life, happy wife." I've got friends who can vouch for that fact also. As a matter of fact, there doesn't seem to be ANY situation which guarantees a successful marriage.

To wit:

"The good news for those feeling unsettled, unhappy, or frustrated in their marriage is that all couples struggle with the same issues. According to Esther Perel, psychotherapist, bestselling author of The State of Affairs and host of two popular podcasts, both happy and miserable couples experience the same problems. It is how each couple comes together and relates to each other that defines whether the relationship will thrive or end.

When couples turn toward each other with kindness, understanding, and empathy, they can endure even the worst storms. However, when the couple comes with boxing gloves on, treating each other with contempt, defensiveness and suspicion, the marital prognosis under any circumstance won't be positive.

Our American society is not made to take care of the many—or even its own people, as other so called First-World nations have learned to do. Those countries seem to better understand the concept of trying to keep the individual parts of the cultural body healthy, to be a healthy nation as a whole. And they achieve this goal to greater or lesser degrees via things like Universal Health Care, the implementation of Siesta and Holiday season, or the guarantee of a universal basic income.

Instead, this nation of self-proclaimed "American Exceptionalism" and capitalism-run-amok was created to subjugate and take advantage of all we have to offer one another for the good of only the few at the top. Being on that constant hamster wheel of survival makes it quite easy for us to lose sight of those core values that can truly fulfill our lives and the lives of others, particularly those we claim love and affection for.

Ideally, our lives should be all about life balance. It apparently can be done; we see balance being achieved in those other societies. But unfortunately, we are a selfish, greedy society. Even more sad is the fact that as Black people in America, we are taught to chase the elusive "American Dream," a dream that was not built for us. Thus, we learn to value, or devalue, one another in exchange for trying to achieve a dream that keeps having the goalpost moved away from us. Or in the tradition of the hijinks of Charlie Brown and Lucy, that dream keeps having the football pulled away just as we think we're about to kick a societal field goal.

Black folks continue to play the game by White society's unfair rules. The frequent result is that we keep separating ourselves on interpersonal, familial, and community levels. House negro versus field negro. Light skinned versus dark. High-earner corporate types versus modestly-earning and hardworking entrepreneurs. White collar versus blue collar.

Money versus love.

And all the while we don't seem to notice that when we learn to pool our resources and when we bring all parts of the Diasporic spectrum together, when we collectively and individually work in partnership instead of pettiness, THAT is when THEY notice and become afraid of us, and view and treat us as a threat to THEIR perceived status. Can you say Tulsa, Oklahoma, 1921, among hundreds of other examples? Implementing a spirit of partnership starts within our homes, in our personal and interpersonal interactions. We cannot wait for society to fix the Black Family and to perfect Black Love. We must light that fuse ourselves, starting with our own relationships. We must unlearn our conditioning and relearn what it truly means to support and uplift one another no matter what the outside world throws at us. And as couples, we must relearn how to truly love each other in partnership and in covenant with God.

DATING IN THE TIME OF AVATARS

The act and art of the date is supposed to be about the person, and not the fanciness of the place, or the priciness of the meal. I don't mind spending money on a "traditional" date; that kind of comes with the territory, especially if, as a man, you are the initiator of said date. But I typically try to start my "gotsta get to know you, woman" quest with something as simple as coffee. That way there is nothing BUT focused interpersonal interaction and java or tea-sipping going on. Because personally, I'm not into trying to impress a woman with how much I can spend on her or where I can take her. When I was young and foolish, I thought that was the way to get to a woman's heart. But trust, I learndt. Man did I ever!

So, if you're not impressed with me, the person, that's kewl; I refuse to waste time and money trying to do so. Because underneath it all, I will STILL be the very same person.

Take me straight, no chaser. Love me for my Present, not my Potential.

On the further topic of even entertaining the possibility of looking at another relationship, this is how my inner me feels right now:

I AM TIRED.

I am tired of the dating game. Especially so in the aftermath of these COVID Times. Why?

Well, for me, people are just not honest enough with themselves. They don't know who the hell they are but will eagerly present a healthy and whole package to you, and it all looks great up until that ONE loose Jenga block in their character gets pulled out from their tediously stacked and precariously balanced pseudo-persona. I am tired of perpetually plucking the shrapnel of exploded relationships from my skin, after the other person suddenly has a "revelation" about who they are, and what they want which totally contradicts who their avatar presented as, and what I stated and demonstrated that I'm looking for. All this typically happens after I've purposefully or inadvertently helped those date-mates make that discovery, of course, and after I've put in the blood, sweat, AND tears. You know the story. Some of you have been there too.

And the time—dear God, the time we put into those people. Can't get that back, can we?

But here's the thing many of those people never seem to get: finding and keeping Real Love is more about the journey toward its perceived perfection than it is about actually reaching a destination. It's one of the few things that you can put on life's layaway plan and pay into as you go and not lose the reward/purchase at the end of the payment plan just because you didn't pay it all off. You can only lose it if you intentionally burn up those receipts and walk out of the store completely. Because of our fallibility as humans, we will never reach perfection in Love—that's a given. But we will never even come close to Love's perfection if we don't wholeheartedly do the WORK to pursue Love as an action verb, and not just as a feeling or emotion we have romanticized.

As with any great road trip, the real joy of taking Real Love's journey is not simply in reaching a preplanned destination. Because life is constantly in motion. Because things change. Your route can be altered. Your gas tank can run dry. You may require a few oil changes along the way. You will likely even get a flat tire here and there. Because the pursuit of Real Love has no guarantees. But despite those possible and likely challenges, it is inherently within the experience of the journey to True Love where we will find the real pleasure and fulfillment in one another.

The journey is the part from which we come away with THEE best stories and THEE most profound lessons about Real Love, ourselves, and each other. It is the journey, not the destination, which contains all those precious moments and memories and experiences we share together. And we must always try to be cognizant of how we take that journey. Because the fulfillment of Real Love doesn't look like that idea of the perfect match we've been sold.

The fulfillment of Real Love is about how we respond to one another in times of imperfection. It is about how we use what we have, what we know, and what we learn along the way—both about ourselves and one another—to treat each other when in Love.

THAT is our imperfect expression of Real Love's perfection. And that is what really counts.

Having said that, I wonder: Is it simply too much to ask for two people to laugh, live, and love one another these days?

Are the strings and things of life SO important that they are tradable for the joy of having someone whom you KNOW that you know that you know loves you, as close to unconditionally as these frail spirits will allow us to get? Are those Shiny Objects more important than finding someone who would take a bullet for you or just as assuredly dispense one out to protect you? Someone who knows all your highs and your lows, your lefts and your rights, and yet doesn't judge your value according to your social, or financial status?

Laws, no, I'm not talking about settling, whatever that means. Or being entangled with someone who is doing little or nothing to lift you or themselves up, and who is, in fact, actively dragging you down on purpose. But I speak of someone who is forward looking, even when they are not in fast forward motion. Because sometimes life stops you cold. Sometimes it stalls your engine. Sometimes what drives one person gives another person pause. But the person of strong character will pause and bend. They will not stop and break.

Not one of us is perfect. No, not one.

We all ebb and flow through this miasma of corporeal existence in the best way we can manage at ANY given time. No exceptions. Because trust and believe, you WILL stand on what feels like the bottom rung of life's ladder at more than a few points in your life, looking up for a way out, only to see what seems to be an insurmountable climb back to the top and out of the hole you find yourself in. That is guaranteed. And I'm certain most of us have been there already at least once. If you haven't, as the old mothers of the church like to say, "keep on livin', baby."

But in those low times, wouldn't it be amazing to know that you had someone—a partner in your journey—someone who was waiting at the top of that ladder with outstretched hands or climbing beside you, helping you get to the next rung up, or even holding that ladder steady at the bottom? Yeah, it would. You know it would.

So imagine my surprise when I found out the hard way that loving with Real Love won't keep you in a loving relationship. And before you ask, yes, of course I knew that it takes much more than Real Love to keep a marriage together. Relationships of any value require WORK. They require consistent, conscious, and constant effort. But what I didn't know was that even when you do everything that you know how to do to the best of your knowledge and ability, it can still simply not be enough. That fact truly begs the question of "can it ever be enough?"

Bottom line for me with relationships, and especially marriage is this: It's you and me against the world. If we're in it together, we're in it together. That goes for everything, from faith to finances. My desire and goal will always be to provide a covering for the woman I love and for my family if I am Blessed to have one. Understand, the man as the primary breadwinner is what most men strive to be, and what most women expect from their men. And that is a fair expectation, if based solely on either sheer biology and physicality, or on long standing ancient religious doctrines. But I also personally believe that part of the equation for a successful marriage, especially within the Black Diaspora, is the marriage being a pure and balanced partnership, and that whoever can get it done, at any given time during that partnership, is the one who gets it done. And the other person does what is needed to support and uplift the heavy-lifter in that moment. The ideal circumstance is, of course, that both partners are bench pressing one thousand percent, firing on all eight cylinders, all the time. Crushing life together.

But that's not real life.

For Black people, those traditional roles have not been as clear cut and accessible as the American Dream would have us believe they are. Traditional male/female relationship roles are nice to aspire to as Black couples, but that so-called American Dream was never built to include us.

Now, this won't be a popular stance, but here we go anyway. Stay with me.

Let's start with reiterating the fact that both genders within the Black Diaspora have been abused and conditioned in different ways by White society. That abuse has led to each sex often turning on the other when we express the anger, frustration, and feelings of futility that result from the abuse and conditioning.

To elaborate on the idea of Black Americans attaining that elusive Red, White and Blue American Dream (did you see "Black" amongst those colors?), we as a Diaspora constantly try to adapt the moires of Anglo culture, i.e., traditional male and female "roles" as laid out by the typical American tradition of family. The man does this; the woman does that, etc. And while many of those assignments, such as men being the singular family providers or women being the keepers and builders of the home, are typically culturally universal to one degree or another, we as Black people in America have NEVER existed under the ideal conditions that would support our ability to consistently achieve those supposed cultural norms. We have never been afforded the resources to fully allow us to live out that "white picket fence/2.5 children/man work and woman stay home" existence. And we keep falling for the okey doke, believing that we have "arrived" and have fully taken possession of those cultural norms and that Faux Dream.

I'd hazard to say that since the 1980s, America and the Corporate Industrial Complex have done their best to emasculate the Black Man, especially in the eyes of the Black Woman. This was akin to a technique perfected during Slavery Times that is related to what was then known as Buck Breaking.

During slavery, Buck Breaking was a directly violent and physical act which also employed psychological and emotional lynching, meant to break Black Men's spirit, subvert their strength and authority, steal their hope, and destroy their standing as men to their wives, their children, their families, and to their community of other slaves. It was done to teach Black Men our "place" and to condition us to live as less than, and in the fear of the consequences of ever trying to achieve freedom or a life beyond our assigned stations and conditions.

Today Buck Breaking is achieved not only through systemic violence against the Black Man via law enforcement, the justice system, and the threat of death or incarceration by both, but also through societal and economical lynching, and through the suppression of educational and career-based opportunities. And for that reason, you often see households where the Black Woman eventually becomes the primary breadwinner because the man has been sidelined from either the workforce or from the family equation altogether. This pours salt into the already deep wounds inflicted by a sense of failure or lack of meaningful success for many Black Men.

The other scenario that arose from this issue has the Black Woman not only becoming the higher earning partner, but quite often becoming the only breadwinner, if not on a permanent basis, then for an extended period of time. This again has been done by design. And all these factors in concert with modern-day Buck Breaking were where the trouble within the Modern Black Family began.

The fact is that Black Women have been major players in this American workforce in one capacity or the other, whether enslaved, free, single, or married, since the Diaspora was forcibly brought here. So Black Women have never had the opportunity, as a whole, to truly live that Anglo-suburban housewife dream because it was never truly theirs to have. Yet within the last forty to fifty years, opportunities have been created by and for Black Women to excel within a White male-dominated workforce. Oftentimes, Sisters have been given opportunities and have made great advances career wise. They have risen from cleaning lady to CEO. And that is a very good thing. Again, that is, in part, also by design.

The sad fact is that Sisters are perceived by White corporate America as "less of a threat" to White men and their careers than Black men are. And so the corporate world doesn't appear to have as much of a problem hiring qualified Black Women, but it is often at the expense of their rarely being paid their true worth. Because even when Black Women are promoted and successfully rise through the ranks of titles and pay scales, they are still almost always paid less than even their White female counterparts. And always far less than their White male contemporaries:

"Black and Hispanic women are most affected by the wage gap, especially when compared to non-Hispanic White men, who make up the largest demographic segment of the workforce...

...Asian women face the smallest wage gap—they earn 91.4% of what non-Hispanic white men earned, resulting in a pay gap of just 8.5%. Non-Hispanic white women earn 78.1% of what non-Hispanic white men do, while Black women earn 61.1%. Hispanic women earn 53%, or a pay gap of 47%. When compared to Black men, Black women earn 90.7% of what men earn, and Hispanic women make 80.6% of what Hispanic men do."
—Business Insider, Sonam Sheth, Madison Hoff, Marguerite Ward, and Taylor Tyson Mar 24, 2021, 10:51 a.m.

At the same time, Black Men who truly strive to be the primary providers have often struggled disproportionally to do so—not due to lack of will, skill, or ability, but due to lack of opportunity and support:

"There is abundant evidence that Black Americans and especially Black men face systematic discrimination in the labor market and in other walks of life, such as schooling. This discrimination limits their ability to accumulate skills and education credentials as well as work experience.

For instance, Holzer (1996) provides survey evidence that Black men receive fewer job offers than any other race/gender group as job applicants, especially in the lower-wage service sector. Several audit studies (which send out applicants of mixed race or gender with identical resumes to apply for jobs) provide evidence that Black applicants receive fewer callbacks from employers than white applicants. Devah Pager (2003) also shows that Black men without criminal records receive such callbacks at only approximately the same rate as White men with such records. And Charles and Guryan (2008) show that Black male earnings are relatively lower in states where whites express racial prejudice (as measured in the General Social Survey), and that such prejudice can account for a fourth of the Black-white wage gap among men.

... Declining employment among less-educated men in the U.S., and especially Black men, has been correlated with a decline in marriage rates. It is hard to determine exactly to what extent this relationship is causal; and, if it is, in which direction the causation works. What seems most likely is that causal effects work both ways – on the one hand, a lack of effective employment opportunities renders many (Black) men as less "marriageable"; on the other hand, lower marriage rates reduce the incentives of men to work to support their families."
—Brookings.edu: "Why Are Employment Rates So Low Among Black Men?" Harry J. Holzer, Monday, March 1, 2021

Sadly, when many of our women buy into those false guidelines to judge how much of a man we are or aren't, they don't consider these CONSTANT external obstacles and struggles we as Black Men face on the daily to achieve that singular breadwinner status, even amid recognizing their own struggles against American society as Black Women. In addition to the aforementioned stats, there are a myriad of macro and micro-aggressions which are always at play against Black Men. From the act of simply walking out of our houses each day and safely arriving at our destinations, to getting an education that gives us the proper tools to navigate a White-centric society. From surviving our own Brothers' and Sisters' misguided and misdirected anger and frustrations in the form of gun violence, to any random encounter we may have with a "bad" law enforcement officer. From finding and keeping a career or any type of gainful employment, to being constantly and purposefully passed over or held back from promotions or opportunities. From the very real challenge of acquiring loans from banks to instead pursue entrepreneurship, to fighting against the "illegal" practice of redlining when we are simply trying to provide a relatively safe environment for our families.

There are exceptions to these circumstances, of course, but they are far too few and far too between, and those exceptions that should be norms come at a MUCH greater sacrifice for us than they do for our White counterparts. Thus, the extra roadblocks and pitfalls created specifically for the Black Man in America to keep him from becoming a successful provider to those he has sworn to protect and provide for only fuel even more anger, frustration, and feelings of futility, which in turn create the ticking time bomb that most often causes the implosion of our relationships and our families. And it ultimately adds to our inability to achieve Real Love, let alone take the journey towards it.

From the abundance of social media posts I see on a daily basis, and through actual conversations with female friends and relatives, quite often many Black Women have taken the "Ain't Nothin' Goin' On But The Rent" mindset and ran with it. Remember ALL those Oprah episodes of male bashing? We sure do. Of course, no woman wants or deserves a trifling man who isn't working or bringing in money. And a good man won't stand for that being him. Yet overwhelmingly, the bank account/status for us became the de facto measuring stick of what has defined a "Good Black Man" for Black Women.

If you stop to think about it, it is in fact an extension of how White American society has always viewed Black Men.

By our monetary value.

On the auction block.

With a checklist of attributes. "Check his teeth. He has a strong back. He looks like he can breed well."

Just take that in for a minute.

And because of that viewpoint, Black families, Black Love, Black Women, and Black Male worth have become the victims. Whether it is completely accurate or not, Corporate America has appeared to readily "give" Black Women jobs and careers; it has always been funny to watch how our women could more often than not, leave one job, and have a new one within a month, tops. White Male Corporate America (WMCA) knew that they could safely allow Black Women into their ranks, in a very well-controlled manner.

They opened those pearly White gates just enough for Black Women to make some decent money, and to outwork, and sometimes out earn, Black Men who were/are seen as a threat to WMCA. At the same time WMCA made certain that Black Women did not become elevated enough to make equitable incomes as their White female contemporaries, let alone White men. Meanwhile, Black Men began to have fewer and fewer opportunities to move into and up in corporate America. So trades, entrepreneurship, and the illegal hustle have become the way we are able to put food on our family's tables.

All of this creates an atmosphere of frustration on both gender sides within the Diaspora. As stated earlier, Sisters very often become the major breadwinners in the family through no fault of the Brothers who are actually working to do better, thus allegedly demeaning the traditional cultural roles assigned to Black Men. This further erodes the male/female dynamic that, depending on your spiritual belief system, was designed by God—or by nature, if religion is not your thing.

So now you get internal chaos because Sisters are trying to hold down both the corporate and the domestic. Hard working Brothers are trying to be leaders in the family, but that leadership is being defined by dollars and cents, not spirituality, fortitude, quality of character, protection of wife and family, or—wait for it—quality of love given to his woman. Now Sisters are confused and frustrated. Brothers are angry and frustrated. Children are caught in the middle. And the whole dynamic of the Black family becomes unraveled. And the results are usually a broken family, a broken relationship, broken trust, and two emotionally—and sometimes mentally—broken people.

With all that said, who can really know how we should treat each other? Because love and respect and loyalty and support and dedication don't seem to carry enough weight. And the understanding that we're only going to survive and thrive if we're in this together no matter the "balance of power" that may be on display at any given time is often hard to conceive and achieve on both sides of the sexual divide. Because life can change in a heartbeat. And the one lesson we absolutely must learn to survive the cycle of broken Black families is that we as Black Men and Women cannot live by the edict of conditional love. We are called and required to strive towards UNCONDITIONAL LOVE. That means—short of someone intentionally hurting the other one emotionally, physically, mentally—if there is real love for one another, stick it out and fight the system TOGETHER. Stop falling for the preprogrammed roles we are taught to play; roles that we within the Black Diaspora rarely ever have the benefit of fully realizing in the same way that the non-melanated do.

And THAT is how we can treat each other well, both Brothers and Sisters. Like lovers and friends. And like partners in covenant and together within the struggle. Because Black

Women like Kathleen Cleaver, Fredricka Newton, and Elaine Brown knew that the time for traditional roles never existed within the Diaspora. It was all hands on deck to achieve the goal, by any means necessary.

CAN YOU RELATE?

Because of the way I'm built, people and things that are important to me get my FULL attention. I'm not one to split my loyalties. It's not that I can't; I have tried with mixed results here and there in the past. But I don't expect any single woman to be perfect, to "complete" me, or to be everything I've always wanted. So, I have no problem being committed to a single, uniquely beautiful woman. Because if you pay attention, there will always be so many, many layers to that one person you can explore and learn together, that you should never truly be bored with one another. And for the things that may not readily be part of who that woman is, if she's the right person, she'll be willing to explore and learn more about what life has to offer you both together, and what wonderful things you have to offer her as a person and a partner. And I am a more than willing and able teacher/student.

I once heard a quote in an old movie that said something like, "when I am truly in love with a woman, when I walk into a room full of other women with her on my arm, my Love is the only woman I see."

How can you truly know the full potential of a relationship without being fully committed? If I cannot be focused and fulfilled by an intimate relationship with a singular woman, then I have likely chosen the wrong woman. Again, relationships for me are not about perfection. They are about being committed to an action from start to finish. And not being concerned about "missing out" on something (someone) else. If I decide to ride my favorite bicycle, I'm not going to do it in a non-committed manner, with one foot dragging the ground...all the while wondering if that motorcycle I see over there would possibly be more fun to ride. I'm here to fully experience and enjoy each of life's unique moments...one at a time.

There are many wonderful people who exist somewhere in the middle between what is defined as "success" and "failure" who often get ignored or overlooked because those persons "haven't arrived" or some such foolishness. Everybody wants a ready-made, fully fleshed out person, but few are willing to take the ride with someone to help them to achieve that success. I'm not talkim'bout choosing Pookie 'N'em who keep living like they're on "Good Times," saying, "one day we g'wan make it," yet who aren't doing ANY work to get to the promised land.

For many, many reasons, sometimes people are not at their goal destinations when we meet them. But if you pay attention, you can see their forward momentum happening. You can see their passion, their vision, their work. And even in their perceived incompleteness, if you have any amount of discernment, you can still see and understand the intrinsic value they could add to your life; how they could enhance your life experiences. How they could also help grow and support you on your own journey. How they would likely treat you. How they would sacrifice for you. How they would possibly love you.

But if you judge someone from your limited perspective by how they look walking down the street while struggling to carry a heavy load and looking a bit raggedy, and you simply deem them as unworthy and dismiss them, but then you turn around to look again and watch them take that heavy load and get into a Lamborghini at the end of the block, then you have missed out, because instead of helping them, you made a judgement about who they are by how you perceived them in the process of their journey.

You often hear people say that they want to be with someone who is open, who is honest and who communicates. They say they want to be with someone who is vulnerable and truthful; spiritually emotionally, mentally—and even physically. But what I find is that many (most) people don't really want that. And most are not ready for those truths. What most people actually want is convenient truth. Or they want another person's truth to automatically match up with theirs without any effort or communication between the parties involved.

Personal Truths are based on personal experiences, perspectives, and the acceptance of the realities of their current places and spaces. We claim to want truth, but many of us end up either downplaying, dismissing, or outright rejecting other people's truths. Or we will try to force our Personal Truths upon others without understanding the consequences of the interaction of our Personal Truths with those of others. We simply assume that our truths are the correct truths.

But if you don't know how to listen, learn, understand, compromise, and coalesce your truth with someone else who you want to be close to or involved with—hopefully someone who is already not far off base from where you are/want to be—if your truth brings with it immutable prejudgment; if you don't know how to compromise and work towards universal truths you both can intersect at and work together with; if your heart is hardened, your mind made up, and your Personal Truth is infallible and unmovable in your own mind, then you will never find happiness. You will always be at war.

And you will always be alone, even if you're "with" someone.

The point is this: find someone. Or allow them to find YOU. Fall in Love. Stay in Love. WORK AT LOVE. Don't abandon Real Love when you are Blessed to find it. Because I'm sad to say, it may not come back around.

But also, don't stay where your Love is not valued, not appreciated. Don't stay where your Love is abused or taken for granted. Pray about the possibility of having to take a new journey with a new route; but don't just contemplate that new destination simply because the resort you originally booked your stay at didn't put an ice bucket in your room. Leave that unappreciated pit stop in your journey, not because someone lit a match to light a candle that you may not like the smell of, but leave that room you are staying in because it is burning out of control and on course to become what Prince so eloquently dubbed a "Violent Room." And if you do have to leave because that Violent Room is truly burning to the ground and threatening to engulf you and everything about you in flames, then go. Free your mind. Set your course. And knock the dust from your feet.

Love each other in truth, in passion, and in human imperfection. Love hard, love smart, and "love" long and prosper.

FAMILIA

Families are like damn miniature cults.

Think about it; we're indoctrinated in the pervasive culture of our families from birth. We believe in, up to a certain age, just about everything that they tell us we should believe in. We technically cannot escape until we turn seventeen, with the rare exception of a child filing for and winning emancipation from their parents. And when we do leave, we take our indoctrination with us, and we infect our own relationships with it.

We often force our beliefs, ways, and thoughts upon our own offspring. In more extreme cases, we circle imaginary wagons around those doctrines, practices, and other family members, even when we have invited new people into our lives, whether via marriage, friendships, etc. We judge others according to the dogma we've been taught; we measure people's worth by it. And very often, we listen to the words of family, even when those words are meritless, irrational, or needlessly detrimental to the people that we ourselves are attempting to create and nurture a new family with.

This question really pertains more to marriages, but in a few cases, it could also apply to a serious long-term relationship. Have you ever felt like you were marrying your spouse's family instead of the person? I'm not talking about the general vibe of that person via their upbringing, and the typical interactions we all have with the families of people we grow close to or become involved with.

I'm talking to a degree where it feels as if that person doesn't really seem to have their own opinions about many things, or where it feels as though you are constantly being judged against the prevailing family culture, hierarchy, or "status." Or maybe you feel like you have just joined a secret society without your consent. And yet you never quite feel like you are truly on the inside of that society or that you have a true one-on-one relationship with just that person you're married to or involved with.

I've been there. It's weird AF.

WE OWE THEM EVERYTHING

For those of us who are currently or have ever been caregivers for our parents, elders, and family members, this new chapter in our lives can be extremely challenging. Add to it the now constant threat of COVID-19, and the due diligence that has to be taken beyond even the normal levels of caution we ALL need to be taking right now; the lack of viable options for getting those loved ones in and out of the house safely, to at least allow them the pleasure of something other than the four walls around them, and it not only makes things that much more trying for us.

But, as challenging as this pandemic has been for us as the caregivers, just imagine that you are a person who has worked hard your whole life. You have sacrificed, saved, lost, and allowed others to have that which you didn't really have to give, planned, and looked forward to enjoying the time of your life when you should be able to reap the rewards of the work that you put in your whole adult life.

And now, here you are in those August years...and not only are you, out of necessity, having to isolate yourself mostly at home, but you also cannot see those who have been nearest and dearest to you throughout your life.

I'm saying all this to say, if you aren't living with those loved ones who are elderly, and even if you ARE...PLEASE...

Check in on them.

And I'm not simply speaking of checking on their physical well-being. Like many of us, this whole space in time can bring about mild to severe depression and anxiety. Most who are now elderly come from a generation that will NOT reach out to tell us how they are coping...how they are feeling. They likely won't ever broach the subject matter of themselves and their emotions because they are not used to doing so. THEY are the ones who have been pillars of strength and fortitude through so many changes in society, in health, in technology, and in the ways of the world—period.

There's been much conversation about the youth who are experiencing being robbed of those milestones and events we have all cherished in our lives by this pandemic; proms, graduations, college, relationships, first jobs, hanging with friends, and doing stupid stuff. And those are indeed tragic circumstances in the fact that many in this generation will not get the opportunities to experience those things as they should be experienced...in their true and proper fullness.

But not a lot has been said about the quality of life during the pandemic for the elderly beyond their physical health and safety. When suddenly the joy of your "golden years" is being carved hollow because you cannot freely enjoy the things, places, and people you planned to enjoy...think about how that must make many of them feel.

I know this read in and of itself may be depressing to some. But I feel like in our day-to-day efforts to find our own footings in this new—and hopefully temporary—reality, we may forget that our seniors need more than just our physical and emotional support. They need our mental support, which ties the other two things together. Try to see if they are waiting for you to ask them...I mean REALLY ask them...how they are doing. Ask them questions and genuinely engage them. What do they think about all that is going on? What might they not understand about it? Are they fearful about any of it? Sad? Depressed? Angry? Don't force them to talk about it. But find a gentle way to bring up the subject...maybe by talking about how it all makes YOU feel; tell them about your own challenges and responses to it all. Add some humor into the mix as you speak about it so that the focus doesn't totally shift to you. Bring up some fond memories and make comparisons about their memories with today's circumstances.

They may share. They may not. But at least they will know that they can. They will know that someone cares about what THEY FEEL. What they fear. And that even beyond being a loved one and a caretaker, that you are a trusted friend and confidant in these uncertain times. Because they are not just Ma'dear. They are not just Paw Paw. Big Momma. Granny. Grandaddy. Uncle. Auntie. Sir. They are whole grown people. Who have hopes and dreams and fears and wishes. In many instances, they are not the same person they've always been to you. Even more so right now in the face of STILL dealing with the fallout from the COVID-19 pandemic. Many feel that their strength... their independence...has been stolen from them.

And so we will need to be patient with them. Be VERY patient. Be kind. Be thoughtful. Be respectful. And if we do all those things...they will really, truly know that they are not only loved, not only respected, but that they are cherished and valuable to you.

THE BIG PAYBACK (CONFESSIONS OF A STRUGGLING CAREGIVER)

Even though I began this book-writing journey almost two years ago, recent life events have made it very important for me to dedicate a space within its ever burgeoning pages to speak about a NOW moment I am living through. Because this new and current chapter in the figurative book of my life could quite possibly be one my life's most defining ones. And likely, the most exigent and existential life experience I may ever go through. Now, I already know and understand that someday in the future, this LITERAL chapter will possibly be a very painful one for me to look back at. Because it will be a tangible, unblinking, reminder of the pain and heartbreak of going through this FIGURATIVE chapter of my personal journey.

As I am writing these words—my beautiful, kind, loving, long-suffering, strong, God-fearing mother is suffering from what the doctors have labeled as "moderate major neurocognitive disorder due to Alzheimer's disease without behavioral disturbance dementia." That's a mouthful of medical speak. But no matter what name it is called by, the curse of Alzheimer's and dementia is a cruel one. And it is frightening. And it is so very hard, and so very unfair. It's this way by default for the person suffering from the disease, of course. And, as a twofer, it is a life altering booby prize for the eventual caregiver(s)—in this instance, me and my brother.

There are many aspects of caring for a loved one with Alzheimer's and/or dementia which are mentally, physically, and emotionally stressful. And those challenges are as varied from person to person as they are unpredictable. If your family has been Blessed enough to have missed being visited upon by this plague, then please—just take a moment one day to talk to someone you know who has not been as fortunate. Because even if they are presenting as okay—they're likely not. At all.

In the case of my Momma, there have so far been a few standout challenges which have gotten to me the most. The first is her obsessive-compulsive late-night rearranging of things: either objects in either her nightstand, her closet, or in the bathroom. I sometimes can only watch as she moves the exact same things out of their previously organized spaces and then attempts to put them back into the very same space but in a different, less organized manner. And if I don't find a way to stop or distract her, she will do this over and over for hours on end, and into the wee hours of the morning. And make no mistake—she's often very difficult to stop. Attempting to do so almost always ends in a fight. My very unscientific theory is that this behavior is part of the process of her mind trying to reorder itself, but getting stuck in a loop.

The second-most devastating of the new behaviors dementia has driven Momma to exhibit are the broken, circular, and pretzel logic thoughts and conversations. You end up interacting as best you can with a person who has, for your entire life, been alert, witty, and humorous, but whom you now suddenly find yourself struggling to understand. This one is so difficult because as both their child and their caregiver, you must slowly and purposefully learn to let go of your naturally preconceived emotional expectation of talking to the same person you have known and loved your entire life. And you must now force yourself to constantly shift your perspective in order to connect and interact with each new personality which may present itself from day to day—sometimes even several times within the same day. The hardest part is tricking your own brain and heart and emotions into a perpetual state of acceptance that this person whom you love is not purposefully trying to frustrate you by masquerading as a stranger. And you must make yourself accept the new reality that when you're looking into the eyes of that person whom you still recognize corporeally, it may not completely be them who is looking back at you.

And yet another symptom of this ravager of life is the most recent I've experienced: it's when they don't recognize YOU anymore. Just the other day, this one manifested itself out of the blue in the form of Momma suddenly asking during dinner where my brother was—while she was sitting directly across the table from him. Even after he answered her, Momma still did not immediately look at him or seem to recognize him when she did. It was chilling to behold. And it was soul-crushing. THAT possibility of my mother, my first love, not knowing who I am anymore, not recognizing the faces of her children and her family—for me, that is the definition of a living hell on earth.

❖ ❖ ❖

The emotionally brutal preamble to my mom's advancing dementia, and the subsequent task of our family having to deal with the very daunting challenges of this horrid disease, was seemingly laid out with expert skill and timing by the universe or karma or even God Himself, heaven forbid. This, in the form of an all-encompassing, life changing "perfect storm."

First came mom's first stroke. Then, eight months later, her second stroke. One month later came my surprise marriage separation. Then bam—six months after the separation, my unexpected and unwanted divorce from a twelve-year marriage and along with it the ensuing emotional heartache and mourning brought on by sudden and traumatic loss.

And of course, six months later came the seemingly extinction-level, "not seen on this scale in 100 years," world-shutting-down pandemic. Followed by the obligatory year and a half lockdown, which not only prohibited my getting mom out of the house post-stroke—both for her (and everybody's) mental and emotional health and healing—but which also severely restricted us from acquiring the necessary medical and psychological help mom would have greatly benefitted from. Not to mention the accompanying financial challenges of limited employment when the bulk of your entrepreneurial career isn't centered around a work from home type of business. Next up, almost two years after mom's initial stroke—surprise, surprise—kidney cancer for me and the subsequent surgery, recovery, tests, and treatments required to remove and manage it.

Hellalot.

A LOT of people were dealing with "hellalot."

Yet here's the irony, spiritual hindsight, and the divine order of it all: if I had still been married, would I have been as able and available to help my brother take care of my mother the way she needed to be cared for after two strokes? Would I have been in the mindset of self-care and self-renewal which stemmed from the ordeal of my divorce to go for a routine physical exam—where doctors just so HAPPENED to discover the four-centimeter growth on my right kidney? And, most importantly, would I have had the newly fire-forged emotional fortitude and perseverance to deal with the seemingly insurmountable challenges of both caring for and experiencing the trauma of a parent slowly leaving me in a way that is emotionally cruel, physically demanding, and psychologically debilitating?

In clear-eyed spiritual, rational, and even logical retrospect, I don't think so. I really don't think so.

That said, I have come to believe with all my heart and soul that I am EXACTLY where I'm supposed to be, regardless of how painful this place can be. I have been "put back together" even while that perfect storm still rages around me—by the Potter—to be stronger and wiser than ever. Through my faith in God, I believe that I was rebuilt/renewed specifically for this moment. Because that is what my mother and, to a lesser degree, my brother both require of me.

Besides the aforementioned symptoms and challenges, Momma still seems to retain some of the long-term memories of her life, albeit not always very accurately. But she forgets other things daily: whether she has had the breakfast we ate only a half-hour after leaving the table. At ninety-three years young, her body is betraying her mobility and ability to do things and go places because of a concurrent battle she is fighting with arthritis. In spite of these challenges right now, she is, thank God, still mostly Momma, because she still has these three very specific things that are very prevalent in her mind almost daily:

- Making sure her money doesn't get cut off by the government (it won't)
- Making sure her bills are paid (they are)
- Going to church (we try)

Sadly, these are also the three things that most often cause us to get into altercations. Because Momma is still fighting to retain her sense of control and independence. I probably would, too. But also because each one of the things she asks me or my brother to help her with she fights with us about when we try to help her. Mentally she's in a place where—even when we are very careful to answer her questions patiently, thoughtfully, and intentionally or to physically demonstrate the answers or try to help her get ready to go where she says she really wants to go—she fights us. She hears our words, but she doesn't understand that we're telling her exactly what she asked about or wants to know. So she gets angry and says she has no one to help her and that she's going to get someone else outside to help her. Who that is varies; sometimes it's the bank people. Sometimes it's a doctor. Sometimes it's a nameless stranger. She out of nowhere accuses us of raising our voices at her when we are most certainly not. Or that we're telling her that she's wrong when no such statement was uttered. Typically, either will happen when she doesn't like our answers to her questions.

But the truth is, she's not really angry at us. She's angry at herself. She's angry at her mind, and at her body for betraying her. She's still self-aware enough to know that something is terribly wrong; but not aware enough to follow a logical line of thinking.

She's angry. And she's afraid. And who wouldn't be? I can't even imagine it for myself.

And watching my mother suffer in ANY way as she slowly loses herself is the most painful thing I've ever experienced in my life. Even more painful than watching her endure the grief of losing my older brother to gun violence more than twenty-five years ago. And it breaks my heart each and every day.

And more often than not—I feel totally helpless.

❖ ❖ ❖

Because the job/privilege of caring for our Parent-Children includes things like:
- Getting them in the bathtub
- Cleaning and feeding them
- Getting them to their much-needed doctor appointments
- Getting them to events and to people that they say they want to get to—and which are people and places you KNOW will help with their mental and emotional wellbeing—but still having them fight you tooth and nail along the way to helping them to get there
- Even something as simple as convincing them to come to the meal table at home and to eat...

Any ONE of these tasks, and many others, can be daunting mentally, emotionally, and/or physically draining, as well as quite time consuming. They can be (are) full of triggers, moments of losing your ish, and hours of exhausting behavior, explanations, and questions.

I reiterate once again: it. Is. So. Very. Hard.

But love conquers all, along with covering a multitude of sins. Sins of unintentional disrespect via words spoken out of frustration or anger. Thoughts that should never enter or have extended residence in our minds. And feelings that should never attach themselves to our hearts.

So if you are a Caregiver, also give yourself some grace. Pray for God's Grace, His Mercy, and His forgiveness.

Think about the many possible times when, as we were babies, our parents may have had moments of anger or frustration with their situations of parenthood with us. They didn't all have loving spouses, fawning grandparents, responsible significant other co-parents, and supportive family members or well-paying jobs.

Or think about the love and sacrifices of our grandparents. Or our siblings. Or our uncles and aunts. Or whomever your Elderly Dependent happens to be to you. Many of them gave us so much—including the lives we currently exist in. And the character that gives us the strength and the courage to be here, now—giving back to them out of love, respect, and, yes, obligation.

Again—if you are a caregiver, also give yourself some grace. Pray for God's Grace, His Mercy, and His forgiveness.

And keep it moving forward as if your life depends on it. Because in a way—it does. Yes, their lives most certainly do depend on our perseverance and commitment to their well-being and our unconditional love. But OUR lives—the quality and purpose and meaning behind them—most CERTAINLY depend on our decisions to move forward with doing everything in our power to protect those we are charged to care for. With perseverance. With selfless dedication. And most of all—with LOVE.

❖ ❖ ❖

People in my age category (tail end Baby Boomers/Gen X-ers) are more or less the first within the Diaspora that TECHNICALLY has access to the finances, life experiences, education, and advancements in medicine and to properly take care of our aging and ailing parents and loved ones.

But guess what? Even with availability and access at hand—ACTUAL ingress to make use of those resources is tepid at best, a complete illusion at worst. Because of the fact that this nation cares nothing for its elderly and their health/financial challenges. Even more so for those who are minorities. And the nation doesn't care, not just because of either melanin count or age. But mostly because there is no financial profit in taking care of the elderly. Or so they have convinced themselves.

This Un-Commonwealth—these UnTied States™—is all about capitalism, power, and profit. End of story. With all the scientific, medical, and financial resources available to one of the richest nations on earth, they put very little of those resources into taking care of those who spent their entire lives working hard, raising families, profiting corporate and blue-collar America, and helping build a nation, and who now, in many cases, can no longer take care of themselves. This national "disposable people" mentality also extends toward children; the mentally challenged; the homeless; minorities; and even those who have fought for and sacrificed, in some cases EVERYTHING, for their country—its veterans. If the powers that be did care, there would be a solid and viable middle ground between crappy government-run nursing homes and facilities and the 10k/month plush spa-like mental care communities of the rich or those who have no choice but to drain their life's savings in order to be there.

    I mean, listen—they want you to be destitute, lying in a hole, with you neck stuck underneath the poverty line while also choking on it before they will offer any substantive financial assistance. Social Security, you say? Sadly, these days, it's almost a joke and in danger of being murdered. It's a pot built upon the backs of that selfsame elderly populace in need of a well-deserved high quality of life that for years has been stolen from many times over, in order to help make the rich richer. And that help from Social Security is typically barely enough to allow you the ability to even peek over that poverty line. The fact is that there is nothing substantive out there to help us;

no Universal Healthcare or Universal income. You know—like in those other civilized first world nations. It's insane. There should be a very specific type of insurance available for people to put in place when they are younger along with everything else we are told to save/prepare for.

But the difference is that while there's lots of dialogue and info about planning for things like college, child birth, home buying, retirement, illness, and even death (all corporate and academia-profiting life events)—there is very little proactive talk about this in-between space in our twilight years that could include Alzheimer's or dementia or some other debilitating ailment. Nobody really educates or informs us, the eventual default caregivers, about how cripplingly expensive proper care actually is for those who suffer from dementia and Alzheimer's. And the folks you know should be educating us and speaking out on this matter—the doctors, pastors, sometimes family and friends—they aren't really doing it en masse either. And because of that miseducation, we the caregivers and our elderly charges pretty much end up blindsided if or when dementia strikes our families. Because we were never actively made aware of the facts, the stats, the causes, and the odds of those diseases occurring to our family members. Or to US. Again, this is especially true over here in the Black Diaspora. We purposefully haven't been educated like many people outside of the Diaspora have; things such as researching options for care and assistance before the actual time of need comes, putting comprehensive estate plans in place, or having preemptive testing done in order to identify genetic markers for the possibility of getting Alzheimer's as we age.

Nah. Instead, we get NOTHING but heartache and impossible debt. And so here we are. Many of us struggling and stressing. Allowing the trauma to make us as ill as those we are caring for. And in many instances, it may be too late to help those who most needed the help and support of getting through the aging/caregiving process. But, my People. Please. Let's have those uncomfortable conversations with OUR children and loved ones. Let's save and prepare as best we can for more than a cushy retirement. Let's put our own affairs in order and give those who will be charged with carrying out our wishes thoughtful, clear, and concise instructions about how to do so. Draw them a detailed roadmap of the realities of aging and caregiving. Let them know exactly what they could be up against medically, mentally, physically, financially, and emotionally. Let's just do better in preparing those who are coming after us; those who will become the caregivers OF us, for the possibly daunting, and often overwhelming responsibilities of doing so.

Let's make it a little easier for them by properly preparing them for the uncomfortable truths of the circle of life.

Six

BACK ON THE BLOCK: THE DATING GAME
IN SEARCH OF FRESH HEARTACHE IN THE TIME OF COVID-19

    I have been part of quite a few dialogues about relationships these past few years with Social Media friends, as well as some one-on-one private conversations with both men and women about the challenges of dating during these Covidian times, about dating when you are of a certain age, and about the weird dynamics of suddenly finding yourself in that space. And I've read much lamentation of the oft-disappointing state of the current dating pool in general. I've even joked in a post of my own about the possibility of dating these days only seems to lead to my having more future ex-wives.

    And while participating in and writing those conversations, posts, and podcasts has been fun, often quite informative, and even somewhat amusing, something struck me as I typed that post about my imaginary future ex-wives.

It is a very odd and sometimes difficult space to be in when you're freshly post-divorce, or after any long-lived and meaningful relationship has ended, when you have faithfully given your romantic, sensual, and sexual attention to a singular woman (I can truly only speak authoritatively from a man's perspective). It is honestly a little disconcerting to even think about having a full-fledged mind-body-soul attraction to someone else, even though attraction to other women besides your spouse never goes away; it simply gets compartmentalized and stored away in its own little mental room. You may peek in that room from time to time; you may even from time to time threaten to walk into that room and stay a while. But when all is right with the world of your love, you're never even tempted to walk through that door. You may even forget it's there.

And when you are truly in love, the fleeting lust for anyone else besides your heart focus that may pop up doesn't even matter. Because Real Love wins out over pheromones, a woman you may see who is bodied up and your type, unsolicited flirtations and temptations, or any other situations where a physical...even emotional...attraction may present itself.

Finding your footing as a single man after twelve years of not being single...is a bit daunting. And dammit, it would happen to be during a doggone pandemic of Biblical proportions. You KNOW you want to love again. You KNOW you aren't afraid of giving your heart to someone again, per se. And, of course, the level of comfort with dating again always depends on the circumstances of each individual's prior relationship demise and how they handle it. But I'm telling you...this is a weird space, made all the weirder by the tumult the world is experiencing right now biologically, politically, financially, and socially. These are hard waters to navigate.

My job is to make sure I've done everything I can to be my best self for that next great love if it is meant to be. Because there is NO perfect moment for falling in love. There is no "now I'm ready" when it comes to love. There is really no "I've got it all together" finish line. If this pandemic should have taught us anything, it's how fragile and precariously balanced the world is; it should have shown us how unpredictable and fleeting life can be, no matter how prepared you think you are. We should be coming away from this with a better understanding of how we need to value people and relationships over things. As a matter of fact, in my humble opinion, the TRUEST, purest, strongest love between a man and a woman manifests when someone can meet you exactly where you are in that moment...in your imperfection and unpreparedness...and still SEE YOU and say, "you were meant for me".

And then MEAN IT.

A FULL-GROWN WOMAN

I don't know if this is true for other Brothers, but for me, there has ALWAYS been a certain type of Sista who presents as an entire FULL-GROWN WOMAN. It's as if they are directly connected to the Earth—grounded, while also in touch with Heaven—possessing an awareness and a connection to things beyond the immediate and the material.

My famous grown woman crushes who have presented as if they embodied this vibe include Phylicia Rashad; from the very first time I saw her on *Cosby* I was like, "forget dem young gurls...who is SHE?" CeCe Winans. Lalah Hathaway. Simone Missick from the television series *All Rise and Luke Cage*. Rosario Dawson. There's a whole list, lol...but it's not that long. Now, these women may not actually be who they present as to us, their adoring fans. But from what I can see, the F.G.W. Force is strong within them.

When I was younger, I often dated older women because of that type of presentation. But it really had less to do with age or station in life or possessions or achievements. It has always had much more to do with that woman's SPIRIT: her character and how she carries herself. And how she views and treats others. It's a woman with a grounded and well-rounded spirit, confident enough in who she is that she doesn't have to validate herself at the expense of anyone else. Which allows her to be more accepting of who YOU are. It's a woman who finds the character of a man attractive, and not simply his looks, his possessions, or his titles. It's a woman who becomes a true friend, a ride-or-die, and both a partner and a helpmeet in the truest sense of the word. A woman who has her own mind, her own heart, her own life, and who loves passionately beyond circumstance or situation.

And I honestly have to say, I think those type of Sistas are in danger of becoming as rare as unicorns. Sure, I know a few. And they may or may not know that I notice them, because I SEE them—whether they see me or not. And that's kewl with me because the space I'm in is the place where I begin.

But the fact is that, sadly, I know more Sistas who are not that type of woman. The phrase "Strong Black Woman" has been usurped and made into a catchphrase. I say that because guess what? I never heard my mother, her mother, or anyone from those generations call themselves that. And the latest designation uttered by some women calling themselves "Alpha Females" has fast overtaken "Strong Black Woman" as the catchphrase du jour. What THEE hell is an Alpha Female (or an Alpha Male for that matter)? A woman having too much testosterone? A woman having a lack of feminine graces?

Ladies, here's a friendly tip from a decent Brother: stop trying to prove who you believe you are by giving yourself meaningless titles and hangtags. Successful female leaders and go-getters simply lead and go get it; they do not have to announce their comings and goings, act hard, compare themselves to men, or any such thing. True playmakers—both male and female—know how to move in silence, or at least in stealth. Sure—certain types of insecure men will always challenge you when you walk into "their" spaces with confidence and conviction because they feel threatened. So there are going to be those times when you're gonna have to flex and even fight. Because we have yet to reach an equitable and fair society when it comes to the genders.

But none of that means that you must become a woman who needs to be "handled." My good friend and fellow bassist Will Howard says this all the time, and I paraphrase: "Only bombs and situations should need to be handled. People shouldn't want to be handled." Yet that is seemingly what many of my Sistas out here in the Dating Game believe—if a man cannot handle her, then he is a weak man who is not worthy of her attention. But listen—if drama is your mama, me and most other good men don't want any parts of you anyway. Life IS drama—there is enough on tap of its own making to go around for a lifetime. My advice? Go handle yourself. You want to impress me—walk into my space with your ish handled, your mind regulated, your heart healed, and your spirit on lock. Be the best you at no one else's expense. THAT is how you connect with a "good man."

But back to our female ancestors who were true Strong Black Women; boy, were they ever all of that—and so much more! For those women to still have been able to stand strong and even thrive—THEY were indeed the epitome of what it truly means to be Strong Black Women. After all the things that most of them had to endure and survive, more often than not as single women and single parents...that type of strength of mind, body, spirit, and character does not have to be advertised. Because real strength speaks for itself. And again, it doesn't come at the expense of anyone else.

And those...those are the type of Sistas that I admire and respect...and yes...find mightily attractive. They are the ones who have that Full Grown Woman Vibe. And that vibe will always show up before she even says hello. It is amazing to me how some women's beauty will just strike me like lightning when I first see them. It's not always because of physical attractiveness or sexual lust, but it is because of the beauty of their inner being that is manifested in their physicality. Their eyes, their smiles, their aura, and their grace with which they carry themselves will grab ahold of my eyes and my spirit and simply not let go.

These type of women...they aren't always women who are in any way available to me. Most have seemingly been already discovered and are being loved by some fortunate man. Yet and still...they move me. Because their spirit says, "This is who I am, and this is what I have to offer you."

THE UNOFFICIAL "CHECKLIST" FOR THE "IDEAL WOMAN"

One of the most prominent points of contention between the sexes has been the proliferation of "The List": a collection of check boxes, qualities, and qualifications for determining the value of a person. A collection of specific ingredients compiled to help rate whether a person is worthy of being considered as either dating material, marrying material, or just plain old material to be used and discarded. And let's be very honest here: these lists have tended to come mainly from the female gender.

It's true, though.

I don't know if popularity of these lists were birthed from the onslaught of dating apps and services. If the quality of a person has been distilled down to possessions and eye color? Or if these lists simply are and always have been a part of the female psyche when it comes to how men are viewed by women in general as a consumer product. I mean, we all like what we like, right? But these lists go beyond preferred physical traits or ideal characteristics. These are hardline, a la carte human shopping lists that are often all-or-nothing affairs. Fall short in one area? Chopped! Making five figures but just below six? Get ta steppin', bruh! Can't pay for her nails AND hair every two weeks? Done, son! Six foot three instead of six foot five? YOU are the biggest loser, my Brother!

But the whole trend made me wonder: what would a thought-out list of desired traits in a woman look like from a man? Men looking for Full Grown Women don't typically make hard and fast lists to classify the traits or the type of woman he's attracted to—at least not consciously. And that may be both good and bad.

After thinking about it for a minute, this is what my ideal wifey candidate would look like. Keep in mind that lists, by their very nature, invite unrealistic expectations, because NOBODY is perfect. But for me, it's more about the core values and traits than the actual execution of them. You must at least have the CAPACITY for possessing and exercising these traits.

Let the backlash ensue!

The Ideal Woman:
- In true spiritual covenant with God
- Honest with self and with others
- Self-aware and self-evaluating
- A lover of life
- Growth-oriented
- Possesses willingness and ability to take ownership
- Open and communicative, always in a timely manner
- Trustworthy
- Healthy, often silly sense of humor
- Makes a conscious effort to stay mentally, physically, and spiritually healthy
- Believes in the wisdom of never going to bed angry
- Confident, but not arrogant
- Ambitious at no one else's expense
- Intelligent
- Unafraid to be vulnerable
- Supportive

* Nurturing
* Possesses individuality and her own interests
* Generous
* Empathetic
* Kind
* Respectful
* Has an active lean towards organization
* Has the ability to improvise and flow
* An understanding of both the detailed and the big-picture view
* An understanding of the real-world ebb and flow of love
* A non-judgmental spirit led by the desire to first gain understanding
* Open minded and adventurous with a willingness to try new things
* A desire to grow by continually seeking knowledge, wisdom, and understanding
* A desire to truly HEAR and understand the challenges of the Black Man
* Not hung up on "roles," hierarchies, and stereotypes, while still respecting the importance of some traditions
* Beautiful to my spirit, my eyes, and my mind

So, the question we must ask ourselves is:

Is the prevailing mindset that we, as men and women, must EARN one another? Is the only avenue towards finding a relationship, meaningful for its own sake, is how much effort we put into "the catch"? How great of a show we put on up front? How shiny that shoe is on that best foot that we are supposed to put forward when we date and relate? Is it all about the razzle-dazzle and the material trappings that go along with it?

Or...does the actual level and quality of the spiritual interpersonal connectivity still hold ANY value?

❖ ❖ ❖

The bottom line is that I truly love, respect, and value all women. And specifically, women of the Black Diaspora, who deal with and give us so very much and often get so very little in return. My only intent in my conversations about women and relationships from the point of view of the male gaze is to offer an honest male perspective via lived experiences. Not to define. Not to chastise or judge. Not to offend or enrage. Not to hurt. Only to offer a different viewpoint, however flawed it may seem to some. My conversations are never about being right or wrong for me. Because—what does that even mean? Depending on the overall context, such as varying cultures, differing class and socioeconomic levels, religious beliefs, or even down to the individual culture of a specific family or household—it can all be quite subjective. I'm not nearly arrogant or unaware enough to believe that I have all, if any, of the answers. And that minuscule snippet of people on this plane of existence that I am privileged to meet, know, and sometimes have intimate relationships with...I would hope that they would know that about me. I would hope that their firsthand knowledge of me would inform how we interact. Not as a pass. But as a buffer and a willingness to listen and to ask ME questions if something I say or do is off-putting. But as I have learned, using the wrong words or incomplete context is an anathema to intent, no matter how altruistic that intent is.

You know: the road to hell and all that.

Not one of us has all the right answers all the time. There are gaps in our understanding that can never be completely filled in, because each person is unique unto themselves. Each gender (NOT promoting a discussion about defining genders here....PLEASE LORD NO!) has its own set of circumstances and challenges. Sure, there are many overlapping human experiences. But who we are as individuals; who we identify ourselves to be as humans, our characters and the environments we have grown from and continue to exist within, and, will customize the hell out of how we each respond to life. We are educated and informed by our own lived experiences and by the experiences of those around us. We gain information from the world outside of our personal bubbles, and we attempt to fit it into the context of our daily living. We devour and digest what seems relevant to our lives, file away for future reference and consumption what is peripherally interesting, and we discard what is deemed to be of low or no value to us.

At the end of the day, I just want us to all be alright. A challenge for sure, and maybe even an impossibility. But to me it still holds as an obtainable aspiration. It would be lovely if, as much as humanly possible, we could all be alright together.

BUT—QWHAT IS LOVE ANYWAY?

People keep fooling themselves.

They keep believing that living a good life is about the acquisition of things. The false sense of security that wealth brings. The idea that if you have less than—or if you don't fulfill a specific ideology about your "role" in life—then you have not lived a good life. You have not "achieved." You are less.

Yes…we should always strive to be the best versions of ourselves. We should always work towards gaining knowledge and wisdom. We should make it our purpose to take care of ourselves and those we love. We should seek to create a legacy that will benefit those who follow behind us. All of these are good and noble goals for anyone to pursue and to achieve.

But at the end of the day, tell me: who truly loves you? Who do you love? Who will give you their everything to bring you happiness? Who will accept your everything, even when it may not be quite enough—accept it because it is you who are giving it? Who will sacrifice their safety in order to keep you safe? Who will share the quiet, important moments with you—both the joyful and the painful? Who will celebrate the loud and maybe not as important moments with you—both serious and silly? Who will keep your secrets and trust you with theirs? Who will accept your truths without questioning the validity of those truths to your very being? Who will face adversity with you, head on, without blinking an eye? Who will speak uncomfortable truths to you without rendering judgement, without abandonment or rebuff? Who will lovingly correct you when you stray off course? Who will give you both honesty and accolades?

Who will push you to succeed without counting your failures? Who will always respect you? Who will speak on your behalf when you cannot...or will not? Who will take care of you when you cannot take care of yourself? Who will "get" you; who will truly see you? Who will accept your faults and your shortcomings...your idiosyncrasies and your "problem areas"? Who will take on your everything...even if you sometimes have nothing? Who will love you as close to unconditionally as we flawed humans can ever love? Who will lovingly impart their wisdom...their perspective...their patience to you? Who will honor covenants of commitment instead of contracts of convenience? Who will share with you? Who will listen to you with their heart instead of simply hearing you with their ears?

Seek out those persons. Find them...surround yourself with them...and hold tight to them. Their numbers won't be great. If you blink, you may miss them. If you drop the ball, you may lose them. Because they are rare and precious jewels. They are to be treasured and not taken for granted. Sometimes they have to be nurtured. Sometimes they come whole and complete. But rest assured...they are indispensable in the pursuit of truly, truly living a good life.

SELF-MAINTENANCE CHECK

Even though television shows like ABC's *Modern Family*, the Netflix series *Orange Is the New Black*, *Easy*, and *Dear White People*, HBO's horror-based *Lovecraft Country*, Showtime's *The L Word*, and more recently, *Interview with the Vampire* have pushed beyond the boundaries of my own personal "relationship traditionalism," they did provide some interesting insight about how people in relationships think, feel, and interact with one another in specific circumstances. It also revealed how sometimes our lack of insight, self-awareness, and honesty... first with ourselves, and second with one another...affects the course and outcomes of our relationships.

If nothing else, these very strange and trying times we are living through—the lack, the loss, the shifting of awareness about who and what has real value and who and what doesn't— should give us enough of a pause in living the "necessary" lives we have led as adults and allow for time to dig deeper into who we really and truly are. This pause...this Shift should allow us to truly see how we affect those close to us and help us to better understand the realities of our responsibilities to ourselves and to those whom we profess to love.

Love...Real Love...is actually a very simple thing, yet at the same time, it happens to have quite a few moving parts. And that is before you even add in the external influences and distractions. It's like our bodies, or like an automobile; what it does and should do is pretty straight forward. But there are many parts that come together as a whole to make it work correctly. And each of those parts must be cared for, maintained, and serviced individually in order for the whole be healthy.

But just like our bodies, sometimes we expect things to maintain without doing anything that aids in that maintenance. Or sometimes we do the wrong things. Sometimes we forget that things shift and change simply through growth, through use or disuse, and through age. But we aren't often willing to do what it takes to keep things running smoothly or to at least put things back on the right track when...not if...when they derail or break down.

When people in relationships first and foremost truly value the relationship and the person whom they are in relationship with, then they can more easily be honest with themselves and each other with no fear. And that, in turn, allows for honest and insightful maintenance through communication, consideration, understanding, awareness, and actions. Often people are insecure in self or simply emotionally lazy; thus, the relationship will likely end out of fear or selfish lack of desire to do the work.

And yeah...sometimes things just change beyond the point of repair. Because we are all distracted. Ofttimes bamboozled by Shiny Objects and ignorant tongues about what is truly important. By life in general. But that type of drastic change doesn't happen suddenly or without reason (unless you simply one day lose your damn mind and weren't all that stable to begin with). But if we do the real work and if we are honest with ourselves—if we do scheduled maintenance without pointing fingers at others for the faults in our stars and without preconceived notions of how things should proceed...then often we can fix, adjust, and properly feed our relationships when they become out of whack or even broken. Because... why would you invest any significant amount of time and effort into something that you don't plan to keep? That type of investment should mean that it's something which has great value to you.

Otherwise, you lied to yourself, and to the other(s); you were never really into it in the first place. And that is truly a sad thing, and it reveals more about you than it does about the relationship.

DAMN—CAN WE SIMPLY BE?

One final thought on love and relationships...

I recently got triggered by a good friend's FB thread (not his fault at all...lol) about Black Men and our constant battle to be heard and seen, specifically by Black Women, as active, emotional, loving partners in our relationships. It was a topic that sadly doesn't get discussed very often because it is usually ignored by those who need to hear/see it the most: Black Women. And this is what poured into me and then out of me from that post:

> "It's like:
>
> Can we just survive this ish together?
>
> Can we make it as simple as it actually is while understanding the complexities of our hearts? I'm attracted to you; you're attracted to me. We are two imperfect people who have found beauty of body, mind, and spirit in each other.
>
> Can we acknowledge that we are both flawed individuals coming together to create a beautifully flawed relationship? Understand that love changes its stripes during the course of the relationship; it ebbs and flows, and that it takes work to maintain anything that has such high value that it is ordained and Blessed by God?
>
> Can we simply enjoy one another, enjoy what the world has to show and give us, enjoy our unique perspectives on that world, and marvel in how our US ties our individuality together without us losing ourselves?
>
> Can we fight and make up and chastise and support and correct and heal and caress and empathize and share and individualize and GROW together in love?
>
> Can we learn one another's love languages, agree to disagree, and respect and fulfill each other's needs...even when we don't quite understand the whys of them?

Can it be you and me against the world without allowing ourselves to be influenced by what outside people say and think, so that we can be clear to use discretion and discernment when it comes to one another?

Because they don't know what we know. And they're not supposed to when there's real, honest, beautiful love.

Can we—simply—BE?"

Seven
THE CREATIVE SOUL LAID BARE

I know, I know...I do a WHOLE lot of talking about heartbreak, relationships, race, and religion, about life's great struggles and obstacles, from the frame of reference of a seemingly angry and jilted Creative Black Man in America. And I know that the tone of this book may sometimes seem a bit...irate. I promise you, I'm a humorous, cheerfully optimistic, and positive guy to be around! But the truth is that we often speak on the things we know best. And the fact seems to be that I am intimately familiar with these subjects in very personal ways, as are many, many people who don't chose to write books about them.

As I said earlier, part of being a Creative is that we are used to putting our pain on display. We are acclimated to laying our souls bare through our chosen mediums after varying degrees of success in trying to hide the depths of those souls in our everyday lives. Take an artist like Robin Williams, for example. Because of the nature of his creative expression, it was easy to miss when a person like him was expressing his pain, while at the same time working hard to mask the ongoing trauma of that pain. Because he was making us laugh, no one heard him cry.

Then you have someone like Phyllis Hyman; every word that she sang told the story of exactly what she was feeling. But because she was "entertaining" us with her sultry voice, no one truly heard her.

And, of course, you also have the more extreme examples, which would be someone like a Vincent van Gogh, who cut his freakin' ear off, then painted a picture of himself without his ear. You can look also to the many, many tragic stories of artists and performers, especially in the world of music, whose personal implosions we have witnessed in real time—whether it was a long and bloody battle with alcoholism or drugs or a seemingly sudden snap that finds someone running in the middle of the streets with a gun yelling at strangers or walking away from fifty million dollars and disappearing into the Bush of Africa. Creatives often walk a tenuous tightrope of so-called emotional freedom, balancing between spiritual creativity and mental crisis. But the need to express ourselves beyond the need to sometimes stop and take care of ourselves often ends in either burnout, total rejection of our art and gifts, or tragedy.

Donnie Hathaway. Haunted by his own personal demons. We will never know for certain what happened in those last moments of his life; whether by intention or by accident, if his life was given or taken away. But the depths of the passion and pain that he expressed in each and every song he penned or sang was so deep it was physically palpable.

But then you have an artist like Prince. He was, in many ways, the ultimate Creative. It is more than apparent that throughout his life and his career, Prince had NO problem expressing who he was at any given time; as a matter of fact, we were always privy to his personal sojourn whether we wanted to be or not. Sure...for the first few years of his rise into the stratosphere of fame, Prince kept his most secret self close to the vest and used that protectiveness of self to wrap himself in a carefully crafted shroud of mystery—which also happened to work out well as a marketing tool. Yet still, we watched as he morphed, mutated, grew, and reinvented himself over and over again, and in some cases seemingly rose from the ashes of a burnt-out career like a leather and lace covered purple dove—er—phoenix. His creativity did not drive him to excesses of destructive public behavior or to a life of alcohol abuse much as he so poignantly portrayed his father living through in the movie Purple Rain. Prince's personal demons became fodder for his drive and his creativity, and he transmuted his trauma into a body of musical work that will stand unique and unparalleled in the history of music.

And even though Prince's untimely death came at the hands of an alleged drug overdose, it wasn't the overdose of a person who could not deal with the pain of his life and sought escapism in narcotics. Prince's transition to the next plane was not the demise of a Creative who could no longer create using their pain as a catalyst or a muse. But Prince's transition came to pass because, in fact, he could not STOP creating. He could not stop pouring out of himself, even when it became too physically painful for him to do so. And so, Prince, who embodied the epitome of the creative spirit of every creative soul great, small, famous, or unknown...found a means to push himself beyond his body's physical limitations of age and constant unabated expressiveness; he turned to drugs to ease the pain in his body that would never be as great as the pain in his soul from not creating and expressing exactly who he was. Even unto death.

And as Creatives, that is how strong our instinct can be to be true to ourselves. We don't refuse having "real jobs" because we are lazy or because we are no more than dreamers, or any of the misreads and mislabels society likes to heap upon us. We are not purposefully eclectic or eccentric or trying to be different. We, instead, are driven. On a subatomic level. We as Creatives are Blessed/Cursed with a spirit-level calling and a passion that is imbued and enabled within us from birth and without permission. Creativity is our assignment from God... from the Universe. I don't know if our pre-souls purposefully chose to stand in the line labelled "Gifts Of Creativity" thinking that we were getting the fun, easy assignments by doing so. But however we ended up on our creative journeys, that ability to manifest what has been put into us is NOT an easy thing to manage. It often comes at the high cost of what we perceive as normalcy.

But not all of us will have the clarity of vision nor the strength of will to clearly plan our paths and go from point A to point B as someone like Prince did. I cannot count the times I have seen this scenario play out:

Creative creates. Non-Creative notices Creative and becomes smitten with Creative's—uh—creativity. Both Creative and Non-Creative become mutually enamored with one another and soon become hopelessly involved with one another. And their life together progresses wonderfully because the two seem to balance and complement one another in many aspects of their beings.

But eventually, the spontaneity of the Creative begins to lose its appeal and, instead, becomes a negative aspect of their personality to the Non-Creative. Freedom of spirit and the innate drive to create begins to instead become perceived as a lack of conformity to norms, responsibility, foundation, and discipline.

And, in similar fashion, the sameness and conformity to roles and rules of the Non-Creative soon becomes a hinderance to the freedom and spirit of the Creative. The push for the Creative to change and to "fit in" becomes an anathema to their very being. It is not due to a lack of desire on the Creative's part to grow as a more well-rounded person. It's, in fact, because that growth has become a demand from the Non-Creative, instead of a process initiated by the Creative for their own growth and wellbeing.

These are of course oversimplified characterizations of both Creatives and Non-Creatives. Obviously, many Creatives are quite disciplined and able to carry on highly productive and successful lives without self-destructing. And, of course, many Non-Creatives have the spirit of creativity within them which can manifest in a variety of ways. But the basic conflicts that seem to arise in relationships between those called to create and those who are not, are characterized by the differences in how we view life in general, and the things that drive each of us to move forward within those lives. Our definitions of success may have similarities in that both include financial and social stability at some level.

But for many a Creative, that level of stability, as it were, does not carry the same weight as it does for non-Creatives. It isn't that stability and great financial health is not as important to us. But, rather, it is because that type of success does not DEFINE us. It is, to us, in fact, simply a by-product of our hard work, perseverance, and creativity. It is not a destination, but a part of our journey. Our trueness to self and our integrity ultimately holds more value than such things. We work hard to not only create art but to create environments that can support both creation and stability. But that process doesn't always look the way Non-Creatives would like it to look. And

I'll admit, it isn't always a practical or even successful process. But it is what helps us to keep our sanity. It is what helps us to maintain our integrity. Trying to reinvent us by force will only succeed in distancing us from the person(s) who attempt to do so. Meanwhile, supporting us through love, encouragement, and measured guidance if needed will always yield a favorable outcome to both parties.

That is why it is important to understand the heart and mind of a Creative before you try to insert them into your definition of life. We all want the same things. We simply have different paths of going about getting those things. And when done with honesty, open hearts and minds, and in love, the success story of a Creative and Non-Creative relationship can be the most beautiful thing God has ever made; it can be the best of both worlds, bringing the balance of what each of us may desire to fruition.

But when we try to change the very essence of who each person is, the relationship is, again, doomed from the start. Creatives need space, encouragement, and support. Non-Creatives need consistency, stability, and attentive reassurance. The funny thing is that those "needs" are more universal than not. They are not really mutually exclusive to one side of the creative divide or the other. These are HUMAN needs—things that are required to maintain healthy, happy, and growth-filled relationships. More often than not, it is US who create the divides between us. We look at life as an assignment of roles to be played by each other, instead of a partnership in a journey that takes us, no matter whether Creative or non-Creative, to a destination of mutual satisfaction and happiness.

Do not lessen the life and accomplishments of a Creative because you don't find the intrinsic value in what we do. Do not begrudge us the fact that we can both enjoy and prosper from what we do. Do not judge us for our perceived shortcomings or our alleged faults. The beauty of how we view life is that those cracks in the pavement that you may see as mistakes and faults, we see as art. We see the beauty in imperfection. We understand the pain of growth as part of the process of growing. We know the tragedies of life as the muses of our expressions. We accept the seeming chaos of existence as part of God's plan that we don't understand but are invariably a part of. Creatives know that there are no guarantees in life, no matter how that "real" job or that financial stability is packaged and sold to you. We are equipped, by our very natures, to adapt and adopt on the fly. That familiarity and embracing of the unexpected and the helter-skelter of existence is both our perceived weakness and our ACTUAL strength.

We Creatives may not have all the answers when problems arise. We may even sometimes falter or fail in how we respond to those unexpected bumps in the road. But what we get right is that we keep it moving. Forward and sometimes sideways. We embrace the unusual and the extraordinary. We are pre-equipped to make the proverbial lemonade from lemons. We may sometimes need a steady supply of sugar from Non-Creatives in the form of encouragement and support. But we will always make the best damn lemonade you've ever had.

Sadly, for those Creatives such as the ones mentioned at the beginning of this chapter, there are times when even perceived or actual success is not enough. The need to create often does not outpace the pain that may fuel that need. These are the times when allyship and partnership from those around us who are Non-Creatives are most crucial. The anchor of your Non-Creative logic and practicality is often the only thing holding us steady. That is not a situation of someone creative being a "user" or a burden to someone who is not. Make NO mistake: the perfect balance of a Creative/Non-Creative relationship is very much symbiotic. Life would have very little purpose without creativity. We would all be nothing more than drones in a beehive, living only to work. Because there would be no outlet to reward you for all your consistency. No music. No film. No art. No sports. No nothing.

Remember the movie The Matrix? Mostly everyone in the Matrix was simply part of the program and they didn't even know it. They did their everyday things without deviance and without question. They played their ROLES. The people within the Matrix were simply being used, drained, and discarded after their usefulness was done to those who reaped the benefits of everyone else's sacrifices. It wasn't until the few such as Morpheus, and eventually Neo, added the unpredictable into the mix. They used both the expected and the unexpected to their advantage. It wasn't until the concepts of freedom and creativity were enabled to flow freely that those trapped within the Matrix were awakened from their sleep and inspired to fight to truly become free.

In a perfect world, Creatives and Non-Creatives strike a balance between chaos and order by working together. Through unity. Through partnership. Through commonality of goals, and not through the ideology of simply playing roles. Because we as creatives know that those roles are constantly being altered by forces that do not want either Creatives or Non-Creatives to prosper. The bottom line for those antagonists is their own wellbeing. And they are that one percent that many keep ignoring, defending, or making excuses for. Meanwhile, the rest of us suffer. We fight one another. We become distracted by the false security of hollow successes within this system—this Matrix. And we instead, miss all the beauty, fulfillment, and achievement of a life lived in creativity, partnership—and love.

Eight
THE GREAT ESCAPE

A fertile imagination is the springboard to success.

It feels as though there has never been a time in my life where I did not have a love of superheroes and comic books. Marvel Comics, to be clear, thank you very much! But the funny thing is, I didn't get introduced to comics until I was about eleven years old.

But before that fateful moment when my older brother Joseph brought home an *Iron Man* comic book, given to him by his boss at the hardware store he worked at that summer, my overly active imagination had already found other outlets for escapism. The earliest outlet I can clearly remember was not an outlet for imaginative play. It was an insatiable curiosity about the hows and whys of things.

Understand, I wasn't that kid who drove my parents insane by constantly asking why, why, why. FIRST of all—Joe Smith was NOT the type you would bug with a whole lot of ques—

okay...let's keep this real—ANY QUESTIONS. Not if Daddy had a cigarette in his hand; not if Daddy had a cup of coffee in his hand; not if he had a newspaper in his hands; not if Daddy was watching a western or a war movie. Watching a boxing match. Reading a book. Sitting in the shadows. Sitting in the light. Sitting. At...home. Awake. Breathing.

I think you get the point.

Momma, on the other hand, would answer my questions if she could. But the fact was that, as I stated, I didn't have lots of questions. Because I was an observer. Yeah—I was a strange kid.

If there were people, I would sit and watch the room. I would listen to everything I could understand. I would watch people's mannerisms and responses to things that were happening around them. And I was painfully shy, so I didn't say a word unless spoken to. That is, when I finally learned to talk. Even beyond those newly learned walking and talking skill set years, my people-watching persisted. Because people fascinated me so very much.

But it was objects and things—how they were put together and how they worked—that really got my full attention early on. And the very first victim to fall prey to my curiosity about how it was built and what made it work the way it did? A Tonka Truck. More specifically, my wonderful glowing red Tonka fire engine.

One of my earliest and clearest childhood memories is of Momma in her bedroom, sitting happily at her Singer/Kenmore sewing machine. Let me set the scene a bit. The warm hue of the glass-covered wall sconce added a warmth to the room, with just the right amount of light for Momma to make sense of the translucent McCall's sewing pattern overlaying the bolt of material that laid neatly to the side, balanced magically on the open flip-top of the sewing machine. The house was quiet, except for the sporadic whirring of the Singer's motor each time Momma pressed her foot down on that funny-looking black pedal on the floor beneath the machine. And in between the eruption of fire engine sounds made with complete accuracy by my mouth and me frantically driving my Tonka around the room in between the legs of the sewing machine and out into the adjoining hallway, I would stop from time to time and watch as the Singer's long shiny needle would simultaneously bob up and down, piercing the material at hand; each time adding a new length of stitching. That whole process fascinated me, too. I wanted to know what secret inner workings made that needle go up and down. I wanted to understand how pressing that pedal way down on the floor made things way up on that machine do what they did.

But I wasn't touching Momma's Singer sewing machine. No way.

Yet that Tonka Truck of mine—it, my friends, was fair game! Don't ask me how, but somehow with a screwdriver from

Daddy's toolbox I had absconded with (yeah, I knew where that was, too), my four-year-old muscles and fumbling little fingers managed to pry loose the metal tabs which held together the cab of the truck with the main body. Of course, I didn't do this in front of Momma. My older brother was outside playing, and Daddy was at work. The rest of the apartment was gently bathed in a cross between darkness and the waning light of a fall sunset which radiated through the two front picture windows that had yet to be blasphemed by the ugliness and necessity of metal security bars.

A quick history lesson:

These were the early days of the Chicago Housing projects; back before we, the Black Diaspora, and my parents in particular, knew the truth about the purpose of those spanking new white triple towers of concrete that lined four miles of the newly excavated Dan Ryan Expressway—which in and of itself has its own dubious history for being constructed as an informal dividing line between the west side of the infamous "Black Belt" and White/Irish neighborhoods such as Bridgeport. The Robert Taylor Housing Projects were bordered to the east by State Street and to the west by the Illinois Central Railway and, eventually, the Ryan.

The Black Belt was a chain of Black neighborhoods on Chicago's south side, which stretched about thirty or so blocks north to south and maybe eight to ten blocks in width. It came into being because of restrictive housing practices which kept

Blacks from moving to other parts of the city. It was basically a corralling of the Black population by city government due to the influx of African Americans to Chicago in the Second Wave of the Great Migration. More than a quarter million Blacks came to Chicago to escape the racism and poverty of the south. Little did they know they were going out of the frying pan and into a bigger, more sophisticated frying pan. That was when the Chicago Housing Authority came up with the wonderful idea to kill several birds with one stone by building a series of housing communities—some high rise, others row houses—that would not only solve the growing Black population's housing needs, but would also allow the government and the CHA to conveniently compartmentalize us in a specific area of the city where they could control us, so to speak.

Thus, once built, the CHA sold potential new renters like my parents on the initial cleanliness, the newness, and the awesome modernness and pseudo-sophistication of high rise city living. They could stack us high, save on the use of valuable real estate, and save their precious neighborhoods from the "taint" of integration. They rented the apartments from the top floors down, so being one of the first families to sign up for 45th and South State Street, they placed my parents on the twelfth floor. At the time, I wasn't even a twinkle in Momma and Daddy's eyes yet, but Joseph was already here, yukking it up as a chubby, happy one year old. It would be two more years before God and I decided that it was time for me to be manifested in Momma's womb and then to come outside to play. And a few years more before the ugliness of stacking poor, disenfranchised people on top of one another created an atmosphere where Robert Taylor went from shiny and sophisticated to neglected and dangerous to the point of needing those ugly metal bars on those beautiful picture windows.

And now, we return you to our regularly scheduled Tonka take-apart adventure.

With reverse engineering firmly in my four-year-old mind, and secure in the knowledge that Momma was good and busy, I simply found myself a semi-dark corner in the living room and went to work. One of the many benefits of being a naturally quiet child was that whenever I was quiet, my parents didn't feel the urge to come looking for me because their "Spidey Sense" was telling them that I was off somewhere getting into trouble. I was quiet, and I was also, generally speaking, an obedient kid.

But I NEEDED to know where that retractable ladder WENT! Slowly but surely, my plans were falling into place. A bent tab here…a loosened screw there. And once I got the top part of that steel truck off, all my burning questions were finally answered. And I was suddenly giddy with newfound knowledge and power!

That damn ladder never worked the same way again.

Oh sure, I managed to put the top back on in a convincing manner. But somehow, my best laid plans for reverse engineering the ladder mechanism didn't work out quite the way I had planned. I knew my rebuild time was limited to when Daddy walked through that door, so I rushed it and botched the job. And I never got the chance to correct my mistake. But the upside? Momma and Daddy were none the wiser—bwahahahaha!

Next victim was an Etch-A-Sketch.

That was messy.

Then a PAF Viewmaster. A Hot Wheels Powerhouse. The engine of a Tyco train...

My reign of toy-targeted terror didn't end until Momma bought me a set of Lego blocks. It was a toy that finally allowed me to build whatever I wanted to; within the limited confines of a bunch of square and rectangular blocks, that is. I'm not sure what made my parents buy me a Lego set for Christmas, but if I had to guess, I think they knew exactly what I had been doing after all.

THE SPACE-AGED ROBOT

Gigantor was my first cartoon superhero. Then came Tobor, the 8th Man. I then discovered Astro Boy, Marine Boy, and then the bestest of the big head, big eyed superheroes (I had no idea what anime was at the time)—Prince. Frickin'. Planet.

Underdog who?

Between channels 9, 32, and 44, I quickly became hooked beyond reason on super beings and monsters from Japan and outer space adventure. My already overactive imagination had been kicked into hyperdrive upon my discovery of them. But even with my indoctrination into the Prince Planet Geek-out Club, anime wasn't done with me yet. No sir, no ma'am. Those wily Japanese, in cohort with Channels 9, 32, and 44, soon doubled down on enabling my action cartoon cult membership, and mercilessly introduced me to—the Mach 5. They walked me over to my TV one day after school and said, "Kenery, this is Speed Racer. Speed—Kenery".

And suddenly, fast cars, kewl gadgets, impossible stunts, and a Monster Car were also part of my collective imagination vocabulary. And then, without warning, I suddenly got the urge to learn to DRAW those things.

Now up to that point, I had only drawn things like buildings and the occasional attempt at those "Draw Me" contests that were advertised in the back of almost every magazine and newspaper at the time. I was also always fascinated with skyscrapers. Telling my age here, but I remember when the John Hancock building was being completed. The idea of a 100-story building amazed me. And the girder patterns that ran up and down the exterior looked so kewl...like nothing I had ever seen before. I remember seeing Marina Towers before they built Hancock Center, but I didn't like them or want to draw them. They were weird to me—they looked too much like corn on the cob.

So my creative artistic skills were already in place, thanks to Momma. But after discovering superheroes and Speed Racer, teaching myself to draw cars and bodies in action and weapons and spaceships, for the first time, I had a true outlet for self-expression. When you are a reserved child, self-expression is not your norm. Art became my next muse. And I was admittedly pretty damn good at it.

After a while, disproportioned anime characters, cars, and the like were easy to draw. These things didn't have to mimic real-life bodies. Perspective, shadowing, body proportions—none of that was a big deal to get right. Then came my brother Joe and Marvel Comics.

QUWHAAAT?

When I tell you that the course of my life was changed in that moment, I'm not exaggerating.

This was my First Enlightenment.

It was the moment when I was introduced to more sophisticated, more realistic artwork. Marvel Comics was my introduction to real story content, as fantastical or corny as it could sometime be. I learned about drawing human body proportions correctly and developing the use of actual human facial expressions to realistically depict human emotions to help tell a story on another, higher level. I learned how to outline a story and how to layout story panels. I studied the various styles of my favorite artists, like Joe Sinnott, George Perez, John Buscema, Dave Cockrum, and, of course, Jack "King" Kirby. I learned that there was a guy in New York City named Stan who had his name in huge letters printed on the front of his comic books and who wrote a "Soapbox" in the back of his comic books to all his readers. Stan was a guy who seemed to talk directly to me and called me and everyone who read his comics "True Believers." Stan told me, in no uncertain terms, that there was the possibility that me, a skinny little Black boy from the Chicago housing projects, could possibly grow up to become a person just like him. I could become a person who, if I worked hard, could actually someday make a living doing what Stan the Man was doing—writing and drawing stories. I could tell stories of fantastic adventures. And I could finally grow to become the person I had always longed to be: a successful Black man like my Daddy.

A fertile imagination is the springboard to success.

THE NIGHT MUSIC SAVED MY LIFE

While I was soon destined to abandon comic book artist as a viable career, the fire of my Creative soul had been lit. A shy child from the Robert Taylor Housing Projects had been inspired to embrace his creativity. Through art, I was shown that there was a whole other world of possibilities awaiting me beyond those cold, hard cinderblock walls. Inside my home, there was always cleanliness. There was order. There was safety. There was the teaching of wisdom, safety, integrity, and character. And even in its roughest state, in our most difficult times, there was always love. Imagination was like the icing on top of an imperfect cake. But just outside those walls, there was danger and hopelessness. It lurked in the unlit, urine-reeked stairwells, in the inoperable elevators; it waited on the broken glass-strewn playgrounds and in those poorly-managed, patchy, weed-ridden grass fields.

I am almost certain that without imagination and creativity, I may not be here right now. Imagination kept me safe in Apartment 1207 and off the streets. It kept me connected to other "misfit" kids who had likeminded imaginings and out of the company of kids who were troubled or living troubled lives. Imagination kept me happy and obedient at home instead of angry and disobedient in the streets and in the wrong places at the wrong times.

One of the main reasons—the final straw of why my father finally decided to move out of Robert Taylor—was when a childhood friend of mine was murdered—gunned down in cold blood in the middle of the playground in front of my building, just minutes before I walked across that very same playground while coming home from playing music.

Music was my Second Enlightenment.

❖ ❖ ❖

THE GREAT ESCAPE

"Music is my mistress, and she plays second fiddle to no one."
—Duke Ellington

Here is an excerpt from one of my Music Bios:

"As a childhood resident of the infamous Robert Taylor Housing Projects, a young and impressionable Kenery was destined to play bass guitar. Growing up, he would hear nothing but the bass lines of songs coming through the walls of his parents' apartment, as the neighbors would tend to play their music quite loudly (i.e., EVERY WAKING HOUR). And so, by default, Kenery became hooked by the bass grooves of James Jamerson, Verdine White, Bob Babbitt, Joe Osborn, and many other storied bassists.

Already possessing an artist's spirit, Kenery's parents later decided to buy him his first bass guitar at 11 years old, and soon he began to hang around the local bands at their rehearsal spots and going to neighborhood talent showcases, learning what he could from watching…and listening.

At age 12, Kenery made his public musical debut in his 7th grade talent show and became hooked on the allure of the stage. And with no true formal training, he began to perform locally with different choirs, bands, and theater groups, learning what he needed along the way. He has toured extensively throughout Italy, Germany, Switzerland, and Luxembourg."

So, as you can see, I've done a few things here and there, and I have achieved many more high points during this musical journey of mine. Music is not my mistress, per se. But we know each other pretty well. She's more like a great trustworthy friend—with benefits. You may ask, why are music and I so close? Simple. Because Music may have saved my life.

Let me explain.

I don't have a storied or star-studded music career. I have, of course, worked with and met my fair share of famous and infamous people. My goal has never been to become an artist. I didn't want to be a star. I had no desire to be famous. And beyond the times I walk onto a stage, I pretty much avoid the scrutiny of the public eye like the plague. I like keeping my life as drama-free a zone as possible. Life has its own collection of troubles on tap for each and every one of our lives. Don't start none, won't be none. With that in mind, it may seem as though that sentiment runs contrary to the perceived reality of living a musician's life. But not necessarily.

I have mentioned before that I am by far no saint. I have experienced the spoils of life as a musician—at home, on the road, and in the spotlight, dim as mine may be compared to others. There have been hotel rooms shared with women who were strangers. But being that I am a bit of a germaphobe and more than a bit of a hypochondriac, that didn't happen much. Plus, you know—that conscience I spoke of earlier. Doesn't make for a great playa playa resume, does it?

There has been alcohol. But while I can hold my liquor quite well, thank you very much, I don't like the feeling of not being in control of my thoughts or actions. Plus, I'm more of a top-shelf liquor kind of guy, so my alcohol snobbery game is tight. So, no—no wild drunken nights, either. But beyond the alleged spoils of a musician's life, here's the most important plus of my being a musician. Here's how music saved my life.

When I was still living in Robert Taylor, I once accepted a New Year's Eve gig; as a matter of fact, it was my very first gig as a newbie "pro" musician. I was about sixteen years old and had no idea about the wisdom of leaving for a NYE gig long before it got close to midnight. This was/is especially true when living in the Hood. Knowing that type of information is of vital importance to being able to make it to your gig, let alone play it well.

So, there I was, standing outside in the back of my building around 10 p.m., waiting for my ride. When allalasudden, a whole gang—literally—ran past me, guns drawn, apparently not going to a party. They were looking for somebody.

One brother with a sawed-off shotgun was running towards me, and I thought that, of course, he was just going to keep running past because...well...what they got to do with me? But instead, dude stopped right in front of me and looked me dead in the face. Then he asked me, "who you ridin?'

For the uninitiated, that is gangspeak for, "Pardon me, my good man—may I inquire about the status of your criminal affiliation and your organizational allegiance?" But before I could even get the word "neutral" out of my mouth, I heard another voice say, "man, that's Lil' Smith, man. He plays music; can't you see he got a guitar? He don't bother nobody—he cool, man."

Needless to say, at that point I was relieved, but still a little undone. Not so much afraid or shaken, but—if I'm being honest—annoyed. Because in no way, shape, or form did I resemble a gangbanger. I was tight; clean cut, well-dressed in a suit and a long overcoat. And I had been relatively relaxed up to that moment; there had been some early bird random shooting, but nothing I sadly wasn't already used to. 9pm is the new midnight on NYE in the hood, so some fireworks, Dago bombs (it was, embarrassingly, many years later when I learned that the word "Dago" was a racial slur against Italians...), and gunshots were par for the course. I had a bass guitar case—one of those big rectangular black tolex covered joints. And I was minding my own business. And yet, this fool felt a need to step to me with an unspoken threat of bodily harm.

And my ride was late. So yeah—annoyed.

I also never got to see nor find out who the person in the shadows was who had spoken on my behalf that fateful evening. I was a little busy watching the barrel of that sawed-off and looking in that gangbanger's eyes. And I had to do that because he needed to know that I wasn't scared (maybe I was a little), and I needed to see what kind of mess he was on to calculate my next move. I kind of believe I know who it was that gave me the vote of confidence. But I never got the opportunity to ask him. We didn't exactly travel in the same circles.

I will always wonder what would have happened if that mystery person who vouched for me had not known who I was from Adam, or if he'd have had no clue that I was a simple, unassuming musician on his way to play his first $25 gig (hey, no comments on the money—I was new at this, folks. What did I know about getting paid on New Year's Eve?). I wonder to this day if, in fact, music had truly saved my life.

That incident, though, showed me several things. First, I believe with all my being that God was there for me in the gift that He had blessed me with—music. I didn't have to be on my way to play Gospel music to commune with Him. Because He has always been there, even in the very act of playing my instrument. God was there with me when I sat in on bass with a real live professional Gospel choir while attending NIU and I blanked out in the Spirit, because I have no idea what happened during those few minutes I played. But the audience and the choir were applauding me, so I guess it went okay. God was there with me when, on the night my father died, I still had to go to work and perform on a stage in front of people. I was being held up and comforted by God, through the gift of my musicality. Sharing that gift in that very moment was immensely cathartic.

Music also gave me a means to express myself in a way that allowed me to have both vulnerability and security at the same time. There have been many times in my life where

I've felt as though I had no one to turn to. I've felt alone or betrayed or even unloved. I recognize that the point of what I've been stating is that I've always had God in the midst of my musical journey to one degree or another. So how can I also say that I've had moments of feeling alone? The answer is that there are times when even the most faithful person feels as if God is not enough. It's a feeling of human failing and a desire to have a human connection instead of a spiritual one. Because there have been times when God felt so much further away than others. And that was, of course, on me. Yet even in God's perceived absence, He still gave me the music. After all, my true relationship with God began with a prophecy about music, given to me in a dream as a child.

This is why music will always be a non-negotiable part of who I am. There have been those who have tried to separate me from, belittle, or diminish my relationship with music. I have gained and lost relationships over music. People have judged me simply based on the tropes and prejudices of what it means to be a musician. You don't get into a music career in order to become rich. But you do accept music into your life to enrich it. And to give joy, inspiration, and enrichment to others. And even if everyone abandons you, you will always have the joy of making and sharing music. And that edifies your spirit. And it in turn, glorifies God. And really, in the end, that's all that matters.

Nine
TRUST

Trust.

It is the keystone of everything. It is foundational to every relationship of import that we will ever form, from an infant knowing that its mother will catch it when it falls towards her, to God's definition of trust and His promise to us about the nature of His relationship with his people:

"There is no fear in love, but perfect love casts out fear. For fear has to do with punishment, and whoever fears has not been perfected in love."—1 John 4:18

Of course, as human beings, we are flawed little creatures. We live in a world that does very little to instill an overarching sense of trust, not only in each other, but often within ourselves. As we grow older, we lose the innocence of our youthful bliss. We learn lessons of disappointment, betrayal, and lack of trustworthiness.

But what we also seem to lose is a true sense of what trust really is. For instance, if someone purposefully does not fulfill a promise to us, we then become skeptical of their trustworthiness. But should that loss of trust extend to situations where a broken promise is due to a legitimate reason for that promise to be broken? If a person says to you, "I will meet you at 5:00pm," but they instead arrive at 5:15pm due to a delay caused by a sudden accident on the road ahead of them...is that then reason to become distrustful of that person's merit? Do we hold people accountable for things that are out of their control, to the degree that we characterize those person's unintended failings as failings of their character? Do we, in turn, give up on those who have, in every other area of their person and their relationship with you, proven to be loyal, true, and good? What truly is the cost of trust?

Submitted for your approval: God himself gives us Grace to cover our flaws and shortcomings, or as the Bible states, "love covers a multitude of sins." That does not give us carte blanche to behave as we want for self-serving reasons. And it does not mitigate a lack of trust in someone who has seemingly broken that trust. But what giving that type of Grace to one another does do is help us to not be self-righteously judgmental towards one another. It helps us to look beyond the surface of what we may perceive as a failing and to understand and consider the reasons—not the excuses—for why our trust feels to have been betrayed.

When we enter into a relationship as important as a marriage, we are entering into a covenant and not a contract. Contracts bind us through legality to be trustworthy in holding up our end of the contractual bargain. A covenant, on the other hand, is a commitment to trust one another and to honor that trust based on our word being our bond. However, that bond—that trust—is not simply a cut-and-dried matter. Because if it were, we would not have Grace.

When life becomes challenging, people are often quick to give up on even the people and things they have previously deemed to be important to them without trying to understand the reasons why the circumstances of the relationship have changed. It is much less work to simply say "that person has broken my trust" and relegate them to the recycling bin than to communicate a loss of trust to that person and then try to work with that person to resolve the issue. We have become a culture of disposability. If something we have is seemingly broken—even if it is otherwise solid and trustworthy—we often opt to simply throw it away and get a new one instead of trying to fix an otherwise perfectly good thing, even before we understand what is actually wrong with it. And we treat one another in that very same manner.

The thing is, everything and everyone breaks at one time or another. Nothing hums along swimmingly and perfectly forever and ever. We, as humans, break. We wear down. Parts of us need maintenance and sometimes even replacement.

So, what type of persons would we be if, when someone we claim to love loses an arm, or that person has a heart failure, yet survives, or they become somehow incapacitated in any part of their physical being, or a child is born to us with what others may characterize as a defect or flaw—what type of persons would we be if we simply threw that ostensibly broken person away?

We would be labeled as monsters, of course. We would be seen as cold, uncaring, and unempathetic. We would be cast as selfish and possibly even evil. So why, then, do we not feel the same way about the throwing away of those who may suffer from emotional, spiritual, or mental brokenness? I'm not talking about knowingly living with a sociopath or ignoring the fact that a person we may love is also a person who is harmful, abusive, or destructive to both others and to themselves. But even in our need to separate ourselves from the negative effects of those types of behavior, should we not, at the very least, try to understand the things that may have created or triggered such behaviors if they weren't previously an apparent part of their character?

What do TRUST and FORGIVENESS truly look like? Where are the lines that we draw in the proverbial sand when it comes to broken trust, second chances, and opportunities for healing? And what things do we itemize and categorize as broken trust? I mean...do we distrust the lover who suddenly loses their job due to mass layoffs? Do we distrust the spouse who said they want to have children, but who, after the "I dos," finds out that they aren't able to conceive or procreate? How about the partner who falls victim to an unforetold ailment that changes the dynamics of how they are physically, mentally, or even emotionally able to navigate through life? Do they suddenly, all other things being equal and all qualities and characteristics being intact...become disposable? Did they break your trust in who they sold themselves to be, even when they had no clue about or control over the changes that suddenly have affected both your life and theirs?

If you are a person who considers themselves to be of spiritual wellness and wellbeing with God, how do you think you would feel if God treated you in the same manner that you treated someone who suddenly became broken through no fault of their own? If God broke His covenant with you, you'd feel betrayed and hurt—and rightly so. If you claim to be in a relationship with God—or in connection with a higher spiritual and moral power if the acknowledgement of God is not in your wheelhouse—how, then, is it even possible that you would deem someone you claim to love as disposable or untrustworthy when they become the unwilling and unintended victim of this thing called life?

I suppose it is a fact that we all have our individual limits and limitations. No one person has the same amount of fortitude to stand against life's curveballs as the other. We each have unique strengths, and indefensible weaknesses. We each are given talents that allow us to help those who do not benefit from having your specific skill sets. But isn't that the reason why we, as human beings, come together with one another? Isn't the whole purpose of friendship, partnership, community, and fellowship to compensate for, uplift, and support one another? And how about marriage? That covenant we agree to before God is one of the greatest expressions of human trust in one another. But that trust goes beyond what material things we do or don't do for one another. Yes, those things are important, because part of that covenant is the fulfillment of promises to take care of one another. But we are also charged to love, honor, protect, and—often as a point of contention—obey. We humans love our cherry picking.

Trust is a commodity that has far more value than the notion of what we bring to that ubiquitous table that many people speak of when referencing relationships and marriage. The "what have you done for me lately" crowd is alive and kicking when it comes to choosing and keeping a mate. The notion of rating, choosing, and treating one another based on Shiny Objects often supersedes the search and valuation of the character and content of a person's heart and mind. Therefore, we tend to trust in things, and not in people. We value the values that WE ourselves place on items—things of which the value can change with the wind, the flow of the stock market, or the onslaught of a worldwide pandemic. We value these things versus the attributes that dwell at the core of our beings that determine how we respond and adapt to those changes in material values. We often trust that the world will stay level till death do we part, versus hedging our bets with level, solid people. I'm not defining solid people as faultless people. Nor as unfailing, perfect people. But I define solid people as persons actively and consistently engaged in knowing themselves, and in who they present themselves to be, even during great life change.

Instead, many of us chase ideas and lists, and unstable and untrustworthy yardsticks of measurement. And that is why marriage is dying a rather quick and painful death in our society. Instead of trusting in one another, we trust in those Shiny Objects to define ourselves and those we interact with. We lose ourselves in keeping up with the Joneses, instead of maintaining our Love Jones.

Honesty. Self-ownership. Communication. These things equal Trust. And getting that much sought-after "six-figure pay-for-everything" husband or that "stay at home, just be sexy and serve me" wife means absolutely nothing without content of character. Oh, you may think you've struck gold having either one of those types. But if there is flawed character, then who else is he paying for? Who else is she "serving"? What good is having those type of people in your life without honesty, self-ownership, and communication?

Without trust?

Ten

YOU IS SMART. YOU IS KIND. YOU IS BOOTIFUL.

I LOVE me some ME.

I am happy to have been born into THIS time, into THIS family, in THIS country, with THIS amount of sun-kissed melanin, with THIS mind and THESE talents, with this body (okay—I'm lyin' a little bit now. I would've gone to a different parts bin for these knees...), and especially with THIS soul. Despite AAAALLLLLL my faults, and all the problems in all the lands that I have had to and continue to deal with—baby, there is NO place like home! I. Am. Me. And there is no one else I'd rather be.

And I pray and believe with all my heart that you feel the same way about yourself.

But the question is, how do we really learn to love self? Is it achieved at the expense of others? Or is it a self-contained, self-sustained bubble of confidence and assuredness? And how do we know when it is time to break ranks with anyone who might threaten our citadel of strength, versus it being a matter of our simply being self-centered and unempathetic towards those closest to us who are also working through their own journeys towards self-love?

As I've said before, we are all damaged in some way or another. Maybe not shattered into a thousand pieces. It may only be a crack or a hairline fracture we are dealing with, a scrape or a paper cut that we are nursing. Some of us may have small pieces missing—maybe an ingredient that was left out during our formation from childhood to adulthood. Others still have had things added and poured into them that should never have been added, either through trauma or tragedy. The slings and arrows of life are unavoidable tolls we pay for being imperfect humans treating each other imperfectly while living in an imperfect world.

But check it: those imperfect parts of us are the very things that make us so beautifully and wonderfully made. I mean—perfection is BORING. But that journey to achieve perfection that we know we aren't meant to achieve, but we take the trip anyway?

That shit is dope!

The pleasure and pain, the highs and lows, the achievements and setbacks, the overcoming, and the obstacles. It all mixes together and, depending on whether we allow someone else to decide how to "cook" us, or to be our own master chefs, we can turn it all into a life well lived and a life that is worth living.

Because how we decide to live with the card hand that is dealt to us impacts how those around us live their lives, directly and indirectly. Short of the responsibilities of parenthood and relationships/marriage, we are not responsible for how others view us or for the choices they eventually make based on their perspectives of us. I included responsibilities of relationships in that statement because there is a misconception circulating the Diaspora that we can simply "be ourselves" when it comes to how we interact in both platonic and intimate relationships. Many believe that we should simply accept them as they are, straight, no chaser. But let's look at what that actually means.

Your best self should be able to balance your true self with your required self. All actions have consequences. So if you, as an individual, decided that you were going to live as your whole unfiltered self, then that means that you are signing on the dotted line of life to accept every equal and opposite reaction to the actions your "real and woke self" decides to engage in. No one is obligated to give you a pass or any considerations beyond the typically morality-based considerations that should be given to another human being. So, if you are being fabulous at other people's expense, then you should expect to be handed the bill for your narcissistic self-centered over-indulgence. Because your authentic fabulousness should not hurt other people. And all that fabulousness should draw people TO you, not repel people FROM you. Otherwise, you are doing it all wrong.

Being true to self has become the excuse for many to partake in feeding their own insecurities at the expense of others. It is a rationalization for self-hate in the form of malevolence towards the rest of the world. It is a cover story for inflicting pain on those who may represent who and what they are not, but long to become. But they're too lazy or cowardly to put in the work. Or those who indulge in such behavior are simply too broken beyond reasonable repair. The fact is that there is no one who ever was who did not have bad things happen to them in their lives. But it's how we respond to those bad things which determines our true selves and shapes our most basic character.

Except for those who are not psychologically or emotionally capable, we all have the ability to self-examine and self-correct and to take responsibility for who we become after those character-defining flash points in our lives. And it is never an easy undertaking. Finding self is, in fact, a lifelong odyssey, wrought with the dangers of becoming totally lost at every turn.

CH...CH...CH...CH...CH...CHANGES

Man, lissen…

What is up with how we view one another? I mean…we all have prejudices. That is an undisputed fact. But the societal changes that have come about just within the last ten years have presented so many challenges to so many of our learned and preconceived notions of what defines who. Gender. Race (that old trope). Class. Ageism. Hell, even what defines a person legally, as per Citizen's United.

So, as a society, here is where we're headed.

We've got A.I. on the come up; when it reaches self-awareness (and eventually it will), how will we define it? As a new life form? As property, or as three-fifths a person, as we of the Black Diaspora were once, not so very long ago, legally defined? Have you seen some of the advances in robotics in Japan?

We've got the wholesale cultural redefining of what makes a man a man and a woman a woman. I mean, I can't call it, y'all. But let me be honest; I'm a person who was raised with the traditional values of thousands of years of civilization, and a strong spiritual foundation and belief in God, both for better and for worse. Yet I am also someone who respects the individual to be who they want to be, barring that who they want to be doesn't negatively affect me and mine in any direct way. But cultural shifts are going to always affect us all indirectly, both collectively and individually. And there is nothing that we can do to change that. Because change itself is inevitable. And unless you are of the 1%, we do not live in societal isolation from one another. Except where we make the conscious effort to do so.

Or because of—you know—redlining.

Now I'm guessing that every racist person who ever was felt as though their sacred worldview and way of life was in jeopardy when "The Blacks" decided that we wanted to become real-life people and not property. How DARE we upset the status quo and flip over the apple cart of racism, White Nationalism, American Exceptionalism, Manifest Destiny, yada, yada, yada. The point being that change is always painful to those who take comfort in and define themselves by tradition. And though not all change is good, sometimes fighting change in the name of sameness is an anathema to our continued growth and evolution, both societal and individual.

Once upon a time, there was this guy named Jesus who came along and literally flipped stuff over in the name of overturning the laws and the traditions of thousands of years of "religion." And man, did those Pharisees and Sadducees fight against him! They fought against Jesus to the point where they felt that the only way to stop him was to persecute him and his followers literally to death. The priests and the politicians were desperate to maintain their power structure and preserve their status quos. They wanted to keep their grip on the hearts and minds of the people. And murder was an acceptable means to that end, in spite of their self-proclaimed "holiness."

Now, is this new societal movement toward redefining gender that same type of world-defining movement?

Aaaand, pause...

Before ANYONE loses their religion or their minds, I am not comparing the LGBTQ+ movement to Jesus bringing the world the New Testament and salvation.

Chill.

What I am saying is that human history is spattered with upheaval, conflict, change, and enlightenment. It's obviously what we do. We have growing pains and painful setbacks, all in the name of redefining who we are. We are constantly discovering new things about ourselves and the world we live in. We are blessed/cursed with curiosity and the intelligence to pursue those lines of questioning which result from our inquisitive, God given nature. And we have been given the mental and emotional capacity to assimilate and grow from what we learn.

Well, maybe not ALL of us.

There are many who are incapable of learning from or embracing change. Doing so does not mean that we will all come together in a spiritually aware kumbaya moment, and suddenly believe the same thing in a quasi-group minded manner. We'll leave the uni-mind stuff to Jonestown...or the Republicans. But what our inquisitively based change and growth means is that we cannot force-feed our beliefs upon those who are not feeling the same way. Being totally transparent, for my part, I'm very much a heterosexual male who believes in the male/female order of nature with, of course, exceptions to the rule being in existence. Does that mean I am homophobic? No. Does that mean I am not respectful of others' lifestyles and beliefs? No way.

As the chapter title suggests, you—whoever you are and however you identify.

You are smart. You are kind. You are beautiful. And you are a person, one who is due every iota of respect and love and happiness that anyone else in this mad, mad world deserves to have. It is not my place to define you. It is most definitely not my place or purview to judge you. And I most definitely have no Heaven nor Hell to put you in. I am far too busy trying to keep my own feet from getting an eternal singe.

AN ANALOGY ABOUT HOW I FEEL OTHER PEOPLE'S GENDER AND SEXUALITY CHOICES

I don't like lima beans. I have a very visceral reaction to eating lima beans. I have very little control over what my tastebuds do when they are confronted with tasting them. It's really the texture more than anything. And no one can change my body's response to lima beans. It is what it is.

But what I don't do is HATE lima beans. I don't go out of my way to express disgust towards them. I do not go into grocery stores and angrily knock cans of lima beans off shelves because they taste so bad to me. I don't protest them. I don't create FB pages of hate-filled rants about the yuckiness of lima beans.

I'm fine with people who do like lima beans. I have many lima bean-eating friends and family. I love and respect them... and their choice to eat lima beans. I think no less about them (and also their okra-eating friends) than I do about those who eat string beans. Lima bean eaters can even feel free and comfortable eating their lima beans in my presence. I don't judge them.

But they cannot MAKE me LIKE lima beans.

AN OPEN LETTER TO THE MILLENNIALS, XS, AND ZS

Dear Millennials, Xs, and Zs,

For many of us who are aged between the vast majority of Baby Boomers and your generation, we have learned that the life which the "Powers that Think They Be" tried to sell you was a lie even when WE were your age. That American Dream life they were selling us all is a Post-WWII propaganda Hollywood/corporate/government construct.

When chasing suburban living came into existence, and interstate highways were created, and the 2.5 kids and a white picket fence vision was being sold to us as something we all could achieve if we got educated and worked hard, it was already a lie.

It was the end of the industrial era, when being a skilled laborer was still a great career. But if you did get lucky enough and educated enough to move into white-collar career path,

YOU IS SMART. YOU IS KIND. YOU IS BOOTIFUL.

it was at the beginning of the age of information, technology, and service. I feel that the WWII Generation (the self-proclaimed "Greatest Generation") reaped the most benefits from those newly manufactured dreams. Admittedly, Baby Boomers (I'm on thee very tail end of that generation) continued the idea of equality and a great life for all. But then greed, corruption, hate, glass ceilings, and all the upheaval of the 60s and 70s conspired to expose the lie. Those times of upheaval and enlightenment exposed all the evils that this country already had as its true foundations, hidden and denied from the uneducated, uncaring, and the unaware.

Then, suddenly, everyone seemed to forget the aspirations of ushering in the Age of Aquarius and the protests against a corrupt government and its corporate minions and the Summer of Love. And false hope in a hopeless nation was once again generated as technology took giant leaps forward in the 80s/90s. New opportunities for all were being touted by industry and educational institutions. A brave new world was once again painted as being just over the horizon for everybody. That's why you see all the partying, happiness, bright colors, racial mingling, and 'We Are the World' type of music, TV, and movies coming out during that period.

"We're all together as one, y'all—Clinton is our first Black President and he played sax on Arsenio Hall...!"

But the truth was that if you weren't established yet or weren't connected to old money, you began to see the opposite of new opportunities. You began to see the beginnings of the latest class, social, political, and financial divides. Rich became richer. Poor became poorer. The disenfranchised (minorities, women) as a whole became more unable to move up the corporate ladder.

The "Powers That Think They Be" have always fought to maintain classism. But when they plotted to kill the "middle class," they were trying to take us back to the 19th and early 20th centuries. "Making America Great Again" is really the One Percent's war cry against the lower and middle classes. And many in the lower and middle classes are unfortunately drinking the Kool-Aid. The One Percent are telling each other, "Let's fool everyone else into spending thousands of dollars on college for careers that they will never get rich in—aaaand keep them on the hamster wheel, in debt to us—aaaand sell them so much consumerism that they keep spending what little money they are making instead of saving and investing like we do. We can continue to get rich and keep them poor, all at the same time! Especially those minorities and rural people!"

But guess what, Millennials, Gen X, and Gen Z? You don't have to drink the Kool-Aid. You are now actually in a place of unimaginable power, and not one of indebtedness and dependency as they would have you to believe. Because you have access to great knowledge and awareness. You have more power than ever to use your voices, your votes, and your vitality to stop the madness. You can speak to and move ten, or ten thousand at the same time—all from the comfort of your coffee house. You can organize protest and change on a dime. You can direct policy, create awareness, and instill confidence on grander scales than we ever were able to. DO NOT let the One Percent fool you into believing you HAVE to work for THEM. You have more opportunities for entrepreneurship than ever. Don't let them convince you that you have to do things the way THEY did. Don't allow them to tell you that you are replaceable and unqualified and unremarkable. Don't let them use misinformation, sleight of hand politics, hate-mongering, and empty promises to divide you or destroy your ambition to achieve a truly great life. Don't let them ravage your future and your planet with their greed and carelessness. Cause they old, y'all. They WILL eventually need YOU.

BUT at the same time: be sure to also honor the elders who have taught, raised, and taken care of you. Be sure to take care of them in their mature years, because many have sacrificed everything to hold the line for you, and to give you a fighting chance and a light of hope and confidence in an ever more dimly lit room called life.

As for the rest of the ancient greedy Post-WWII and Boomers who continue to get their obscene congressional salaries (remember, most are already millionaires), even as the rest of the government employees are struggling to make ends meet because of an unnecessary government shutdown or some such thing; as for those who get million dollar bonuses as CEOs of million and billion dollar corporations, yet continue to price gouge the rest of us; as for those who continue to divide us with rhetoric, hate, and false narratives...

Go out and TAKE THEIR POWER.

And then use it to save this country and this world. Remake this nation into a REAL light on a Hill...a truly fair and equitable country. Use that power wisely. Take back your lives. Make things better than what they want you to settle for. Go above and beyond even your own expectations. Do it for us who are older yet have always supported and believed in you. Do it for yourselves to have life, and more abundantly. Do it for your children and their children. And do it for your own better future.

P.S. Just my two cents:

If you believe in God, keep Him close and nourish that relationship. If you don't believe in God, you owe it to yourself to at least try to find Him. If you're lost in the isles of the Big Box Store of Life, He's always waiting at the front of the store for you. And failing that as being an ideology which appeals to your current sensibilities: live by a set of standards that are higher than yourself.

GROW AND TELL

Sometimes, as we age and the responsibilities of life feel as though they outweigh the possibilities, we can fall prey to losing our connection to the beauty of simply living life. But no matter where we find ourselves on the spectrum of our individual journeys, each new day we are blessed with still holds the promises of recommitment, revitalization, reevaluation, and examination in its purview. The days simply work as distance markers between one set of goals and the next—a point in time designated as either a measuring stick, or a timekeeper.

One thing I know for sure is that I am not going to allow myself to be defined simply by the passage of time. Recognition of a new decade beginning is still only a marker, a signpost. Age is part of growth. But age in and of itself is not the thing that should define whether we should or how much we should grow. The saying of "you're never too old to learn something new/follow your dreams…" is a pearl of wisdom and inspiration we should all keep in our hearts and minds.

What I also know is that taking care of self must be priority numero UNO. The flight attendant on every plane instructs us to put our oxygen masks on first because we're no good to anyone else if we aren't okay ourselves.

Because when we love self, self will love us right back by allowing us to have the strength, fortitude, peace of mind, and clarity to be able to take care of those we love who still need us. Loving self will sharpen your discernment about those who are in your life adding negativity who no longer need to be there. Loving self will give you even more purpose because you are doing what God desires for us, which is to be better, stronger, and healthier in our spirit, mind, and body.

"DEPRESHE" MODE

For anyone who has ever suffered from moderate to severe clinical depression—

—and was/is involved with or interacted with someone who allegedly cared/cares for you—

—and has been told in some way, shape, or form that you need to "do something about it" or take care of your own health or "snap out of it" or pull yourself up by your own bootstraps: here's an analogy that comes to my mind about how to explain to them that beating depression is not as simple as "go do something about it."

Have you ever had one of those bad dreams where you are either trapped somewhere or trying to get away from something/someone? And in that dream, you KNOW that you are in danger. You KNOW that you must do something to escape that danger. You may even know exactly what you must do.

But then you try to get out or to get away. And you realize that you can only move in the very slowest of motions...as if you are stuck in molasses. You can't even see where you are trying to escape to because it is also dark where you are trapped. Or the road to get away from the thing that is chasing you is long and dark, leading into a dark, dark forest or tunnel.

And while you are moving in slow motion, fighting for your life, the monster or whatever is chasing you is moving at normal speed. Sometimes even faster than normal. And you simply feel as though you cannot move an inch, or at least not far or fast enough to escape your fate, no matter how hard you try. You see no light at the end of the tunnel, no sun-filled opening between those tree boughs covering the forest, and no clearing or meadow up ahead.

All your energy, your force of will—the strength that would go toward boot strap-pulling up—is being used simply to hold your position, to keep from being dragged backwards.

If you've ever had one of those type of dreams, then you now know how to describe to the ignorant what it feels like to try and just "snap out of" or "do something about" depression.

And if those who claim to love you still don't understand—if they mischaracterize you or make light of your struggle or even abandon you—

—then understand: that wasn't love. Understand that it isn't your fault that you are where you are. You didn't choose to feel this way. You aren't "not trying hard enough". Or faking it. Or imagining it.

With depression, you are almost perpetually at war. With yourself. With your own mind and spirit. With powers and principalities in high places. With chemical imbalances. And if there is anyone in your life who is choosing to fight on the wrong side of your personal war instead of being an ally or beacon of positivity and hope? Then you are, sadly, at war with them, also. So, you may need to cut. Them. Lose.

The truth is this: you have it within yourself to win this battle. But in order to successfully do so, you must find a worthy and TRUE ally outside of yourself to help you. Someone who truly loves you, wherever you are in your journey. Or, barring that possibility, someone who is QUALIFIED and COMPATIBLE with you—someone who knows how to teach and guide you through your storm. Someone who can help lead you to a victory that you surely CAN win. For some, that help is God. For others, a more visceral ally can be found in a counselor or mental health professional. Or why not both? Spirituality and psychology, they aren't mutually exclusive.

Also, ASKING FOR HELP DOES NOT MAKE YOU WEAK. Indeed, there is no greater show of strength than when you acknowledge to self and to others that you have reached your current limit and that you need HELP, even as you are STILL striving, moving forward.

But you MUST cast your anchor to latch onto someone or something that is outside of your storm. Something or someone that is solid and strong. And when you do, "be sure your anchor holds," as that beautiful old hymn says. If you are already Blessed to have someone close who truly loves and understands you, then so much the better.

So please. Don't give up. Don't stop moving forward. It's always worth it to get to the finish line, no matter when/how you get there.

Life, my friends, is truly worth it.

Eleven

I'M BLACKETY BLACK AND I'M BLACK, Y'ALL

THE PURPOSEFUL MISEDUCATION OF P.O.C. (AND WHY SOME OF YOU HATED BLACK PANTHERS 1 AND 2)

A friend and I were recently talking all things Marvel Cinematic Universe, and he rightly lamented the lack of enthusiasm, apathy...even downright bashing...of the historic, symbolic, and cultural significance of the Black Panther and Black Panther 2 movies by some P.O.C. when they first premiered.

His frustration was with the fact that while many of us laud and uphold creative works such as Empire, when presented with an extremely positive, awe-inspiring, and uplifting movie like Black Panther, many of us have chosen to criticize the movie for having "too much dialogue, not enough action." Or laugh at/ignore the culturally significant depiction of the African Diaspora in all its glory and variety. Or make light of the fact that our strong Black women play not only a prominent role in the films, but that they are highlighted, empowered, and beautiful in each of the character depictions instead of being presented as one-dimensional caricatures of the African Female Experience.

Indeed, Black Panther/Black Panther 2 encapsulate so many aspects of not only African culture, but the Black Experience so well that it's possibly overwhelming to those who are used to simply being entertained. And what about that? Why, very often, does a laugh seem to win out over an education in our culture? Why do many of us seek more violence, poverty, ignorance, and foolishness in our entertainment, when we most def have enough of it here right'chere in real time, in real life? What makes us go for the okey doke and the folly over the wokefullness and the self-awareness?

Escapism? Sure. We all need that from time to time. Lord knows this is not an ideal world these days for most of the Melanin Dipped set.

Fear of the truth? What is this TRUTH we always speak of? Complacency and blissful ignorance have always been a problem within our communities.

Apathy and disregard of who we are/were/can be? The "keep your head down and be quiet…don't make no waves…let me be a big fish in this tiny pond" mentality? Yeah…there's that.

But the truth is, the answer is all of the above. And more.

The problem at hand is all about the Purposeful Miseducation of P.O.C. And I do mean PURPOSEFUL. If you don't know that this is an ongoing campaign against our unity, you'd better slap yourself and "woke" up. Because this nation was not built for us. From the foundations. Don't believe? While you are feeling all "Wakanda Forever-y," y'all need to check out a very well done, very informative podcast called Seeing White, a multipart podcast series produced by Scene On Radio via NPR. That's "National Public Radio" for those of you who only listen to music and fading comedians on the radio. It will truly educate, inform, and enlighten you about who we are to this nation. Knowledge is power.

Ah, those damn Shiny Objects. We love 'em. And we're fed them daily in twenty-four hour news cycles full of aspirations of quick rises to wealth and fame. Easy paths to fame and fortune.

Become a "reality" TV star! Act a fool, and YouTube your way to fame! You, too, can make it as a Hip Hop rapper because, well, your wordplay is gonna be better than that last famous rapper!

How about the allure of becoming a "leader" with "power"? Start a storefront church—uh—even though you don't really believe in God all that tough. Go into politics! Oh wait—you're not doing it to elicit change for your people. Nah, man—so you can be da man (or woman) and get perks and kickbacks and accolades! Be a sports superstar. But please, whatever you do, don't use your platform to stand up by taking a knee for a cause! Stay enslaved and safe with your millions!

Listen, there's nothing wrong with most of the above paths to self-fulfillment if you are truly following your heart. Because let's face it—those corporate glass ceilings may have been raised a little higher, but they are still there. And we keep bumping into those same transparent ceilings that allow us to see what's available and what's possible, right there, just on the other side. Each and every day, there are brave and tireless souls fighting to shatter those very well-reinforced security glass barriers. And I thank God for those warriors. Many, many of them are my family, my friends. I pray for them. I fight with them in spirit and in truth.

And yet, we keep smacking into those glass ceilings because we keep trying to climb (no elevators for us—we must take the slow and arduous route) to the top floor in the same house.

Repeatedly.

Hey, here's a thought.

Build your own house.

Why not truly come together and create a Wakanda?

You know, it HAS been done before, in a fashion. In the Greenwood district of Tulsa, Oklahoma, 1910. In Rosewood, Florida, 1870. In North Brentwood, Maryland, 1924. In Weeksville, New York, 1838. In Mound Bayou, Mississippi, 1887. Glenarden, Maryland, 1910. Blackdom, New Mexico, 1908.

Yeah, yeah, I know how a few of those stories ended. But why haven't we tried it again? Fear? Lack of resources? Lack of community and togetherness? The defusing of common goals by the culture of assimilation?

I submit to you that The Miseducation is the true problem. We are constantly being fed information and entertainment through the media—both social and mainstream—that will gladly help us to be back stabbin', money grabbin', sex havin', bling nabbin', infighting tribes. We are depicted as "thugs" and "terrorists." Meanwhile, "they" are described as "mentally disturbed", "very fine people on both sides," or "kids just being kids." And we seem to keep buying that bill of goods.

For our part, we scream about the misappropriation of our culture, but we don't support those who strive to continue the traditions or create the next cultural or social contribution to the Pan-African Diaspora. That's why art forms like Jazz, Blues, dance, storytelling—and so many other great parts of our heritage—that's why we've lost them or are losing them to others. That, and we don't learn our own history. 'Cause—you know. It's the past. Irrelevant. Lame. Right?

We undercut each other. We steal from one another. We are lacking in trust within the Diaspora because we are not always trustworthy or truthful with one another. We fight with each other about small things but won't fight together for big things. We don't create legacies. We often don't reach back without charging a "cost of doing business." We sell each other short and don't pay one another our worth because we have been taught to devalue ourselves.

We live only for the pleasures of today. Sure, many of us have allowed ourselves to be forced onto the "paycheck to paycheck" treadmill. Again, miseducation. Misinformation. Lack of vision.

"My people perish…"

Understand, I truly don't expect everyone to love everything the same way just 'cause it's got color attached to it. And I don't expect everyone to love Black Panther/Black Panther 2. Or Black-ish. Or Hidden Figures. Or Fences. Thirteen. She's Gotta Have It. Luke Cage. Atlanta. Insecure. The Underground Railroad. Watchmen. Lovecraft Country. Kindred. Etc.…

We, the Pan-African Diaspora, are not a monolith. We all have different needs—different viewpoints, different goals, and beliefs. That's why we have many faiths. Various denominations of churches. Harold's, Popeye's, and Church's. Natural hair spas and weave salons. An endless variety of tribes, cultures, hues, and views throughout the many countries of the Diaspora. We have variety, folks. And we should embrace that variety.

As was depicted so beautifully in Black Panther/2, even the different tribes that made up Wakanda came together for a singular cause: the protection, security, progress, uplifting and empowerment of them all. Even the brothers and sisters in the mountains came together and played by rules established by the collective community. And even Killmonger's misguided hate had relevance; it was valid hate. He had VALID points about how Wakanda treated the rest of the African Diaspora in not helping by sharing those technologies and cultural enlightenment that made Wakanda great.

Think on that the next time you ignore someone in need who looks like you. Naw, not the scammers who have their "kids" with them in that car that won't start or is perpetually out of gas at a different location every day. I'm talking about a child who needs mentoring. An Elder who needs some company and a helping hand. A friend who just wants an ear to listen to their troubles. A young woman who says she's being abused. A kid who comes to school hangry 'cause there's no one adulting at their house. A person who walks into your church in tattered clothes, smelling like urine...who sits in the back waiting for someone in the congregation to show them this "Love of Jesus" y'all keep shouting and singing about.

And with a little inspiration from the likes of T'Challa (RIH), maybe we can begin to heal the African Diaspora. Maybe we can aspire to create a Wakanda in the real world. Or maybe we can start by working to make Black America GREATER.

Again.

NOT ENOUGH "SOUL" FOR YA?

And in that same line of thinking, let's take it backwards in time a little bit more; here's my unsolicited opinion about the feedback which the Disney movie *Soul* seems to have garnered within the Black Diaspora (I LOVE that word!). These thoughts came to mind after hearing and reading what others have said about it, including some of the official reviews from "woke experts."

SPOILER ALERT: Potential spoilers if somehow, in these past years, you haven't seen it yet.

When something artistically Black Diaspora-centric comes out, whether it's via film, TV, or music, I'm not one of those people who believes "you ain't Black if you don't like it." Everybody's entitled to their opinions.

But IMHO, *Soul* is not a "Black" or a "Jazz" film, per se. It's a film about life and death that happens to be centered around a Black male lead character who is a Jazz musician. And that's refreshing, especially being a Jazz-adjacent musician myself. The life struggles, concerns, and personal challenges portrayed by Joe Gardner not only hit close to home, but came in my house, stood in my kitchen, and slapped me around a few times. And I was okay with that mild assault, because it was a reminder of where I've been and an inspiration for the constant move to challenge, grow, and adjust where I am going.

The funny thing is, the Diaspora often wants two seemingly contrasting things to happen with our stories and our representations on film and TV, all at the same time. We want a normalization of having Black lead actors in films that are not specifically Black, i.e., Idris Elba as a James Bond, or some type of Black version remake of quaint, traditionally all-White stories. But, at the same time, we want to have the realest, most authentic, to-a-tee representation of our "cultural purity" to be accepted as mainstream media and to not be mishandled, misappropriated, or misused by the pervasive whiteness of America. Take that any way you'd like. Now, equal and fair representation in film is not a bad goal by any stretch of the imagination. However, the full realization of those two very contrasting ends of the culturally representative creative spectrum can seemingly pose a bit of a dichotomy and a dilemma.

While I've never been a fan of making an originally White character into a Black character just because (a series like *Raising Dion* is proof enough that we have many, many original ideas waiting to be tapped into), I understand the desire to flip the script on the well-worn cliché of forced American societal norms. We, the Black Delegation, have been battling many, many hard-fought battles for many, many years to, first, be seen as human. Then to be respected. And THEN to be seen as "equal"—whatever that means. And then to simply be SEEN.

We made our way up the ladder and into the institutions to dominate in sports of all kinds because—well, let's be honest—there's nothing we can't do well given the opportunity. And while that dominance shows up all over the playing fields and courts, it has yet to barely scratch the surface in the C-Suites that own and run those institutions.

The same can be said with the rest of corporate and political America; doors have been kicked in, places have been taken, and some glass ceilings have been cracked and even broken. But, in contrast, try to start or buy a cannabis business while Black. How about a major TV or radio network? Start or run a major tech company? Get a SECOND Black president elected? Okay—we've got a Black VP in place. Even though many people thought she was simply "diggin' her potatoes" for that top slot cause—you know—Joe is old. Others only find her to be Black-ish. Whatever.

When it comes to the Arts—film specifically—there were those who, here and there, paved the way for inclusion. The McDaniels, Belafontes, Dandridges, Hornes, Poitiers, and Carrolls kicked in the doors for the Cosbys, Washingtons, Bassetts, Davises, and the Freemans, who held them open for the Chadwicks, Mahershalas, the Michael Bs, the Elbas, Lupitas, and the Tarajis.

The Quincys, Ellingtons, and de Passes made way for the Spikes, Townsends, Wayans, Hudlins, and Singletons, who punched way up above their presumed weight classes to clear the path for the DuVernays, Rhimes, Daniels, Peeles, Barrises, Waithes, and the Issas.

But still, as with everywhere else in American life when it comes to Black people: lots of nominations, but far fewer wins. Even fewer executives owning or running major studios, both in film and TV. Like him or hate him, Tyler Perry is one of the few outliers and exceptions to the rules that govern Hollywood. Define that as you see fit.

So I GET it. When something comes out of Hollywood that even slightly touches on the Black experience, we want our representation to be authentic, not cliché, and to have the happy endings that, contrary to popular belief, we DO often experience. We're tired of the pimps, drug dealers, gang bangers, pregnant Black Women, and incarcerated or dead Black Men. We're tired of being the Redshirts of American society.

But when it comes to *Soul*, I got more of a "Black" story than I expected from Disney. And, at the same time, it was a very universal story. I didn't expect to connect with the character of Joe Gardner in any way, shape, or form outside of the love of music. Even the drummer in jazz saxophonist character Dorothea Williams' band reminded me of a drummer I know (I won't say who...lol). As to the original premise of this thread...that the belief by some viewers and critics that the movie "missed" its opportunity for Disney to finally do a fully fleshed-out Black character and instead killed him off in the beginning of the movie, at the pinnacle of a long-fought battle to achieve his life's dream...well. Life DOES that to us sometimes. The bottom will both literally and figuratively drop out of our lives in a way that, while it may not actually kill us, can make it feel as though life's problems are a dark, bottomless pit...a Sunken Place, if you will...where we, too, can feel detached from our bodies, our lives, our souls. It doesn't just happen to Black middle-aged Jazz musicians, though. It happens to people from all walks of life; all colors, creeds, cultures. Didn't The

Shutdown kind of do that to us all to one degree or another? Hell—didn't those FOUR YEARS of socio-political madness interrupt the mess out of many of our lives?

Life interrupted is often a major characteristic of our lives. But the good news is that many of us get the opportunities to get back on track. Sadly, many others do not. But, if you watch the movie Soul not only from the perspective of a Black person in America, but simply as a person participating in This American Life...and this life on Earth in general, then you may come away with some wonderful life lessons, some inspiration, a little bit more joy, and the realization that the lesson here is that as long as there is still a spark of life available, there is a reason for hope and a purpose for living.

STAND BEHIND THE YELLOW TAPE, PLEASE

Good people...the answer is not A or B.

There are forces that are constantly creating the circumstances that affect us. Our life in America is an ACTIVE CRIME SCENE. There is not a one-size-fits-all "it's your fault, Black people; don't do this, don't do that" type of situation.

Yes, we are accountable for our own actions, and many of our own circumstances. We cannot constantly blame "the man," the system, God, whomever. BUT the fact remains that there are many forces at work against us that are constantly in play. Many institutions, laws, and "powers and principalities" that are engaged in our destruction, deconstruction, and in the continued state of captivity of the Black Diaspora. Not only in America, but throughout the world.

From the ever-present and unaddressed lead poisoning in our lower income homes and schools that affect the minds of our children at an early age, which strips them of their moral centers and conscious ability to reason; to the lack of adequate preventive and general healthcare for those caught between poverty and making just slightly too much to receive assistance from the government. The very same government we are supposed to pledge some type of cult-like allegiance and respect to by not kneeling in protest of its centuries-old abuse of our bodies, minds, spirits, and values.

We are hamstrung by subpar educations and nutritional food deserts; by homes and families without a positive male influence, thanks to the outright murder of our Black Men, the unlawful incarceration of some, and the lack of real due process for others. Our cultural roadblocks include the nonexistence of opportunities to make a legal and fair wage and the miseducation of our people through the manipulation of the media. We are crestfallen by the failures, with some notable exceptions, of the Black Church Industrial Complex using its power and influence to work at creating better lives for us in the here and now; and the caricatured narratives and distracting brain drain of "reality TV" fed to us as entertainment.

We, the Black Diaspora, are up against everything from the blind consumption of "social" media to the deterioration of social skills that said social media creates. We're sick with a love of those oft-mentioned Shiny Objects and America's culturally nurtured need for instant gratification. We are afflicted with everything from not being taught the skill sets to save and grow wealth to the constant glorification of the almighty dollar over the value of a human life.

From the state of "Woke-ness" misappropriation to the blanket monolithic "solutions" to racial injustice that many of our own would-be self-proclaimed intellectuals and self-righteous "voices of the people" keep dishing out in the media. From the emasculation and demonization of Black men and the de-feminization of Black women (not all coming from outside the community y'all), to the lack of true engagement about the full spectrum of EVERYTHING that affects and impacts us daily.

Let's face it. It's complicated. By design. Pick a problem and start creating a solution. Everyone doesn't have to protest. Everyone doesn't have to wear a dashiki or a kufi. Everyone doesn't need to think like you think in order to be right, cause there's enough wrong to be fixed to go around.

IT AIN'T MY FAULT

If you are a Black person...or even if you are non-melanated: how often have you thought or said that it was a person's responsibility to overcome their past and take responsibility for their own actions? What is the point of fighting the outside forces to secure freedom and equality if we cannot even control our own on the inside of the Diaspora? As things stand today, we will have a generation of youngsters (and obviously some who are not so young) who believe lawlessness is the way to go. They won't know how to build anything because they won't value anything. Condoning the bad actions of our own people in the name of "they made us this way" is a weak excuse and doesn't bring about good results.

When it comes to the events of a year like 2020—with its pandemic and the protests by BLM over the murder of George Floyd—I don't care one bit about these megaretailers and their stores with mega-insurance coverage. But what about the Black owned businesses who don't have those type of resources and who DO service our neighborhoods? What about the companies who DO reinvest into our people, provide jobs, and help us recirculate that almighty Black dollar within the neighborhood? What about those small businesses owned by non-Blacks that do respect us, few and far between as they may be?

Sadly, when the outside agitators and then inner fools infiltrated our legitimate and peaceful protests, there was zero distinction made by those looters between Black owned/managed businesses and any other business. Because for the young and foolish, as well as the old and selfish, there is no sense of historical context about what happened to the South and West Sides of Chicago after the 1968 riots protesting the murder of MLK—no knowledge or concern about how there was NO reinvestment by anyone because they could not afford to take the chance on putting their businesses in our neighborhoods again.

And it would be somewhat different if waiting in the wings had been a whole slew of quality Black businesses, ready to fill in the vacuum of the white/Asian/whatever businesses that divested. But that is not the case. Know why? Because potential Black business owners cannot get business loans from financial institutions due to either systemic racism and redlining or because of a fear of investing into something that will end up looted, destroyed, or not making a profit.

At the end of the day, WE bear our fair share of the responsibility for the vicious cycles we, the Diaspora, endure. Because we damn sure should already know that the cards are stacked against us. The question then becomes: when will we transform ourselves into the dealers instead of the players and reshuffle the deck? The good news is that we've done it before. And we surely can do it again.

THE BLACK MAN, THE BLACK WOMAN, AND THE ART OF THE BLACK PARTNERSHIP

As a Black Creative—as a Black Man, an entrepreneur, and a musician—I am all for the hustle. It comes with the territory, and you must know that before you dive into these treacherous entrepreneurial waters, untethered to a guaranteed paycheck that comes at regular intervals. Indeed, you must love the hustle almost as much as you love the art. But I cannot tell you how often someone has propositioned me for my professional musical and event coordination services, how often I have been asked to put together a group of talented, professional musicians and vocalists, and then get hit with the most insulting pay offer since Pharaoh told the Israelites how much he was going to pay them to build his pyramids...

There is this misconception out in the ether that Creatives simply enjoy doing what we have been gifted to be able to do simply for the sake of doing it without the need for fair, professional compensation. Whether this ideology comes from people being cheap or from the utter lack of respect for what we do FOR A LIVING, there is always someone who is ready to lowball us into oblivion and the poor house.

It usually goes thusly: the potential client will first ask your availability. Once you answer that you are possibly available, said client will often ask how much you charge. The typical reply by us as professionals should be to ask these vital questions: what the total event time is, location, number of attendees, expected time and length of performance during the event, parking situation, required attire, size of venue and performance area, food and beverage allowances, special song requests. And, of course, the method of payment. All these factors will determine the rate that said potential client will receive. I mean, c'mon; no matter how it looks in the movies, musicians don't simply magically appear, ready to play any song ever sang, while gleefully carrying tons of expensive equipment just because we love music and killing our cars and our backs. Yeah…knowing a variety of music and carrying the required equipment are part and parcel of what we do. We know that. But know this; it ain't cheap.

Sometimes, that potential client may skip straight to the laundry list of everything they require and desire from your services. Often this to-do list is quite elaborate and time consuming in the prep time it would require before even playing a single note on the day of the event. You, as they client, are paying for that also.

"What?" you may exclaim. "Why are you charging me for all these peripheral things that don't have anything to do with the day of the event?"

Well, that, my friend, is where the "professional" part of our titles kick in. This is the part where people misconstrue what it means to be an entrepreneur, a small business, and a professional. See, what people fail to realize is that when you desire professional services, you are requesting all the experience, preparation, dedication of time specific to your needs, and usage of resources that are not always readily available to us as they would be for a large business. You are requesting the services of persons who will be prepared, punctual, and performance ready. As a client, you are not simply paying for a stellar musical experience. You are paying for everything that makes that stellar musical experience possible. The care, maintenance, and feeding of a human jukebox requires money. Fair, equitable amounts of money. So, often, as an entrepreneur, consistent work isn't always consistent. Why?

Sadly, we also will do damage to ourselves. Here are the facts: as professionals, we are swimming in a sea of other musicians that has its fair share of lowballers, Judases, and thieves. Again, that's just fact. So while we are fighting the forces on the outside who devalue our talents and try to pay us unfairly to, in their minds, "smile and dance," the forces on the inside of our community help to perpetuate that climate and behavior. And, woefully, those types of "co-workers" are gonna always be with us. Whether it's because they really need the work or because they want to steal gigs that others have worked hard to build, we simply must be aware of who they are, and then call them out.

All these facts and factors are simply stated to demonstrate that there is no straight line from failure to success. In the world of "real" jobs and careers, the guarantees and security that have been promoted and advertised to every high school and college student ever are also non-existent. And again, add into that equation race—and you've got a cruel running joke about the existence of any real pathway to success.

We see, time and time again, people going into debt for life to acquire educations that often fail to pay off in opportunity. That does not mean that we should not acquire knowledge; that should never be an option. Knowledge is the beginning of wisdom. And opportunities can only be created through the combination of both.

Now, add to the equation of Creative Entrepreneurship the factor of being Black. And the whole formula for success shifts dramatically. Gone are the simple prospects of acquiring bank loans or the startup Angel Investors or the generational wealth that allows Uncle Bill to throw you a few grand to get you started or on your feet. We, as Black people, cannot depend on a system that was not created with us in mind to cater to our efforts and achievements in the same way that it has for our White counterparts. And the irony of that is the fact that these days, they too—especially Millennials and Gen Z—are beginning to feel the seeming futility of fulfillment from going through the traditional educational pipeline to a successful career.

Except not really. Their stumbling blocks are based on corporate greed and class separation. These are things that can theoretically be overcome or compensated for. But you add on top of those class challenges a bias towards melanated skin; that is not something we can overcome being (we have no desire to do that; most of us love the skin we are in) or compensate for. You cannot really compensate for an unjust system while existing WITHIN that unjust system. We as Black Creatives and entrepreneurs, both men and women, learn to navigate, adapt, overcompensate where we can, and glue everything together with spit and elbow grease. But it does not come without a price, typically one that is far beyond what our White contemporaries pay.

We pay with broken families. We pay with seemingly unconquerable debt and poor credit. We pay with hypertension, diabetes, and other stress-related health issues that, in a twist of irony, we also cannot afford to take care of preemptively or otherwise. We pay with unaddressed mental health issues that stem from those oft-referenced macro and micro aggressions eating away at our opportunities, confidence, and trust of those we love and have the responsibility to take care of, and at our souls.

I'll reiterate: I know that we, as Black people, are not the only peoples who are or have ever suffered at the hands of shining American Capitalism. The system is operating as it was created to operate. But here's the lick: that system was imagined to keep US on that bottom rung, and on that hamster wheel of dependency. Other ethnicities have come into America and eventually gotten their "comeuppance" as a culture, apart from the original occupants of this land. The system simply chose to try and eliminate them altogether and outright, with varied degrees of success. On the other hand, we as Black people were instead used to build the very system we are oppressed by. And we are still trying to overcome that oppressive system 400+ years later.

I submit that we cannot do it alone. But the fact is that we never could, really. For Black Men in particular, we have been conditioned to carry the weight of the world on our shoulders, no matter what. We get most of the blame for the ills of the Black Diaspora, but rarely any of the glory. That is not to say that some of my Brothers have not earned the ire and contempt of my Sisters, and of the rest of the Diaspora. There will always be clowns and fools who seek to destroy instead of build within every cultural society. But the reality is that we as Black Men simply cannot carry the weight of the burden of being the only (sometimes, according to statistics, even the main) breadwinners within a system that loves to snatch our bread. And that challenge is compounded when we are forced to strike out as entrepreneurs, Creative or otherwise.

We cannot afford to simply continue to exist from generation to generation, barely making it through our lives and telling stories of how we got over. Because we do not have the luxury of the American Dream being a given reward for playing by the rules. We have to improvise. We have to reeducate. We as Black people have to reimagine how we interact with one another, beyond the Anglo traditions that have been foisted upon us from our arrival on these shores.

We must learn truly to understand the reality of our existence—and then change that reality to fit the narrative we desire for ourselves. We have done it many times before. The most popular example, of course, being Tulsa, Oklahoma 1921. But somehow, somewhere—we lost the script along the way, either through distraction or dissuasion. We get so busy trying to survive in the present that we neglect to learn from the past and to build for the future.

And to effectively build that future, we must think outside of the box as this society tries its dammy to keep us inside. At the center of that solution, Black Men and Women must become true partners in our collective success. We must stop allowing others to dictate HOW we succeed. The rules are constantly being changed in favor of the supposed game masters BY the game masters. We cannot change the way the game masters manipulate the rules. But we built the damn game board; we built it, and we can flip it over. But only if we re-imagine who we are. Only if we truly embrace the best of our past from both antiquity and modern times. Only if we make our own new rules. And only if we truly embrace each other as partners in the success of the retooling and the rebuilding of the Black family.

To highly paraphrase W. Shakespeare:

No Black Man or Woman is an island entire of themselves; every person is a piece of the Black Diaspora, a part of the main; if a clod be washed away by the sea, The Diaspora is the less, as well as if a promontory were, as well as any manner of thy friends or of thine own were; any person's death diminishes me, because I am involved in our kind.

Please indulge me as I reiterate a few important points:

The rules keep changing, but the game is still the same. There are, of course, still Black Men who can and will provide comfortably for their families without the wife having to be an integral part of the equation. But they are not quite as abundant as one would like to believe. I said this earlier; the system has always been designed to emasculate Black Men, and to manipulate Black Women, starting from birth.

Let's begin with Black Women historically having little to no access to prenatal care. Then add environmental, physical, and psychological challenges while growing up in less-than-safe or stellar neighborhoods. Hard working parents...or parent... trying to the best of their abilities to raise children the most informed way they know how. A lack of healthy, knowledgeable mothers who know how to care for themselves before, during, and after childbirth. Fathers who are imprisoned, killed, or are absent physically and/or emotionally. A lack of positive male mentorship on how to become a man, a good provider, and a loving father and husband. Slumlord-operated places of living and other subpar living conditions rife with lead poisoning and disease carried by pests that stunt young minds and bodies. Food deserts that yield less-than-nutritious options for growing bodies. Lack of access to preventive healthcare. Subpar educational options. Children dodging the school-to-prison pipeline bullet. Or simply dodging a bullet, period.

Then we move on to an absence of interest or ability to pursue higher ed, or the acquisition of higher ed, but without the benefit of being prepared to make the most of it. Graduation (maybe) into a job market that rejects even the most qualified of us. Absence of educational and career counseling, mentorship, or apprenticeship opportunities. Which leads to fewer long-term career choices. And when a good career is captured out in the wild, there is typically unequal pay and even less opportunity for advancement as you get to watch Unqualified Bobby get the promotion you deserve.

Meanwhile, Black Women are usually, but not always, more likely to graduate than Black Men, go on to higher ed, do well, graduate again, and go into a great job/career. Again, it's been designed that way. But they still must deal with even greater disparities in pay, in addition to both racial AND gender bias and discrimination. And if those Black Women inadvertently have children out of wedlock with one of those irresponsible, uninspired, or unemployed Black males (not men), in many instances those Black mothers also must raise those children pretty much by themselves.

All of this leads to women who are now used to taking care of themselves. And in many instances, it creates a type of Black Woman who won't settle for what they deem to be less of a man if that man cannot do demonstratively more for her than she has already done for herself. This judgement often comes at the cost of their potential opportunity to meet a solid, hardworking, loving, and responsible Black Man; one who is doing great things for himself, even if he has not seemingly "arrived." It comes in lieu of them finding that "good man," and then creating a partnership with him.

And to a degree, I get that.

I get that it may seem counterproductive for a successful Black Woman to involve herself with what they designate to be less successful Black Man. Less successful is, of course, a relative designation.

The actual truth is that the days of single-income households being adequate to create a very comfortable living environment for a couple—let alone a family—are long gone, if they ever truly existed. The Middle Class is dead; long live the Upper Lower Class. In fact, we as Black folks, both entrepreneurially and traditionally employed, never truly had those days to begin with. We just got bamboozled into thinking that we too, could have that shiny "American Dream" if we did everything the "right" way. But folks, there is no right way, at least not for us. Even entrepreneurship is under attack, from both outside and inside.

Brothers and Sisters, the times, they have a-changed. And as with any species, survival of the fittest is all about adaptation. So, it is incumbent upon our continued survival and growth that we as a culture, enact and embrace change. We must be open to rethinking how we do things, especially if the things we are doing are not working for us individually and as a whole. We must not only war against being a slave to a system that means to continue enslaving us for its own benefit. but we must also learn to not be slaves to the doctrines of roles and traditions. Order, hierarchy, and gender-based roles are still valuable and important concepts and precepts in Black society. But we cannot allow those ideas to become self-made stumbling blocks to our own success.

Twelve

WORDS FOR THE LEVITES
AND A FEW FOR THE HEATHENS, TOO

Musicians. What is there to say about us? We make THEE world go 'round. Or at least we keep it spinning in rhythm and in beauty.

But man, can we be interesting. Some call it eclectic. Others call it eccentric. Still others will slow fight you and call it weird. Unreliable. Irresponsible. Unrealistic. I have been told by an ex that the reason that we are exes is that because I am a musician or creative spirit, that I am a "bird," versus her being more like a tree. The obvious implication here being that as a musician, I am flighty and not grounded. Meanwhile, her tree-ness made her well rooted.

Okay.

While that is simply a fabrication of the imagination, I must admit: the freedom of mind that comes with being a Creative often comes accompanied by a struggle to be seen as—what is a good word for it?

Responsible. Respectable.

This is especially true when it comes to musicians. And now, let me define "respectable" in the context of non-Creatives' effort to define Creatives—and let me tell you, you really have no clue how prevalent this is.

There is a stigma—not wholly undeserved, but overly stereotyped and mos def NOT exclusive to musicians—that we are dogs. Broke, irresponsible, carnal-minded, daydreaming dogs. And doggettes; equal opportunity is in effect here for the ladies! Everybody loves to come see and hear us perform. Everybody loves the spotlight factor, the allure, the mystery and fantasy of what it MUST be like to be and/or be with a musician.

"Oh. My. God. It MUST be exciting and wild! It has got to be risqué and sexual. Adventurous and uninhibited. IT. HAS. GOT. TO. BE. FREEDOM INCARNATE! MAGICALLY DELICIOUS EVEN!"

But also, "please don't bring one of their asses home with you."

Why? Well, of course, because musicians are broke. They will spend all your money. They will bring you STDs with a smile. They will use you up until you are a dried husk, then abandon you by the roadside...and not even in a well-lit area. They will steal your joy and crush your soul.

Musicians will break your heart.

Now, here's the real-world version.

- I personally know more musicians who have had their hearts broken by non-Creatives than I can ever hope to count, me being one in that number.
- Most PROFESSIONAL musicians desire and achieve stability, love, and family.
- Most professional musicians are hard workers, who hustle constantly and hone their craft JUST as hard as entrepreneurs in any other given legal vocation. And often for far less financial reward. But that does not mean that they are broke.
- Most professional musicians work to establish multiple streams of income...just like any successful entrepreneur does. It just not always as simple to do.
- Professional musicians are real people, with real world problems, concerns, and challenges that have zero to do with hooking up.
- The only true "freedom" most professional musicians achieve, beyond having more control over our daily schedules, is the freedom of self-expression when we are on that stage or in that recording session. Those moments are often our only moments of reprise and renewal. They are the moments we live for.
- We are not "dreamers" or untethered birds. We are

solid, beautiful, loving, giving people, who are most likely far more versed and grounded in the hard realities of life than many "real job" workers.

- We are the creators of the sounds that help you keep your sanity in this world. We create the music that helps to usher in your worship. We are the purveyors of the melodies that keep your memories and emotions, both good and bad, alive and accessible to your mind and heart. We create the art that defines the soundtracks of your lives.

- Musicians are the second most important source of Heavenly praise in God's hierarchy.

- Musicians are flawed human beings, simply trying to be happy, and to make others happy, both through utilization of the same medium. Music.

Those preconceived notions about us do not end at the secular doorstep. They follow us, full-throatily, into churches, temples, and synagogues. Very often, those false characterizations and sentiments are even expressed by those who are supposed to be our spiritual covering. We are not any better or any worse in our behaviors and proclivities than that well respected doctor of lawyer. That law professor or that scientist. That politician or that pastor (oops...).

It is true that Creatives, musicians specifically, are very much unfairly maligned by the public. But, at the same time, let's be real; there are certain aspects of that reputation which are, sadly, well deserved...even if they are sustained only by the actions of the few bad who overshadow the many good. We cannot allow a reputation perpetuated by others whom we have no control over to define who we are as individuals. It is our own responsibility to be our best selves, in musical execution, in business dealings, and in interpersonal interactions. Because we have a sacred responsibility. Musicians bring life.

Musicians change the world for the better—one note at a time.

I GOT "PUT ON" BY GOD

It is hard being married to a musician.

It is hard being a married musician.

It is hard being a musician.

Those are just a few of the perspectives about life as a Creative, and specifically as a musician. In most cases, music is a calling of sorts. It chooses you and not the other way around. Case in point:

When I was eight years old, before I had ever even picked up a bass guitar, I had a dream...a vision, if you will. It wasn't the first time I had experienced a vision; my childhood was riddled with them, both good and bad. Most actually saw fruition in the real world in some form or fashion. Others were simply either a pleasant or painful experience that I never grasped the meaning of. All these visions felt quite real. And they were always presented to me in high definition for their clarity and realism, which is what differentiated them from my normal everyday dreams. I mean...the clarity of those visions was the equivalent of putting on virtual reality glasses and participating in the most advanced VR game you could ever imagine.

In this particular dream, I "woke" to find myself standing in the middle of a huge and beautifully elaborate hotel lobby. And in that instant, I immediately knew that in this vision, I was clearly playing the role of myself...but not quite myself as I was in the woke world. Here in this vision, I was an adult. I never actually got to catch a glimpse of myself, either in a reflection, or in my dream mind. I simply KNEW that I was older. I felt taller, stronger, and more...mature, whatever that meant to me at the time.

As I was standing there in that dreamscape lobby trying to gain my dream legs and acclimate to my newfound adult status, I became suddenly aware that there were other people present who were busy doing their tos and fros and bustling back and forth between the grand hotel entrance and the concierge desk. An endless variety of interesting people flowed in and out of any one of several banks of oddly narrow yet ornately inviting elevators which stood off to the right side of the lobby area. These people were of all shapes and sizes, colors, and characteristics, moving almost in unison, as if they were traveling together on an unseen assembly line conveyor belt; their ultimate destination being the long marble check-in counter where smiling hotel employees waited to engage their eager guests. And most notably, there were people traversing up and down a wide, elegant marble staircase framed in finely-embellished gold-hued handrails and lined down its center by a warm, plush forest green stair runner dotted with bright specs of red and gold, all of which greeted hotel guests with their opulence and old-world magnificence and an aura of welcoming invitation as they continuously pierced the veil of revolving and handled doors stationed with attentive and sharply-dressed doormen.

The realization soon came over me that I was apparently standing in that lobby waiting for someone, but at first, I didn't know who. Suddenly, a small group of people emerged from one or two of those narrow elevators and were instantly familiar to me...but at the same time unfamiliar. My woke mind did not know the faces. But my spirit and dream self seemed to know these strangers quite well. And as soon as they walked up to me, I was overwhelmed with a sense of family and belonging. There was an innate knowledge that I was MEANT to be there, at that specific moment, in that specific place. I immediately gave off a broad, inviting smile, and we all proceeded to laugh in concert and greeted one another with hugs and handshakes.

We then proceeded to walk towards the hotel entrance, with the sole intention of departing on an adventure. I could feel the anticipation and the joy of it all; even at eight years old, I knew this was going to be a wonderful day. And stepping through those brass-adorned lobby doors, I was instantly transfixed by what I saw: aged, yet beautifully maintained streets built of cobblestone, brick, and cement. Sidewalks covered with arches that were a flowing, natural part of the architecture of the hotel itself and of each and every building as far as the eye could see. The infinitely varied hues and textures of the stone and concrete that made up the beautifully-aged and intricately constructed façades. Colorful lights, strung up like a never-ending ode to Christmastime celebration, forming a canopy above a teeming, lively open air market whose borders were encircled by a canyon formed of even more gleefully inviting places to shop.

There was seemingly nothing you could not purchase when it came to food, clothing, and bric-a-brac. As our small group walked down those cobblestone streets, alternating back and forth between navigating those arch-covered shops and the draw of the marketplace, I was enthralled and intrigued that such a place as this could possibly exist. And even through the experience of all these amazing sights, scents, and sounds, in my spirit, I knew and recognized that the reason I was even there in the first place—the reason I was one among this lovely group of unfamiliar friends—was because of music. It was because of a gift that I had not yet manifested in my waking world, but one that was as inherent, natural, and God-given as my ability to breathe the fresh and invigoratingly clean air of this magical dreamscape. And I was being told by God—in NO uncertain terms—that this unmanifested, unrealized talent was ready and waiting for me—waiting to take me on a journey, both physically and spiritually, that would continue for the rest of my life.

The places that music has taken me, the people that I had been Blessed to meet, interact, and perform with, and the joy of discovering that God's gift to my life would also serve as a gift to others—if you look at your life and you realize the magnitude of the wonderful things that you have been Blessed to experience, none of which you felt deserving of—THAT is when you know, without doubt, that you are exactly where you are supposed to be. And no matter who it is that tries to steer you on another path for their own selfish reasons, no matter when those who claim to love and support you only doubt and abandon you, no matter when even YOU begin to doubt yourself and your purpose—NEVER let anyone or anything cause you to stray from the path, the gift, and the Blessing of what God himself has manifested within you.

Even before you knew that gift was even a thing.

BE GLAD THAT YOU ARE FREE

There is no direct and clearly mapped-out path to success. To be honest, I don't believe that there is even a true definition of success. For every person alive, from the seemingly poorest farmer, happily working his crops and livestock from sunup to sundown, to the CEO sitting atop the ivory tower he or she has managed to climb with hard work but at great personal sacrifice, each person must define their own idea of success.

Here in the United States, we have been conditioned by culture and capitalism to define success in strictly monetary terms. And to be fair, it is damn near impossible to achieve and maintain any reasonable quality of life without meeting this Westernized yardstick of success. The system here is built that way on purpose. You say you're not reasonably successful, American style? Well, then, no basic human rights or dignity for you. No healthcare. No housing. No support. No protections. Just the hamster wheel of work. Day in, day out. Paycheck to paycheck. Stressful crisis to stressful crisis. Broken family to broken family. All the while, never truly moving forward…only treading water. All the while the well-heeled one percent keeps creating artificial waves and adding water to the shark tank they call "democracy," making it progressively harder and harder to even effectively tread that water to avoid either drowning or being eaten alive.

Can you afford to eat? Do you have gas in your car, if you even own a car at all? Can you pay your bills? Do you have money in the bank? Those are typically seen as some of the lowest on the totem pole measurements of success. Yet in many places outside of these "Un-tied" States, the fact is that there are people who are genuinely HAPPY living very simple, seemingly meager lives. They are far less stressed. They enjoy a quality of life that brings them joy and happiness. They value the things that matter the most: love, health, laughter, and peace.

For instance, why has Finland been ranked for the last four years as the "happiest country in the world" by the UN's *World Happiness Report?* It's because they value the simple things, and they value each other. And, apparently, their government values these things as well. So, their people feel supported and secure. Not because they are individually successful. But because they are successful at simply living. And letting others live. Finns reportedly have a high amount of trust in their fellow citizens. That trust stems from a respect of person and a true sense of self within each individual.

So, as Creatives—as musicians—why do we believe that we continue to voluntarily endure the seeming struggle to maintain this life of never-ending gigs, late nights, road weariness, fighting to get paid fairly, if at all. Often living in a way where, on the surface, the quality of our lives is only as good as our last gig? My response to that question is this; as Creatives, we tend to have a truer, more realistic sense of self than most people. The reason being is that daily we are required to tap into our souls—our very essence—in order to create. We must not only tap into our souls, but we must also put what we find within ourselves on display, in broad daylight or under a glaring spotlight; more often than not, in front of a less-than-captive audience. Baring our souls for all the world to see, scrutinize, and judge.

When we as artists are truly performing at our best or in our "zone"; in our live and full-on moments of expressive creativity, we cannot hide ourselves. Our true natures come out when we are giving our best presentations. Sure, many artists are performing, in the sense of playing a role, for the enjoyment of those who come out to see and hear us. People want to be entertained. Period. They come to experience the creativity we have been blessed to have, to find escape from the lack of creativity and self-fulfillment that they themselves may be restricted from expressing or experiencing in their non-Creative daily lives. Sometimes we even act as catalysts which spark the nascent self-expression that is living within seemingly non-Creative people. In other words, Creatives move people. We touch hearts, minds, and souls. We inspire and remind.

For those of you who get to experience the baring of our creative souls, you'd better believe that, in most instances, what you as an audience member are seeing is not simply a part being played. What you are seeing is a part of who we truly are. A sliver of our true selves. Sometimes magnified or exaggerated. Sometimes tamped down, ever so slightly, as to not completely overwhelm the recipients of our gift and self-sharing. But make no mistake: you are seeing part or all of what we truly have and feel within us. It is the most freeing, self-aware thing that a person can experience. The ability to express our inner beings and have that expression connect viscerally, emotionally, and spiritually with others is everything. I have heard it said that music bypasses the conscious mind and goes directly to our central nervous system. I'm guessing this is why you may often find yourself unconsciously tapping your foot or moving your body to a beat playing in the background. Or why you may quite suddenly blurt out the lyrics to a song that wasn't even playing. Or why a song will suddenly transport you emotionally and mentally to a moment, space, or time—joyous or sad—with or without your permission.

Imagine experiencing that each and every time you step on a stage to perform. As musicians, as artists, as Creatives—we don't have to imagine. We live it, almost daily. And we embrace the reality of it.

It makes us free.

It unbinds our souls.

It manifests power.

Music puts us in direct communion with both God—and let's be one-hunne here— sometimes with the ungodly. Because both, neither, and ALL aspects of divinity and chaos exist within us all. It is why music is so very powerful—and, when misused, so very dangerous. After all, Lucifer was God's "number one": in charge of music and the eternal and constant praise and exaltation of God Himself. I mean, next in line behind words, spoken in complete faith and power (God SPOKE the universe into existence—size of a mustard seed, y'all), music is the most powerful thing in Heaven, even after the Fall. Especially after the Fall.

This is why, as Musical Creatives, we have responsibilities. We have obligations, realized or not. It is why "church musicians" were originally Levites of Old Testament Biblical times and were valued and anointed. But see, back then, Levites were taken care of, completely and wholly (holy) by the church or temple. In essence they may have been seen as "owned" by the church. This is an oversimplification of their relationship with God and the church, of course. But essentially, Levites wanted for no shelter, food, or clothing. They also didn't do club dates, so there's that. No judgement. I'm literally preaching to the choir here. Or at least the riddim section. As Michelle Obama so wisely said, "it is what it is."

But in a non-Biblical context, our responsibilities are not all that different than those of the Biblical Levites. We have the power to "usher in" spirits of all types. In our acts of self-expression, we experience the aforementioned freedom of spirit from within. We can disengage from worldly cares, albeit temporarily, and take audiences on our out-of-the-moment experiences right along with us.

And if all things are working as they should, musicians are also simultaneously having "conversations"; we are speaking our truths to one another through our voices and/or instruments. And we are there, on stage, to include the listeners in those conversations. The audience typically responds in kind with their feedback—their accolades, rebuttals, or even non-responsiveness—to what we are speaking.

Our responsibilities, then, are to speak clearly. To speak honestly. To say only what is necessary to convey a sentiment, a vibe, or a "spirit," as it were. We are responsible for which spirits we escort into every room, space, and venue we perform in. And we are responsible to act accordingly to the appropriate spirit is for the specific space, event, client, or circumstance. Our responsibility is to speak in excellence. Some musicians adhere to the idea of playing "as if this were your last night alive...." That generally translates to giving each performance your all; don't leave ANYTHING off the table.

I get that. And I'm down with the sentiment of that statement, if not always the actual execution of it. But sometimes we are there, on stage, playing, to simply heal ourselves. Sometimes we are barely present, struggling to even be there, physically, mentally, and emotionally. So, every time that I am Blessed to step onto a stage, or into a music pit; every time I go to lay tracks in a studio, or to enter musical worship in a sanctuary; it won't always be amazing. It won't always be a rip-roaring, "it's the end of the world as we know it," throw-up of notes and amazing musical moments, or perfect musicianship and solos for the ages. Sometimes it will be a solemn reflection. Sometimes it will be a silent cry for help. Sometimes it will be anger and frustration. Sometimes it will be pain. Any given moment of sharing music can be a rock-solid, feet-planted-firm testimony or declaration. Or it can be an unravelling rope, with us barely hanging on by that one good thread left.

But even when my situation or my vibe is any one of those things, my responsibility doesn't simply become about giving a perfect performance or entertaining an audience. It becomes about introducing that audience to who I am. In that day. In that night. And in that moment—

I am truly free.

Thirteen
OH, THE (IN)HUMANITY!

The Human Condition.

What is it, really? Can it be easily qualitatively and quantitatively defined? Much has been said about it in prose and in literature, in song and in film...about our lust for knowledge or our capacity to love. But there is also that other quaint trait of humanity: our invariable and seemingly inescapable leanings towards self-destruction. Honestly, I have quite often wondered to self and aloud:

"How the hell have we made it this far?"

Thousands and thousands of years of progress, innovation, and discovery stand right alongside and in stark contrast to thousands and thousands of years of the most horrific events and behaviors manifested and enacted by human beings against human beings.

The Bible itself speaks of the fact that humans, at one time in our history, were so horrific to one another—so "sinful"—that

God had to literally clean out the toilet bowl that Earth had become. He put some clean water in that mug along with the soap of righteousness, and he washed the sinful away and started over.

Now one would think that events such as the Coronavirus pandemic or the war in Ukraine—or anywhere else for that matter—would become a kumbaya reset moment for humanity. It is, after all, a not-so-existential threat to mankind on a planetary scale, which affects practically everyone from every walk of life. As a kid, I used to daydream about earth coming face-to-face with one of those type of extinction-level threats, playing it out in my mind where such a worldwide catastrophe would finally unite all of humankind against a common enemy, and humanity would then elevate to a higher level of existence through working together and defeating our shared adversary.

But Hollywood has always known better. As purveyors and manifestors of our darkest and innermost imaginations, they knew that humanity would constantly fail at reaching its lofty goal of spiritual, moral, and cultural elevation and enlightenment. Because in every damn movie ever made about aliens invading, giant monsters attacking, continent-sized meteors striking earth, viruses infecting us all, the sun exploding, or some such tragedy—there have always been humans portrayed who, even amid our mutual destruction, found it within themselves to make matters worse by attacking and destroying those who were different, or the most vulnerable among us during the given catastrophe. Those wayward humans always found their way towards greed, hate, violence, and destruction, even as the entire world crumbled around us all.

And as a child, I never believed that humans could be that terrible—that selfish and evil. And yet, as an adult, I've seen that human flaw manifest itself time and time again. And never more in my lifetime than during these last few years of being a Black man in America. Of course, it is a phenomenon which is evident worldwide. But always seemingly in allegedly "less developed," non-democratized, or less-civilized nations.

Alas, just as with COVID-19, this human virus is everywhere. No place is immune to its manifestation. No culture does not have the pock marks of its past infections by hate, evil, and greed.

Fortunately for humanity, many of us stand as natural antibodies against the forces of our own self-inflicted demise. Whether through nature or nurture, there have always been those of us who have stood against those others who would drive the whole damn bus full of us over the cliff simply to be in charge. Or be right. Or be rich. Or simply to be perceived as "better" than someone else.

Fragile egos, rampant narcissism along with psychopathic and sociopathic tendencies, underdeveloped self-awareness, damaged brains, inbreeding, total spiritual disconnect from the world and the universe. Greed. Fear. Stupidity. Ignorance, both willful and societally reinforced.

"How the hell did we make it this far?"

WE'RE ALL WE'VE GOT

I'm going to be honest: if it weren't for my chosen profession of music (as stated earlier, it chose me. Actually, God chose me), I likely wouldn't be on social media much...if ever.

I mean, I do enjoy being in touch with friends who are not easily seen or heard from due to time, distance, or simply life. I very much enjoy meeting new people, sharing thoughts and opinions, ideas, and life stories. And I'll be the first to admit that I love a brisk and healthy debate. Nothing stimulates the mind and spirit more than honest and passionate communication between deeper thinkers and open minds.

And just as stimulating to the mind and spirit are bouts of shallow silliness, laughter, and witty (sometimes not so much, though) commentary with both friends and strangers. But sometimes, in this day and age, social media platforms are the only spaces we have access to that allow us to enjoy these things, although my undying preference will always be enjoying communicating and sharing with people up close and in person. There is NO substitute.

Even though I, for the most part, don't share and air my personal life on social media when it involves those who are close to me, I will say that these last few months have been some of the most awfully trying times of my life. When your life gets "flipped turned" upside down, you find that underneath that rock, things get exposed. People get exposed. YOU get exposed. Very often not only to others, but to yourself.

I've said this many times before; depression is real. The toll that loss and/or drastic and unexpected change takes on people is real. Smiling faces...our own, and others'...sometimes they don't tell the truth. The struggle to stay in forward momentum—to stay relevant, to stay happy and healthy, and on top of your game, and strong for others, and balanced, and joyful, and peaceful, and debt free, and successful, and pay your bills, and stay on task, and stay spiritual in commune with God, and find a job, and keep a job, and be supportive for family and friends, and—did I say stay sane?

The. Struggle. Is. Real.

So many of us have unexpectedly lost people over the last few years whom we never expected to lose so soon. Family, friends, people we work with and knew both intimately and in passing. With so much loss and tragedy, why then do we not value each other more? Why do we willingly throw away people who truly love us, support us, care about us? All in the name of material gain or irrelevant and temporary disagreement or even misunderstanding? Before God gave us material things, He gave us life. Then purpose. Then each other. Then guidance (you may call them rules, but I don't see it that way). In that order.

The true goal of life is love. The distraction of life is material gain. Do we need "stuff and things"? Absolutely. Is it okay to want and work for a good life that includes things we don't need to have to simply survive? Absolutely! But what happens when the values get twisted? What happens when the stuff goes away?

I know that I often opine strongly about the world we live in--the climate of divisiveness, hate, and rhetoric. I talk often about race. About politics. About religion. And it is never my intention to offend anyone with my words. I will ALWAYS speak my truth. But I will also ALWAYS listen to and HEAR the truths of those who respectfully share theirs with me. And as much as I don't like most humans these days, I still love people. And next to my love of God, Life, Music, and the last slice of pizza, I will always respect and value people who respect themselves. And, more importantly, I will respect those people who respect me.

But those who manage to find their way into the deeper recesses of my life, my heart—those who show me that, without a doubt, they strive to UNCONDITIONALLY love me: those are the ones who are priceless to me. Nothing on this earth has more value to me than they do.

So, if you have some of those people in your lives, hold them close. Don't trade them away for the Shiny Objects of life. Love up on them while they are here to be loved. And don't allow life's foolishness to separate you from them.

'Cause, at the end of the day, we're all that we've got.

DINOSAUR BRAINS

Observation:

The same people who have denied the existence of the COVID-19 pandemic, and who constantly decided to NOT wear masks or social distance, who worked hard to debunk the death tolls, protest about "rights" as if the scientists, medical professionals, and government officials who are trying to do what little they know to do to save lives, are doing so simply for some imagined diabolical political reasons. The same people who have no empathy towards anyone affected by the virus...of course, until it actually affects their lives directly... and who would rather breathe in your face, throw bitchy fits in stores and public spaces that are trying to keep everyone safe, repeat lies, call you names and spout conspiracy theories—they would rather do all that than to simply think about the common good and act accordingly while the body count continues to rise in real life.

My friends, those are the EXACT same people who do the EXACT same thing when it comes to racism.

Like the pea brain of a Tyrannosaurus Rex, their minds are literally incapable of thinking beyond their next meal. Critical thinking for them means being critical of anything or anyone they disagree with, even in the face of blatant and real time evidence to the contrary.

These type of Gumbies can only see two feet in front of themselves. Because that is the limit of their world view and their views of humanity. Even horses with blinders on will look at them like they're stupid. Because they are. They are willfully blind, because seeing anything beyond their peripheral vision would challenge their own fragile Jenga constructs of self-importance and place in the world. It's why they use words like "snowflake" and the like. Because they share the same damaged mindset as those "bullies" in life who are determined to beat down everyone else and have their gotcha moments first before anyone exposes their own failings and weaknesses. Feeling "superior" to others is the only thing that gets them out of bed in the mornings. It's what defines them. Because wisdom, uniqueness, honesty, and character certainly do not. They simply go with the mob mindset because it's easy. It's herd mentality.

Ladies and gentlemen, these types of people are the Tofu of humanity; they have no flavor of their own. They are only as good as what is mixed with them. They will steal "flavor" from everyone else. But they don't want to acknowledge who the original sources of that flavor are. And so, in their minds, the only options are to either control or destroy the sources and the narrative.

And that is why these types of beings can only define themselves when someone else is being made to be perceived as lesser than them. And I'm here to tell you, I don't believe that they have the brain, heart, or soul capacity to behave any other way.

❖ ❖ ❖

As a species, we humans are certainly seeing, in real time, that there are some definitive subdivisions of humankind in as far as how we think and respond to situations and circumstances. It seems to break down as follows:

Those who thrive on chaos and anarchy and who care little about the wellbeing of others.

- » Those who crave power and a sense of self-importance at any cost.
- » Those who make purely emotional and fear-based decisions, and who respond accordingly.
- » Those who follow the herd blindly because they have no individual strength of identity, and so they simply go along with the group mind because it's easy.
- » Those who divide the world into "us" and "them" and respond to life on those terms.
- » Those who make rational decisions based on clear and proven fact-based information.
- » Those who actively seek out solutions to problems for the benefit of not only themselves, but others, as well.

Of course, there are our own unique and individual responses to life. But to me, what this pandemic has truly made apparent—that clear, practical, and rational thinking is not a given or automatically inherent to our race.

I am always amazed that we have survived this long.

❖ ❖ ❖

Black Diaspora. White, Hispanic, Native, Asian, Middle Eastern Accomplices ("we don't need racial equity allies, we need active accomplices"): don't let the whataboutism get pulled over your eyes.

Some people will keep trying to use slanted and outdated statistics to "win" arguments. Give them all the shade you can muster. Those type of people will never see things for what they truly are. They are only here to placate their own guilt and Privilege. Their self-righteousness and narcissism are all that matters to them.

SLEEPWALKING

As I've stated before. I'm kinda tired. I know MANY of us are.

I really don't believe that people know how to truly interact with one another anymore. And while Social Media of course has its limitations, drawbacks, and pitfalls when it comes to engaging with people, both familiar and unfamiliar, the truth is, we know is that Social Media is anything but truly social. And the problems with Social Media have only been highlighted, heightened, and exacerbated by the concurrent pandemics of C-19 and political, race-driven irrational hate.

I tell you: I truly miss good old in person human interaction. Being an introvert by nature, I was more or less fine being on lockdown. But what I did miss was meeting new people in person organically...honestly. Outside of family and close friends, we as humans really aren't always interacting. Sure...we talk AT one another endlessly. But we are not, in large part, having CONVERSATIONS. People are "hearing" but are not "listening".

We've seemingly lost, as a society, the art of meeting new people. The fun of getting to know someone. The skill of conversation. The gift of openness and honesty. The essence of discernment and trust. The beauty of love, loving, and being in love. The depth of real and lasting friendships. The sincerity of supporting and holding up one another through crisis and tragedy beyond "praying hands" emojis and "sincerest condolences" statements that we are now regulated to and which have now become more ubiquitous than genuine.

I'm a fairly simple person. I don't need a lot of things—although, YES, I love my basses, my A/V gear, and my books. In the words of Steve Martin in The Jerk, "...and that's all I need." See, all I've ever really wanted is to enjoy life for the gift that it is; that includes using the talents that God Blessed me with of painting life's truths with words, and moving souls with music, to express to and communicate with others. To share ideas and musical conversation with other musicians, on stage and in studio. To be surrounded by and involved with family, real friends, and loved ones. To fall in love with the love of a good woman, and to love her pure, hard, and true. To laugh, cry, hurt, heal, support, fight, and grow together. To connect on a subatomic level to likeminded people with similar honest goals and wants and needs.

But on the real, we live in a world that works to actively suppress and destroy light and joy. This we know. God has long ago told this fact to those of us who have listened.

Powers and principalities in HIGH places. That's what we're fighting against. Active and ongoing soul-snatching. Greed. Hate. Murder. Evil. And, of course, there are some (many, actually) who willingly and voluntarily give their souls up for sale and barter with those High Powers. Judas would be proud.

Instead of getting better, we've apparently gotten worse. Are there pockets of resistance to the darkness? Are there warriors, both young and old, fighting to hold back the slow roll towards the cliff of human destruction? Absolutely! And I am holding on to that fact—that hope—that we aren't quite yet done. Because otherwise, we've seemingly lost our collective and individual ways.

Many claim to be "woke"—but in actuality, they are simply sleepwalking.

We've lost morality. We've lost respect and honor. We've lost honesty and sincerity. We've lost love...traded it for status, false security, and a misunderstanding of what love is all about. We've seemingly lost the best of our humanity. We've lost God. We've lost ourselves.

But hopefully, prayerfully, the search and rescue parties out looking for our lost humanity will succeed in finding it and bringing it back home safely.

DON'T BELIEVE THE HYPE

I strive to not be judgmental when looking through my own flawed lens at other people. You know—that whole mote and beam thing.

And then there are times when people hide behind the phrase, "it's my personal truth." Well, the problem is that while we all live within our own personal universes, which must, by necessity, interact and intermingle with everyone else's personal universes daily, there are simply some things that are not personal truths for most of us; they are convenient lies we tell ourselves to achieve whatever goal we're going after. They are true lies by measure of any critical way they are looked at. Yes, we all have put protections in place to protect ourselves from past hurts and failures. But often, many will weaponize those protections and convert them from offensive protections to defensive weapons.

Sadly, people who do not enact periodic self-checks and inventory maintenance will not recognize or acknowledge the fiction that supports their "facts." They won't look at that crap stuff packed waaaay at the back of their mental and emotional warehouses. Because it's too hard for them to climb over the wall they have erected to hide the garbage pile. And they subsequently begin to believe their own hype, their own world view, and their own lies. And then they pass that toxic crap on to others.

THE SKIN WE'RE ALL IN

Every nation that ever was has had people who were indigenous to that nation, who worked hard to build it. Unfair labor existed…yes. Child labor? Sadly, that is most certainly the case. The poor, the powerless, and disenfranchised have always been cannon fodder for the elite.

But the next level below that is revealed by the question—how many of those workers were brought to a country NOT of their origin by force? And I'm not talking about using criminals to do the work like Australia did. I'm talking about pillaging and genocide. How many of those workers were beaten, lynched, and desecrated on the regular? Sold as property? Had ZERO human rights? Separated from their families for the purpose of breaking their spirits? Sold at auctions like animals? Abused as the norm? The truth is that the horrors of slavery far surpassed anything that white laborers suffered, even in light of the fact that we all originally met on the field of indentured servitude. The elites saw that Blacks had formed connections with those whites who were indentured along with us; that is when we attempted our blended revolts against the elites.

Those self-proclaimed elites could not have any servants working together for freedom. And so, Blacks got relegated to the very bottom of the human pecking order—actually, below human—in order to make whites who were being used by elites feel at least superior to Blacks and to separate us by skin.

Of course, we all know it's the very same playbook used today, that somehow keeps effectively working. Because the poor whites don't recognize that the poor Blacks' struggle will always be one rung below them due to the fact that, for us, economic poverty is only a subset of racism, as opposed to simply being kept poor. Poor whites have at least the opportunity of becoming a middle class, or rich white person, and no one would know their humble beginnings and judge them by it. It's the story of every white immigrant that came to these shores and made something of themselves.

We cannot hide our skin, no matter how well-off we become. And that skin will ALWAYS, first and foremost, define us negatively to the prejudiced and racist non-Blacks of the world.

TAPPING OUT

I was today years old when I first heard "Allyship Fatigue." I get that if something doesn't seemingly directly affect your life (but if they paid close attention, it actually does) that it is hard to sustain an active involvement with it. Oh wait, how about those animal activists like PETA? Or Greenpeace? Or...

But we have another name for Allyship Fatigue that is all-encompassing: White Privilege. Because, if so inclined, White people have the PRIVILEGE of being able to walk away--of jumping in on the double Dutch game, then quitting after they feel that they've played long enough...before the "game" is even over.

"Travel T, cross your legs, turn around and out...!"

Thanks for playing.

THOUGHTFULLY UNCRITICAL

Fact:

Some people just say and repeat what they hear without thinking about the things that they actually see. They don't look at the 'big picture" because they already have false images formed in their own minds based on personal partialities and prejudices. They become ideologues based on feelings, not facts. It's what you are now seeing on both far ends of the current sociopolitical climate. Despite what they may believe, they are NOT "critical thinkers."

Because thinking critically requires a person to take ALL aspects of the situation into account, to weigh the pros and cons, and to be objective about the possible outcomes and the viable solutions that will be the most effective, practical, and logical ones for the given circumstances. Critical thinking creates sound strategy based on ALL the information that is available...if you're looking for it.

Critical thinking requires one to step outside of one's own biases and preconceived notions, to arrive at an elucidation and a panacea which resolves the issue at hand, and not simply a response that may work in the most ideal of circumstances.

Fourteen

WHITE LIGHT
DIARY OF A MAD BLACK MAN

To be VERY CLEAR:

No one alive today is responsible for the creation of the scientifically and biologically false concept of "race" in America. No one Black is blaming anyone non-Melanated for that.

But—and please hear me clearly with an open mind and heart when I say this:

The majority of non-melanated people who are alive today benefit directly or indirectly, purposefully or passively, in one way or the other, from its existence. This is not an indictment. It is simply a fact.

In the case of America, non-melanated people benefit from the creation of a false hierarchy created to justify, specify, classify, and label people for the benefit of the controlling group holding the power to make these prejudiced distinctions; and ALWAYS to the detriment of the group not in power; all in direct conflict with the beautifully worded edict written into this nation's foundational doctrine, The Declaration of Independence. Words that claim belief and allegiance to the ideology that "all men are created equal."

Thus, when basic human rights and protections are controlled by those in power who have a lesser view of those who are not in power, those basic rights and protections are made to look like…and meted out as…privilege. In this case, "White Privilege." We know that they are actually basic human rights and considerations. But we didn't make the rules here. So we call it for how it is put into practice: as things allowed and not natively owned and deserved by everyone.

These privileges are subject to the whims and wiles of those who have deemed themselves worthy of enjoying them, unencumbered by their skin tone or points of cultural origin. Yet these same privileges are regularly and conveniently rationed out as seen fit to those who have been designated as not only less than worthy, but as even being less than human. Thus effectively making the unworthy incapable of being represented by the words "all men" (and let me point out that women have their own sub-detriment under this ideology; yet Black women must live with the double whammy; the sub-SUB detriment of being MELANATED women).

Many like to believe that Black people falsely see race in everything—that we often "cry wolf"—when, to them, there is NO wolf. But here's the thing: if you don't live in the wilderness, you are likely to never see a wolf. And even if you do see one, you'll probably not believe your own eyes, and maybe even call it a dog instead. You won't get stalked, preyed upon, or even killed and eaten by the wolf if you exist in a beautifully constructed bubble, made not BY you, but most certainly FOR you, to not only protect you from the wolf, but to blind you to its very existence. To make it seem as though the wolf is only a fairy tale—an "urban" legend, if you will.

And many of those same people express that they grow weary of talking about race.

But if you are tired of hearing about race...then how do you think WE feel having to LIVE it each and every day?

To those of you of that non-Melanated life who are not in true allyship with us: please check yourselves when you don't get why someone who is Melanated is offended or put off by something you may intentionally or unintentionally say or do. Or when you think you have all the answers. When you unilaterally decide a melanated person is making a big deal out of nothing. When you get tired of hearing about race.

Want to know why we as Black people are seemingly triggered by any and everything?

It's because the gun attached to that trigger is constantly pointed. Directly. At. Us.

And trust and believe—that gun is ALWAYS loaded.

❖ ❖ ❖

My existence, well-being, and prosperity is only a threat to you if your own self-worth is lacking. That's it. That's the message.

FEAR OF A BLACKERER PLANET

These are the things that people need to understand and accept before change can happen:

the financial and power infrastructure of America is built upon racism, pure and simple. This country was never meant for POC to be free and equal. Thus, the audacity of someone to create a television show that depicts slavery in the modern day as a corporate business. The Powers that Be don't want change. Period.

Those same powers control politics, not the people. They buy elections. That's what lobbying is. And SuperPACs. And corporate giving to the candidates of choice.

Politicians, for the most part, are not working for us. And those who do try to altruistically work for their constituency and the common good, are typically politically crippled, shut down, or "unelected" by those Powers that Be who want to maintain the status quo that most benefits them. This system has been in place for a long time, and politicians are way too comfortable where they are. That's why they won't take the same healthcare they are trying to ram down our throats.

The middle majority is afraid of change. They too are comfortable, even when they are struggling. They are comfortable because their struggle is based on financial issues that they have been led to believe can be overcome with a better job. Our struggle is based on the color of our skin.

The problem as always is that whenever we as POC speak our truths, there's always someone who wants to tell us not to, because in doing so we're adding to the violence by saying "Hey XYZ, we need to stop bringing up race, or slavery." Or anything. Just be mute and humble and go on about your business. AND, many times, such a sentiment has been expressed under the guise of religion and healing. Often. And always with self-aggrandizement and self-righteousness. Contrary to what you seem to be implying, God HAS ALWAYS been our sustenance and sustainer. Not the god small "g," who was forced down our throats during slavery. But the God we already knew centuries before our forced migration from The Motherland. The God of Abraham, Isaac, and Jacob. That God that we were made to worship—that's not the same god. Because the god who everyone— from the colonizers of the past, to "conservative White Christians" of the present continue to reference; that god is a false god and a scapegoat, created, crafted and morphed as needed in order to serve as weak justification for those who worship him. That god allows the non-mlanated and others of their depth of brokeness, to sleep better at night—covered by a blanket of their own fabricated self righteousness, hatred, judgement, misdeeds, and sins against humanity. All under the guise of religion and "manifest destiny. Let's just call them children of a lesser god, shall we?

I'm sorry, those of you who are those children of a lesser god. We the Melanated, will NEVER not speak out; NEVER not fight for our own justice, and remind the non-melanated that we are here to stay. Because when the wound never heals because the vultures continuously pick at the scab, how can the patient not cry out as they experience continuous pain? These wounds we as POC carry, these stripes—they haven't healed in more than 220+ years. Because the world keeps ripping those scabs off and applying the wrong medicine—or at the very least, administering only temporary relief.

So, until those who do not live our lives and experience our struggles actually get down and dirty into the muck of fighting against our oppression, discrimination, racism, classism, glass ceilings, innocents' killings by cops, outright dismissal by the "powers that be," and experience the heartache and Groundhog Day-like lives we have to face each and every day—

You don't get to tell us to be silent.

MOVE ALONG—NOTHING TO SEE HERE

Here are the degrees of racism in America from my humble point of view:

1. Outright hate against Black people by White people based simply on our melanin content being different

from theirs and their desire to feel superior through the subjugation and destruction of others

2. Less active, yet just as pervasive hate against Black people by Whites, based on their discomfort with their own hate for those who do not look like them. Thus, the backlash we receive whenever we "play the race card." Even though white people created the deck and the game itself

3. Active disdain (not quite outright hate) towards Black people by Whites based on having to share anything they deem belongs exclusively to them, and that we are "taking away" those resources or opportunities from their exclusivity

4. Passive, generally dormant, yet trigger-able disdain for Blacks by Whites when the notion of institutional racism or white privilege is mentioned, thought of, discussed, attributed to, referenced in passing, acknowledged, or Blacksplained to a White person

5. Offense expressed when Whites feel "excluded" any time Blacks create anything that caters to the specific needs of the Black Diaspora due to a lack of those needs being met by the Unmelanated Industrial Complex. In other words, NAACP, Black Wall Street, Rosewood, Black Panther Party, BLM, Black Institutes of Higher Education—hell, Jazz, Blues, Gospel, Hip Hop—whatever.

6. Active annoyance, denial, and defensiveness by Whites whenever Blacks call out Cultural Appropriation or any of its related iterations (our declaration of being the creators of anything they like, use or need, etc.). Up to the point when someone says something about it, we're all one big happy see-no-color, melanin-less, kumbaya-ing family.

Until we aren't.

A person cannot "get over" what is still happening to them. A people cannot "move past" what is still being perpetrated against them. A nation cannot "come together" standing upon the two sides of the rotten foundation which still supports it.

THIS IS HOW THEY DO IT

Dig it...

What do you do if, in the most powerful country on earth, you are part of a small, yet rich, powerful, and influential percentile of the dominant culture...and you see the data which informs you that your "race," as it were, was on track to becoming the minority race in said country in a few years?

Well, that's simple! You create "The Others." You create an environment where you make those of your race who are not so influential, not so powerful, and not so rich believe that every other race in said country (specifically those who don't look or speak like you) is out to not only take over your jobs, your neighborhoods, your schools, your women and children, your "purity," your privilege—but that they are also coming to destroy you. You make them believe that The Others are here to challenge your very existence and your dominant position by the power of their acquisition of equality and by their sheer numbers as they invade "your" lands and multiply.

You create laws to punish, suppress, and control the females, including those of your own population, blocking them from having pregnancies that are aborted for any reason, taking away their right to make decisions about their own bodies. Not for some real and altruistic moral or religious belief. Or for a deep-seated belief in the sanctity of all life. But you create these laws in order to simply build up the progeny of your race, and increase its population for the grand future of your dominant race to secure that dominance, that power, that influence, for the far seen future. And, of course, the "unintended" fringe benefit to these laws would be that those women of the other races who are poor, who are helpless, who are without access to proper medical care or financial stability—they are the women who you believe will break these laws far more often than those of your race. And so, you can prosecute, imprison, and further suppress the growth of these non-you populations.

You change the laws that regulate the criteria for citizenship in your country to be "merit based," favoring those from other countries whose migrants are born looking just like you, who have in-common cultures and heritages with your great and wonderful dominant culture, and who are more likely to be well-educated and well-adjusted, thereby limiting the entry numbers of those who seek to escape the poverty, war, persecution, and ravages of their not so well-adjusted nations because, well, they're less likely to look like you anyway. And those are usually shithole countries to begin with. So, there's that.

You even mislead those who are the poorer, less empowered, less socially viable, less educated of your ilk—the lesser—into believing lies, deceits, and misinformation about things that you say will be better for them and make their proud and wonderful nation great again. You tell your followers that "they" are taking "your" jobs. That the others are driving up your insurance costs. That they are all terrorists, gang members, drug addicts, thieves, and murderers. You create an enemy for your followers to focus on while you steal from them and keep them in the societal class that you need them to be in for your 1% to maintain your positions at the top of the heap. Because, truth is, there are no real enemies except for the ones within your own tribe.

You use their blind hatred and fear of the differentness of The Others and their blind faith in your sameness with them to keep them complacent, obedient, and loyal. Without ever offering a way for them to truly be just like you. After all, every hive needs its worker drones, right? Hamster wheels can be fun and fulfilling too, right?

Those of your sameness who maybe by chance believe in the right of "The Others" to have the opportunities to enjoy the equality, prosperity, freedom, and justices that you have always enjoyed? Well—you discredit them. You dismiss them. You frame them as sellouts to your sameness. You define them as being misguided, uninformed, and, at worst, traitors who have aligned with the Others against the sameness of your race. They become a threat to the purity of your race, and so you convince your supporters to treat them as they would treat the Others—as enemies.

You play the victim. You dismantle any achievements made by powerful Other-Lovers who have come before you. You become Pharaoh Rameses, scratching out the name of Moses from every monument and temple that you can.

You destroy a nation in order to build YOUR world in your xenophobic, narcissistic likeness. And in the process, you also help to destroy the very same world you desire to rule over.

We ALL have, to one degree or another, implicit biases. We all tend to relate more easily to and favor those whom we have more in common with than others. It's the tribal aspect of our human nature.

But implicit bias is not hate. It's not even racism, which, by the way, the dictionary definition of is being updated, thanks to a beautiful young sister, Kennedy Mitchum, who went directly to Merriam-Webster and fought to make that oft misused word's definition more accurate. However, implicit bias IS a jumping off point for prejudice. Implicit bias is the spark that makes some happily judge a book by that proverbial cover.

And if you can work out all the rationalities safely within your own head without research, facts, or knowledge—well, that just makes it easier to believe the lies and assumptions you have told yourself to feel your self-righteous indignation. And you do this so that you never have to face up to the fact that you are end-justifying your own means. All in order to plug up the gaping hole of insecurity in your own soul. All in order to help you feel superior to another group because of...get this...melanin count. That's it. Melanin. It's not even about the cultural differences we have. It's skin color. Do you understand how asinine that sounds when you say it out loud?

I have friends from many walks of life, friends with different melanin counts. Some with much more than I. Some with different hues of melanin altogether. Some with little to almost none. And I see ALL their respective colors, shades, and hues. Because that is part of what makes them who they are: the people that I know, love, and respect. Yet—to a fault and to a person—I consciously try not to allow my implicit biases to predispose me to a certain idea about who these people are. What they think. How they behave. What they believe. Or how they feel about me in their secret spaces. And I try to extend that same courtesy to anyone new that I meet. I'll circle back to this point in a bit.

Yet, first and foremost, that act of self-monitoring requires a will to see beyond that first physical impression we have of one another, which is usually the only thing we have to initially go on when meeting someone for the first time. It takes a desire to acknowledge and understand. A thirst to learn and a healthy respect for that which is not intimately familiar to us.

None of that takes away our implicit biases. Many of us watched "one of these things is not like the other" on Sesame Street. So we know everything is not supposed to be the exact same thing. But what it does achieve is to give us the equipment and the tools to overcome those preconceived notions. It moves us in a direction of true self-awareness via some self-imposed mental and emotional checks and balances and some real and meaningful soul-searching.

We mostly tend to like who/what we like. And even as individuals, we tend to gravitate towards the familiar, the comfortable. But when you decide to actively oppress, hate or kill the unfamiliar and the uncomfortable, then that goes far beyond implicit bias. That is The Sunken Place in your own soul. That is self-loathing, insecurity, and broken morality, manifested as lashing out at the Others. And, sadly, there may be no hope for you. Satan has a contract with you. And you willingly signed on the dotted line.

MELANIN

I mentioned it earlier—but lets get into it a little deeper.

So colonizer—lets talk for a sec.

Now I would think that you'd have something better to do with your time, effort and money than spend it all in a futile attempt to destroy me. Like—I don't know—at least maybe helping those of your own tribe who have less than zero.

Really. It's the dumbest thing ever when you break it down to basics: you hate me because I have more melanin than you.

That's it.

Not because my tribe killed your tribe. Pillaged your village. Stole your children. Kidnapped your men, women, and children, packed them into the bottom of ships under the most inhumane conditions for weeks. Threw you overboard into the sea to become shark food if you tried to escape. Enslaved you. Raped your women. Destroyed your identity. Stole your land. Committed genocide against you.

Reneged on the promise of reparations once you were symbolically "freed" from enslavement. Terrorized and denied the rights of every human being. Lynched, burned, dismembered, disfigured, beat, and shot you for sport to be displayed to children and whole families on a sunny Sunday afternoon after church with said events photographed and made into commemorative postcards with your smiling evil faces.

It's not like we beat, arrested, fire hosed, or dog attacked you for peacefully protesting for your God-given rights. Or like we burned, bombed, looted, destroyed, and razed to the ground the towns and neighborhoods that you created for yourselves through sheer force of will and ingenuity in spite of our oppression of you.

It's not like we stole farms, businesses, patents, or money from you when you worked hard to gain them. Or that we actively created groups specifically to impose fear, harass, and destroy your will and your ways. We didn't change gun laws on you or anything. It's not like we changed many other laws, gerrymandered maps, closed voter polling locations, required payment and ID that were unavailable to many of your people because of lack of opportunity and access, simply to stymie your voices and limit your power and influence.

It's not like we destroyed the whole middle class because you were becoming a prominent part of it, and we needed to keep a healthy income gap between us and you to perpetuate your lack of generational wealth and our societal and financial "dominance" over you. Or that we only see you as entertainment for us; that we want you to just shut up and dribble. Or dance and sing your way out of poverty—if you can. And even then, it's not like we want you to stay in your lanes. It's not like we give you poor educational opportunities, and concurrent to that, we also create a pipeline to our prison system by giving you beatings and arrests instead of books and apprenticeships, cops instead of counselors, and apathy instead of access.

It's not like we put guns and drugs into your neighborhoods—I mean ghettos; guns and drugs you could not possibly have gotten ahold of without our help, because you can't even get ahold of a decent grocery store in your hoods. Or like we then police you and arrest you and hustle you through the legal system often on...trumped...up charges, incarcerate you for inordinate numbers of years compared to us for even the slightest offense. Or like we make lots of money off of every one of you we can imprison because we privatized the penal system to be Slavery 3.0 ('cause you know...it's not like we created Jim Crow laws and indentured servitude and sharecropping to enact Slavery 2.0 or anything).

It's not like we have created privilege for ourselves out of the most mundane of rights and freedoms and put self-sustaining systems and institutions (that, by the way, your enslavement helped to create and finance...no, nothing like that), redlines, checks and balances in place in order to make it a lifelong struggle for you to achieve and even hold onto any modicum of those rights and freedoms. It's not like we get fragile when you want to have a discussion...ANY discussion...about race inequality and injustice. Or like we lash out like crazed toddlers when you try to tell us that your lives matter, too, because the "all" in our original and ongoing laws did not include you.

It's not like we shoot, choke, kneel on your neck for 8 minutes and 46 seconds (or 9 minutes and 26 seconds depending on who you ask), or kill you any way we see fit, whether or not you peacefully comply or struggle to breathe; or when you inform us that you have a license for your legally issued weapon; or when you simply ask why our law enforcement is stopping your vehicle for a broken tail light; or when you are coming home from your run to the store for Skittles; or when you are going for your morning jog; or when you are checking on your mother's house; or when you are in your own home eating ice cream about to go to bed; or when you were already asleep after a long shift of saving lives of your own AND ours; or when you are simply accused of passing a counterfeit $20 bill that you may not have even known was counterfeit…if it was ever counterfeit at all; or when our law enforcement can't tell a motorcycle from a van and lay you and your children out on the hot asphalt face down, with hands cuffed behind their backs simply because of the color of their skin (because it's not like if it were us arresting us, we'd have taken our own to Burger King instead…even if we had just mass murdered people).

It's not like we elected an inept and insane monster as president simply as butthurt backlash to your electing a first of your kind: a history maker; an intelligent, capable, and real human being. Or like we publicly and boldly proclaimed that we would oppose EVERYTHING that your first-of-your-kind president tried to enact...even if it was something that would benefit us.

It's not like we separated families, most simply seeking a better life away from oppression, poverty, and danger (kind of like why most of us came here), put your children in cages for indefinite periods of time, lost some of them, abused some of them, and sent you back to the horrors of your homeland without your children. It's not like we are content watching you die as you work to save our lives, feed our families, power our cities, move our mail, build our infrastructure, teach our children...during the worst worldwide health crisis of our lifetimes. It's not like we are withholding funds to the states where you are seemingly more valued and more protected than in others—-funds that would help keep you safe and healthy, get you tested, keep you cared for in hospitals, keep you from starving, being evicted, and possibly losing everything. Nope...not us.

It's not like we've done anything like that to deserve your hate and disdain.

So...why do you hate us so passionately again?

Oh, yeah.

Melanin.

SHUDDUP AND DRIBBLE

Certain groups of people keep espousing about how "disrespectful" kneeling in protest of police brutality during the national anthem at the Super Bowl was. They keep going on and on ad nauseam about how disrespectful peaceful protest is to their privileged norms.

You know what's disrespectful?

* Genocide.
* Slavery.
* Internment of Japanese-American citizens
* Lynching
* Land and property theft
* Reconstruction
* Jim Crow
* Marrying into a Native American tribe in order to murder their newly acquired spouses for their oil-rich land that YOU displaced them to before you knew it was oil-rich
* Forcefully uprooting and destroying a Black village in order to build a park
* Segregation
* Declaring a human being to be 3/5ths of a human being due to having more melanin than you
* Classifying a person by race when there's no such thing

* Coming up with a "one drop" rule in order to discriminate against a group of people
* Conducting medical experiments on Black men without their knowledge and watching them die from said experiments for the sake of "science"
* Using Black women as lab rats in order to perfect medical procedures that white women would benefit more from
* Bombing, razing, and pillaging Black neighborhoods and towns because they became self-sufficient
* Lying on a twelve-year-old boy about an "affront" to white womanhood, then brutally and wrongfully murdering him
* Setting off atomic bombs near a populated South Pacific island to test the effects of radiation on a population
* Redlining
* Anti-Semitism
* McCarthyism
* Putting a delusional, racist, paranoid schizophrenic crossdresser in charge of one of the world's most powerful police and spy forces
* Bombing Mosques

* Mass-murdering school children, Black church goers, and concert attendees
* Pulling a Black woman over for a broken taillight and then committing Law Enforcement sanctioned murder of her while in jail
* Law enforcement-sanctioned murder of a Black woman in her sleep in her own home
* Law enforcement-sanctioned murder of a Black man in his own home while eating ice cream
* Law enforcement-sanctioned murder of a Black man in front of his woman, who did everything "right" by telling you he was licensed to carry a gun and that he had it with him
* Taking a mass shooter to Burger King after he was peacefully arrested, yet taking a knee on an innocent Black man's neck for 8 minutes, 46 seconds
* Forced labor by colonizers to build buildings, monuments, and infrastructure that you will never benefit from
* Child labor and seven-day work weeks forced upon the poor by the elite class before unions came into being
* Buying of a president and an election by the elite class

* Not allowing women the right to vote
* Blackballing a Black athlete for exercising his right to protest police brutality against Black and Brown people peacefully and silently...

In the words of Captain America (the irony CANNOT be lost on anyone here), "I can do this all day."

CAN WE ALL JUST GET ALONG?

I really wish things weren't the way they are today.

I still want to believe that a good majority of people of all cultures in this nation simply want to live good, safe, happy, and fulfilling lives. And even though there are a myriad of cultural differences that make up this "melting pot" that the United States has always touted itself to be, those differences are mostly ones which don't hurt or hinder any other group's lives in any way. As a matter of fact, the opposite has proven to be true; we are all enriched when we are able to freely coexist and share with each other the unique cultural beauties from each of our diasporas. In those moments when we are able to do this, we are actually fulfilling the true promise of American exceptionalism, as it were.

Sadly, there will always be those who are not satisfied with peaceful and prosperous coexistence. Their own insecurities, self-hate, envy, jealousy, fear, and moral bankruptcy will always drive them to view everything from an "us versus them" perspective. There is no common ground in their minds and hearts. There is no space or place for "other" in their worldview. They will always be driven by the desire to feel "dominant"—to vilify anything and anyone who is different from them. They will always desire to loot and steal from others, to refuse understanding of anything that is not within their comprehension, and to suppress and/or destroy that which is a perceived threat to their status quo.

These are the types of beings who are devoid of common sense. Rationality is overridden by irrational hate. It doesn't take much for them to turn from pleasant neighbor to angry frothing-at-the-mouth Karens and Bobs (no offense to you actual Karens and Bobs). Because the thin veneer they front with on a daily basis, the facade of humanity they display to us, to themselves, and to each other, is just a click away from tribal, animalistic insanity and antipathy. And again...most of these beings don't even honestly know why they feel the way they feel.

They are simply the Manchurian Candidates of racism, just waiting to be triggered.

There is this combination of generationally-indoctrinated hate, mob mentality, and simply a desire to be part of the "in-crowd" as it were, i.e., it's fashionable to hate Black people. If you could ask some of these types of people why they honestly hate Black people, 99% will not have a valid, personal negative experience with any of us. It's literally what they've been taught. It's what they consume information-wise. And it's what makes them feel better about themselves, which is the original reason that the misguided ideology of "race" was created and nurtured in the early days of this nation. Before that, it wasn't even a thing.

"If you can convince the lowest white man he's better than the best colored man, he won't notice you're picking his pocket. Hell, give him somebody to look down on, and he'll empty his pockets for you."
—Lyndon B. Johnson

❖ ❖ ❖

When a person's entire existence—their perception of their place in the world, and how they got there—is challenged, exposed for half-truths and untruths…then they are not going to go willingly into the light. And to some small degree I can understand that.

If you have never had to deal with the circumstances and consequences that others have had to deal with—if the quality of their lives hasn't even been in your purview, let alone within your consciousness—then understanding and accepting the realities of "those others'" lives…and how the values and circumstances of YOUR life directly benefit from their challenges and tragedies…is a very big pill to swallow.

BUT it is ABSOLUTELY the necessary medicine that MUST be taken for this nation to truly heal and move FORWARD. We must come to terms with our past (and, sadly, some of our present) to create a real and viable future that benefits EVERYONE EQUALLY.

Unless, of course, you are a person who is comfortable with racism, fascism, lies, and deception. And apparently, many, many people are.

BUILT TO LAST

Human beings will always have biases and prejudices. No amount of bias or sensitivity training at our jobs are going to change that. We don't live in a world where you cannot learn about anything you care to learn about anymore. Information is literally at everyone's fingertips. So, while most White Americans will never experience the totality of the Black experience, it is more than possible for people to educate themselves if they are so willing.

The reason why systematic racism is a major factor is not because it is being fed by people who don't know any better or who need more education and awareness. It's because the whole system is built to profit from it—ALL of it—from law enforcement to the judicial system, to the prison industrial complex; from education to corporate America, to healthcare. They ALL profit from misery, lack, and the suppression of those who would otherwise prosper as much as the next man or woman.

So, the people in the middle are continuously trained to believe, generation after generation, that their way of life is good, and that any imbalance brought on by something as terrible as equality or justice would jeopardize the way of life they have been trained to value...that lovely American Dream™. America has been, is, and always will be fueled by profit for the wealthy...rebranded as capitalism to be sold to the White middle class and dangled in front of the White lower class. And simply teased at as a possibility to minorities and immigrants.

The system did not "become." It was built this way. Those hallowed "founding fathers" didn't come here and start a nation because they were tired of King George's oppression. They did so because they got tired of not being the ones on top. Because they brought the very same elitist hierarchal mindset to these shores, replete with the idea that any human being that did not conform to their ideologies of being "civilized" became subject to being "converted", enslaved, subject to genocide, and kept in a place they deemed fit by way of "manifest destiny." "Life, liberty, and the pursuit of happiness" only applied to White European male landowners. Everyone else was cannon fodder, surfs, or property.

Look at history through the 20/20 eyeglass lens of reality... not the faraway telescope of idealism.

Redlining still exists. Jim Crow still exists. Slavery still exists. It all still exists. It simply gets rebranded by those with the power, money, and influence for every generation. Citizen's United is the epitome of America's priority of wealth over general welfare. The common good is only good when "greed is good." The bottom line is that for America to exist in the way that the White top 1% needs it to exist, it will always require someone's necks to be underneath their boots; equality, liberty, and justice for all be damned.

Tag, Black Man, Black Woman.

You're it.

Fifteen
IT WAS THE BEST OF TIMES; IT WAS THE WORST OF TIMES...

When I was in a better emotional space in my life (just continuing to keep it real; no shame in my game), I used to have this visualization exercise that I would do when attempting to alter a mindset I was seemingly stuck in or when I was making plans to change a specific set of circumstances within my life. I would visualize a giant electronic switch in the back of my head which was labeled on each side of its toggle with the words "stagnation" and "change." Whenever the situation that required my mental or emotional attention was seemingly nonproductive or harmful to my well-being, I would visualize that mental switch, and it would invariably be set, by default, to stagnation.

And so, whenever I realized that there was no other recourse, I would simply mentally "flip" that switch from "stagnation" to "change," the result of which was usually an instantaneous and genuine change of mind and/or heart within myself. It worked like a charm ninety percent of the time. Now, sometimes those labels would instead read "on" and "off" or "stay" and "go"; it really depended on what the nature of the challenge was. And, in recent times, I have begun to work toward reimplementing that strategy within my life.

Because this pandemic and social climate has elicited so much uncertainty, fear, and anxiety within so many of us, I'm certain that most of you would agree that an overwhelming sense of stuck-ness—a Groundhog Day movie effect—has been in play in your own lives during the past year and a half. Of course, I'm not implying in any way, shape, or form that you or I were simply standing still, doing nothing during all that shutdown time. Many people have been able to achieve many hard-fought goals during a time when setting goals may have seemed like an impossible task. After all, adversity typically REVEALS character. And many of us were unafraid to take a closer look at our characters, take a deeper dive into who we were in the Before Times, and try our best to assess who we aspired to become for the After Times.

But I mentioned that feeling of stuck-ness more so because prior to the development and announcement of the very first successful COVID-19 vaccine, the future of everyone in all the lands seemed so very uncertain in how it would eventually unfold. I mean, it's hard to make plans when you have no clue about what you will be able to do.

Most of our lives have been filled with a myriad of defining moments, both large and small. And some of those defining moments were not even recognizable to us as such when we were experiencing them. Unenlightened people often like to ask other questions such as, "when did you know…" or "how could you tell when…." But unless the unenlightened are inquiring about moments that are blatantly and obviously self-defined as important—a wedding, a job promotion, a funeral, or maybe a graduation or a breakup for instance—how can we ever really know which moments out of all the seemingly more mundane moments we experience in life will have lasting and profound effects on our lives?

A major part of my own healing processes—my switch-throwing moments—has been having the ability and the fortitude to rewind my life in my own mind, to find, identify, and define those flash points. Some may see this as dwelling in the past or rehashing mistakes and reopening old wounds. And I am thee first to admit that this process can be painful beyond painful. But I see the process as reconciliation. I see it as a cleansing. I view my mental rewinds as mental and emotional forensics. I must resolve my past in order to build my future. And if that means taking a cold, hard look at past traumas, then I would much rather do that than to have something consciously or subconsciously controlling or negatively influencing who I am without my permission.

Going all Back to the Future with myself won't solve all my Momma/Daddy/broken heart/familial/me issues. That's what prayer, meditation, counseling, and friends are for. And that is, for me, in part, what the process of writing this book is for. Because as a Creative, writing—whether it is writing music, prose, poetry, or journaling—is very cathartic. For me, writing down the pain, and speaking the pain aloud, has the same power as writing the vision; you are taking those thoughts and feelings that are on the inside of your mind, heart, and soul, and you are acknowledging them and releasing them. You are facing your inner demons. You are manifesting the path for your own healing. Writing the pain is putting a name to your pain so that you can see your enemy face to face instead of having that enemy bumping around all willy-nilly inside of you, affecting you on a physical, emotional, and mental level, visiting you in your dreams or haunting your waking world with vague feelings of hopelessness or helplessness. That is the catalyst for depression, among other things. And it is the very reason why I always have so many damn words.

Here, then, as an example, are some of my personal BEST times, and the subsequent WORST times that are directly related to them. I mean, you've got to look at the whole thing, right? I decline to be that person who lives a life of false identity and delusion. I deny myself the luxury of allowing myself to lie TO myself for the sake of my own solace and conformity. I REFUSE to avoid sorting through my own REFUSE in order to make others comfortable with my misery.

I choose instead to rip the band-aid off. To order the emotional enema and be stuck at home for days while it runs (pun) its course.

BEST: The moment when I knew I had finally established the bond with my father that I had always longed for when we completed a home repair project together and he told me, "good job, Kenny." (Never Kenery...lol)

WORST: The moment my family and I received a call from the VA hospital that my father had passed.

❖ ❖ ❖

BEST: The moment my big brother called the morning of July 4th, 1996, saying that he was going to handle the barbecuing that day, and that he wanted the whole family to come over to his place later.

WORST: The moment immediately following my brother's declaration of manning the grill for the day when, suddenly, in the pit of my stomach, I felt the uncontrollable urgency to convince him that he and his family NEEDED to instead come over to our place, and that he could use both grills to cook, and it would be better that way. And then...the subsequent, all too ubiquitous in the Black Diaspora phone call which came later that afternoon...stating that my big brother had been murdered in front of his own home...in front of his children.

❖ ❖ ❖

BEST: The moment I stepped off a tour bus in Basil, Switzerland for the very first time...and had the instant realization that the fulfillment of a prophecy given to my eight-year-old self was now in full effect.

WORST: The moment during that very same tour when I received an early morning phone call to my hotel room, stating that a beautiful and amazing spirit whom I had only just met days before—a woman who that night before, had spoken some of the most encouraging words that any stranger had ever spoken to me before or since—had suddenly passed away, far from home, as we all peacefully slept.

❖ ❖ ❖

BEST: The moment I said, "I do," when I FINALLY decided, before God and a house full of family and friends, to become a married man.

WORST: The moment I said, "I do," when I reluctantly agreed before God, a judge, a singular friend, and an early morning courtroom sprinkled with strangers— to accept the terms of my surrender, and to end my marriage.

❖ ❖ ❖

BEST: The moment I felt as though I was going to be able to help my mother have a wonderful quality of life in her golden years because my life was coming together so damn well.

WORST: The moment my brother called me while I was in route to choir rehearsal to inform me that our mother had just had a stroke.

❖ ❖ ❖

BEST: The moment I realized that my life was handing me an opportunity to start over with myself.

WORST: The moment I realized that my life would have me starting over by myself.

❖ ❖ ❖

BEST: The moment when I was smelling myself, feeling self-righteous, and believing that I was simply a victim of circumstance in the demise of my own marriage.

WORST...BUT ODDLY, ALSO BEST: The moment when I realized and accepted the fact that I wasn't simply a victim, but that I was, in fact, in one way or the other...a willing participant in the demise of my own marriage.

❖ ❖ ❖

Honestly, I don't believe in pity parties. That doesn't mean that I don't plan, coordinate, throw, and host them from time to time. Each one of us has lived with and battled our way through self-doubt and self-pity at one time or another. And the last time won't be the last time...not by a long shot. Life doesn't play fair, and it is no respecter of person. Those constantly appearing bad times guarantee that we don't become comfortable in those cherished good times. Saying it out loud, it only sounds like a raw deal when it comes to how life works and the price we constantly pay to be here. I mean, why would it be a bad thing for us to just have a pleasant, smoothly-running, balanced life? No muss. No fuss. No loss. No pain. You know...Heaven.

But that balance is, in fact, the value-add to our lives. Those bad times define us. Good times only show us who we are when everything is at its relative best. And that only presents us with a half-complete idea of who we truly are. To expound on what I said earlier, adversity doesn't build character—it reveals character. And in order to be any good to anyone, including ourselves, we must know and own our WHOLE selves. Because that other part of us that many don't want to see or acknowledge—it WILL show up. You cannot hide from it, nor hide it from others. At least not for long:

Luke 8:17 (NKJV)

"For nothing is secret that will not be revealed, nor anything hidden that will not be known and come to light."

Folks, that's just the way it is, whether you believe in the Bible or not. It's a universal law. And we are denizens of the universe, and, as such, subject to its laws. So, unless your name is Stephen Strange, or you've been holding out and possess the Reality Stone, then you can only hide that purposefully hidden part of yourself for so long, even from yourself. Wouldn't you rather be ahead of the curve by cleaning your own house before guests arrive? Knowing yourself intimately and honestly—taking OWNERSHIP of your you, both the beautiful and the uglay, and everything in between—is the best way to move through this life.

Some will try to redefine transparency as weakness. They will insist that owning your shit is unnecessary. Because the past is past. Why revisit it? And, of course, if you have, in fact, made true peace with past failures or traumas, then sure; pack them away in the life experience box of your soul. Those files will still be available if, for some reason, you ever need them again for reference material. But you should only pack those files away after you have thoroughly read them, all the way down to the fine print.

Because being transparent isn't weakness. It is, in fact, the greatest manifestation of your strength you can do. Because it demonstrates the confidence that you have in yourself and who you truly are. It says that who you are is more than good enough, warts and all. Honesty and ownership guarantee that you will never have to defend yourself while unarmed. Because lies, deception, and denial make poor weapons. They can be disproven, dismantled, and discovered in the blink of an eye. But the truth? That shit is solid through and through. Just like those Universal Laws I spoke of. And whether your truth is for everyone or not (I'm not talking about that "personal truth" BS that you make up on the fly to win an argument on Facebook), it doesn't matter. It is truth, plain and simple.

Explore your truth before someone exploits it. Embrace it until the right person accepts it. Fulfill it before it loses its luster. Manifest your truth…in power, and in confidence. With no redactions. No omissions, with all acceptance, and stamped with your seal of approval. Explore and know your truth—all the pleasant and the disagreeable—before your truth becomes a lie. And that whole person you keep trying to hide only exists as a half of a person for the rest of your life.

Sixteen

STOOPID GOOD-LOOKINGS
Fannee Doolee Loves Peeps, but Hates Humans

Okay…I have a theory about people. And it's not something radical, or something that you likely haven't heard before in one form or another. But my theory focuses more on the drivers of those theories.

Basically, there are two types of people in the world, with a few gray areas scattered in the mix, and a kind of pit, or "Sunken Place" right in the middle. Some have termed the two polar ends of types as "good" and "evil", although those terms oversimplify and mythicize the actual underpinnings of their subsequent characters. Don't get it twisted; I believe in God, Satan, and spirits. But I also believe that there are human traits already in place in each of us that, without the proper guidance or nurturing—or with the wrong stimuli or environments—will attract those "dark forces" in the universe to us. Thus, temptation. And the old Biblical adage from Proverbs 23:7, "As a (wo)man thinketh, so is (s)he." We attract those things which our minds and our spirits allow to dominate our characters.

My theory then, is that there are people who like diversity. And there are people who do not. And in the middle, are those who are apathetic to both ends of the spectrum, which can make them somewhat of a "wildcard"; never knowing exactly where their allegiances or passions or actions will fall. Or if they even have passions at all. And sometimes…sometimes those in the middle will simply present as…obstacles.

Those who favor diversity are typically more closely related to being "good" people; they are more liberal in their thoughts, deeds, ideas, and tendencies. They generally want good for more than just themselves. They want unity and happiness and prosperity for all, or at least for most. They are seemingly more open to change, more flexible in their thoughts and actions; more generous in their giving, and typically less judgmental of anyone or anything that is different from how they view themselves.

And then there are those who favor sameness. These are the people who crave homogeneity, and what they consider to be "order". This group of people will skew towards having an insular viewpoint of how life should be, with the extreme end being xenophobic behavior, or in terms of cultural and social norms, even racist. We see extreme forms of tribalism that can arise from such groupings of people, with tendencies which lean towards a fear and mistrust of "other", which in turn drives their overt expressions of that mistrust in such things as hate and exclusion.

Of course, those are the more extreme cases. Yet what we have been seeing in these past few years is a dumbing down and coalescence of that fear, hate, and mistrust into more irrational and radicalized thinking on the part of those who skew further towards that misnomer of an "evil" designation. Its often, simply a predisposition for a lack of tolerance of anything that does not comply with their single mindedness, their monochromatic ideology, and their love affair with familiarity as being the only path to inclusion into what they accept as normal. Or good. Or right.

So, the division of how most people can be broadly categorized seems to come down to diversity versus homogeneity. Open mindedness versus closed mindedness. Acceptance versus rejection. Community versus tribe. Good versus evil.

Now, understand—I'm not actually calling those who prefer their "own kind" evil in the traditional sense of the word. As human beings, we naturally desire to associate with those who reflect who we are. Which brings us back to the word "tribe". Some people call them families. Others call them cliques. They can be called clubs, organizations, special interest social media groups, think tanks, fraternities/sororities...you get the picture. Like I said, human nature forms these types of bonds within society. It's kind of how we are built. Natural, with no additives.

But it IS unnatural when the additives come into play; the rhetoric, propaganda, lies, deception, agendas, vilification and classification through prejudice and ignorance, isolationism, segregation, and misinterpretation. It is then that the natural drive and desire to be with sameness is bastardized. That desire for familial bonds mutates into a need to subjugate or destroy anything and anyone who falls outside of the preconceived definitions of family. It's when the broad view narrows to a laser focus, or an ever-contracting tunnel, like a hardening of the arteries make it harder for blood to flow freely. And soon the big picture—the open-minded world view—becomes nothing more than an echo chamber. A self-perpetuating, self-realizing microcosm of limited scope and limited viewpoint.

❖ ❖ ❖

Social Media isn't alone in creating this moral crisis of humanity we are living through—this slow train crash and death of common sense, civility, intelligence. Social Media isn't singularly responsible for the idea and implementation of faux democracy which we saw unfold in real time right before our very eyes under the previous administration. All Social Media is responsible for is giving permission, avenue, and access to the true hearts, minds, and souls of man and womankind. Social Media is like a giant scab pull that is exposing the wound beneath that some of us knew was there but that most others either ignored, futilely scratched at, or simply were busy creating more wounds. The infection has spread fast because Social Media is the perfect delivery system. Better even than religion or politics, although both are incorporated into the viral load. And America—the diseased patient—is dying from an abuse and overdose of Social Media.

But let's not get it twisted...America's sickness has been there from the outset, in the form of its original twin sins of genocide and slavery. And that sickness was indeed in a seemingly symbiotic relationship with those who have been rich enough or White enough to benefit from its spread. But even while the sickness of America has mostly prospered, those elite one percenters—beginning with the so-called founding fathers on through the J.P. Morgans, Andrew Carnegies, and Cornelius Vanderbilts, and all the way up to the Jeff Bezos and the Elon Musks—Social Media has surely fast-tracked the entropy and erosion of the already weakened mental and moral health of America the Patient. In part because those who could/can/should make a difference—those who can help save the patient—are either too few and not powerful enough or choose to stand on the sidelines instead of being an active participant and doing their part. They are comfortable and complacent. And they dwell in that aforementioned middle ground, that Sunken Place.

Horn Blowin' Bill got it all wrong. It is NOT the economy, stupid.

It's you.

And for many, their arrogance, nonchalant-ness, and self-proclaimed "wokeness" is going to be a big part of what puts this failed experiment in "democracy" into its eternal sleep. It's the ones who will throw themselves onto their own dull swords, or who willingly "die" atop empty, irrelevant hills, who are the most pitiful of creatures. And yet, they are also the ones who are the most dangerous to the rest of us.

They define themselves by their desire to be "right" no matter the consequences, often to their own detriment. Their choices defy logic and reason and are even contrary to all evidence of their own eyes and ears.

Yet and still, they will hold obsessively hard and fast to those illogical beliefs and false narratives. Because without their fallacious affirmations and false dichotomies, those who cling to such things so blindly are often simply hollow, empty shells of human beings.

FEAR IS THE GREAT DIVIDER.

Fear of guilt. Fear of accountability. Irrational fear of "replacement" (we like who we are, so we don't want to replace anyone—we simply want access and ownership of the same types of rights and privileges they enjoy); fear of EQUALITY...they can only feel good about who they are if they feel superior to someone else; fear of "other"...they'd rather have sameness than diversity, and are willing to kill, steal and destroy in order to maintain not only sameness, but status quo.

And fear is the sustenance of evil.

Seventeen
BETTER GIT IT IN YOUR SOUL

The universe favors chaos.

Entropy is its natural order. We awaken. We work and live. We sleep. We are born. We live. We die. Nations are born. They grow and prosper. They collapse and disappear. The stars are born. They burn bright. They sputter. They collapse. They die. The universe grows and expands. It stops. It shrinks back upon itself. And it will ultimately collapse and die, too.

Yet there will always be rebirth. The infinite cycle. And there is a force which will always be present throughout the cycle of existence. The spark. The source.

That is why and what God Is.

He/She is the foundation that corrects that imbalance. Once other beings...the angels...were created, they were given self-awareness. And somewhere in the millennia of eternity, that self-awareness apparently began to slant towards self-importance...even though with the angels, God did not grant "free will" as we define it. This is the only explanation as to how and why Lucifer could ever grow to resent and ultimately challenge God. And he did this even when he knew he could not possibly win that battle.

Fast forward to human beings. Those same traits apply to us. God gave us total free will within purpose. And He has placed Himself as the source of our sense of Good/Order/Light. But Lucifer went all in with the opposing force of Evil/Chaos/Darkness in hopes of, if not winning, at least bringing enough of us, whom God loves, into his chaos and ultimate death.

So, you have those humans who embrace the chaos, or at least allow themselves to be led by it. Because it is very easy to hate.

Pause.

As an aside to the existence of purposeful chaos embracers, there are those who fall victim to less obvious attacks on which side of existence we choose. Don't get it twisted, y'all. I said it before: mental illness and spiritual demons are NOT mutually exclusive. Just as God and science are not mutually exclusive. The One who created the science knows how to adjust the rules He put in place to govern it. But I digress.

Next, you have those of us who embrace or, at least, move towards order, and who see the benefit of riding with God, even though it's seemingly a harder, more restrictive way to live. Which, actually—it is not.

My stance on spirituality and my relationship with God is that we are not here to use religion as a weapon against one another. We can express our beliefs—spread the Gospel, if you will. But, at the end of the day, it is all a matter of faith. I have personally experienced things, several times in my life, that science cannot explain. Things which fall under the category of miracle. And my relationship with God is complicated; it's never been a matter of non-belief. More of a matter of lack of understanding.

The atheist will say that there are people who suffer and die every day, and God's seeming absence from those situations belies the fact of his actual existence. But life is life. Bad things happen. The oversimplification of who God is has been that "He saves the righteous from evil and harm and punishes those who are against Him." And so, you may wonder, when bad things happen to good people, where is this God whom those good and faithful believers have been praying to and tithing for all their lives?

The short answer is—yes, He is still here. But there is purpose in the hows and whys of our lives that is beyond our understanding. Again, I have lived through some of those "why" moments, and have seen the purpose clearly revealed to me later down the line. Now, that's not always the case; there isn't always an answer given.

People often say, "what kind of God would allow XYZ to happen." But God is not an intervening superhero who swoops in on every terrible situation to save us. There is a purpose—His purpose—as to why He allows things to happen. We could not fathom the big picture, even if it was handed to us. And we may rail against Him for the suffering we endure. But His main concern is for the salvation of our souls. And if a person doesn't believe in an afterlife, that's understandable. Empirical proof is unavailable. But if that proof did exist, how, then, would faith manifest itself? Everybody would simply be on their best behavior just to get into what they believe Heaven is. It would all be an act, not an act of faith.

And that is what God wants from us. Belief and faith, despite what our eyes and ears and experiences tell us. THAT is the most personal choice of all that we can make. And no one should have it crammed down their throats or judged by others who feel that they have "arrived" in their spirituality.

'Cause none of us are anywhere near perfect.

THE ANSWER IS: 42

Why the hell are we here?

If you have never seen it, then do yourself a favor: go watch… or, better yet, go read The Hitchhiker's Guide to the Galaxy. If you enjoy silly, British-style humor a la Monty Python, then you'll likely love Hitchhiker's. You'll then understand the significance of this chapter title.

What is the meaning of LIFE? What possible reason could there be for us as human beings to seemingly be stranded in the self-proclaimed middle of a vast and infinite universe...with no other sentient life even remotely close to us? Are we really that messed up? Did God put us at the kid's table of existence because we do not play well with others? Maybe the Earth is a giant time out corner, or even a galactic detention room. We humans apparently have Mommy/Daddy issues. We fight with one another constantly, often for no real or apparent reasons. We tear up things, even our own stuff, like wayward, untrained dogs locked in the house when the "parents" are away. We rage, and we posture, and we destroy, and we hate. I guess it's no wonder that we aren't allowed to have any company.

Purpose, by design, is the basis of Christians' and other religion's beliefs as to why we are here; why we exist. In Christianity, when you get past all the fluff, the rules, and the "thou shalt nots," humanity's sole purpose is supposed to be to glorify God.

That is it.

Without getting deep into the bushes of theology, mainly because I am NOT equipped to find my way either in or out of there with any real authority—Christianity's bottom line seems to be that everything we do, say, and achieve is supposedly done to glorify and edify God's glory. Now, no disrespect or blasphemy meant here, but does that sound like the ultimate in universal narcissism to you? If you are looking from the outside in, then that is probably exactly what it sounds like. Its sounds like we were created, in essence, to make God feel good about God. And so we live, toil, and die—all for the glory of a being we cannot even see, let alone directly interact with in the way humans generally understand interaction. We meander through life, suffering its slings and arrows, trying to attach meaning and purpose to everything we experience and achieve, without truly knowing the actual meaning of it all.

Even with that in mind, many of us do in fact, turn to God, or A GOD—or multiple gods—seeking our universal purpose. We plug ourselves into our chosen spiritual equations, and we go about our daily lives with the peace of mind that there is a bigger picture, and that we are chosen—blessed, if you will—contributors to a universal plan. Under God. Apparently not indivisible. And most definitely not with justice for all.

Others, quite understandably, chose to embrace the notion that there is no God, and, therefore, no predetermined purpose. They therefore chose to believe that life is random and chaotic. They chose to live their lives on their own terms, so to speak, and not according to some spiritual or moral edict of a higher power. They don't concern themselves with the possible afterlife-related repercussions of their actions. These people either choose to be good people because it makes them feel good, or they chose to be evil for that very same reason. In either case, morality is ambiguous when you don't believe in a defining moral code. When there is no rulebook, you make up the rules as you go along.

What, then, is the answer? The source of this subchapter's title suggests the absurdity of even trying to find or define an answer. Truth be told, I've got nuthin'. Except—I kind of DO.

When I was a kid, I used to ask myself or anyone willing to listen these questions:

"If we are on a planet, and that planet is in a solar system, and that solar system is within a galaxy, and that galaxy is just a small part of a universe, and if that universe is infinite… then where is the universe? It's got to be inside of something, right? Are we inside an atom, which is inside of God? Is that how God is perceived as being omnipresent (I obviously didn't know that word as a child. I just said 'allover')? And if that's true, then where is God? Is he in his own universe? Or does it all turn back in on itself in an infinite loop?"

I apparently had far too much free time on hand, and because of questions like those, far fewer friends.

As a child, I would also imagine that for God, life was simply like a huge game of chess. I would theorize as much as a child could theorize that Good/God was in a constant game of chess with Evil/Lucifer. Now Evil always knew that Good would win every time. After all, Good created everything, and thus created the rules. But Evil's purpose was never to actually win; it knew that wasn't possible. But Evil's purpose was to see how many of Good's pieces it could gain by the end of each game. Evil knew it would never win them all. But Evil strove to taint and destroy as much Good as it possibly could. And at the end of each game, the board was reset. And it all started over again.

In reference to Christianity, that childhood imagining is how I reconcile the things that are seemingly contradictory in the Bible to many, both believers and non-believers. God does not DO anything to us, as people often bemoan. "Why did God allow this person to die? Why did God afflict that person with a disease or an infirmary? Why does God let bad things happen to good people?"

As children, when your parents made big decisions that affected you, like not buying you a specific toy (unless you were just a terror), not giving you a bigger allowance, moving you away from friends, or sending you to a school that you may loathe, they were not sitting down with one another and saying, "hey, let's do this specifically to make our children lose their friends and be mad at us." Your parents were making those big decisions to serve the big picture. There was usually a larger plan and purpose at work, and those changes to your life were merely a consequence of that all-encompassing purpose. Contrary to what it felt like, you weren't specifically targeted to be messed with.

If you, as a parent, do something to your child that child doesn't like or may even cause that child some emotional or physical pain (taking them to get a shot at the doctor's office, give them a spanking, taking away a bottle or a toy, or even a separation or divorce that separates that child from the other parent, etc., etc.), that child will not understand the purpose of those actions. And they may see it as unfair or even catastrophic to their lives.

But you, as the adult and parent—you who love that child—will know and see the big picture, the reasons for your actions or inactions. Even when something may happen in that child's life that is not the result of your actions, having wisdom, experience, and knowledge, you will know the hows and whys of the situation.

It's the same with God. There will always be a bigger picture with God that we will never have the capacity or capability of seeing or understanding. And if the purpose of our existence is to glorify God with our lives, then how can God accept back into His fold a part of his plan that is tainted by evil? To be clear, our salvation has NEVER been about perfection. It is about the condition and the content of our hearts. If we truly desire to please God, then we are more prone to doing His will. Being flawed humans, we will fall short of perfection each and every time. But God knew this, and that is why he built stopgaps into our imperfect existences. He built in Jesus. Grace. Mercy. Favor. And God simply allows us the free will to live our lives within the parameters of being able to be subject to the consequences of...and to choose to live in service to... both good and evil.

But as I said, God cannot take evil back into Himself. He simply cannot BE God if He were to become blemished by evil—if that is even possible. I mean, He kicked out a whole third of

Heaven because evil had tainted his Number One, and those who decided willfully, to also embrace that evil. We don't have to be perfect for God to take us back into Him when we are done here. We just had to have purposefully worked towards the goal of reunification with Him, knowing that perfection was not obtainable, but that His Grace was sufficient to close the gap between our human flaws and His divine perfection.

A SATURDAY MORNING PERSONAL MUSING

They say "favor ain't fair" when it comes to the Blessings of God. That simply means that there is no understood formula, respecter of personage, or anything like that—at least in terms of what we can understand about God's will.

But favor is also weird. It shows up in the most huge and important situations as well as the most strange and insignificant things.

The little things. The seemingly small "favors" God Blesses us with. The favor of loving family. The favor of true and loyal friends. The favor of a beautiful gift to make music. The favor of relative health, safety, and strength. The favor of technology that allows us to spend some type of qualitative time with those we cannot safely see in person right now or who are far away. The favor and Blessing of life itself.

We have many of us lost SO much during these trying times. Many are still suffering from so many different aspects of this life we are living in these perilous times. And those tiny things I just mentioned are insignificant in the larger scheme of things. They pale in comparison to the losses, the stresses, the pain, the fear, and the challenges of an unknowable future ahead.

But take heed; as long as we continue to have breath and have Blessings both large and small, we must continue to fight fervently against those powers and principalities in high places. But we must also take stock in those "small favors" that God sees fit to Bless us with as we navigate this storm. So, pray. Meditate. Whatever it is that brings you peace. And don't get too caught up in even the material Blessings we may receive. Because at the end of the day, it's not about money. Or things. It's about people. And love. And community. And truth. And life—one which is well lived, and which honors those Blessings and Favor that we have received.

If, like me, you are in a working relationship with God, it doesn't mean that we don't make mistakes. Sometimes we cry out to God; sometimes we curse and turn our backs on Him. Sometimes we say and do things we know don't please Him. And often we say and do things to others that are just as offensive. We cuss and say crazy things on social media, and in person. We get angry at those we love. We disrespect others with intention. So when we are in a working relationship with God, it doesn't mean that we are perfect. But what it DOES mean is that we know He who brings perfect peace. And we know that a contrite heart brings His forgiveness.

A PECULIAR PEOPLE

I've stated before that I used to believe that the world was mostly good. That there were simply a few bad apples in an otherwise delicious apple pie.

And then I became a full-grown adult. And I began to believe that there were simply moments in our collective existences where we had lost our way and where a minority had become misguided, broken, or corrupt.

And then I began to believe that the world was broken, and that those of us who honor and seek out true and honest love were the anomalies. The rest of the world had, sadly, been led astray.

But what I've come to understand is that the world is operating as it was created to operate. Because it was given over to be ruled by one who operates in hate, chaos, and entropy. It is a choice to love. But the norm seems to be hate. Because hate is easy. It is the narrow path. And that those of us who choose love over hate are not anomalies, but simply the exceptions to the established rules.

A peculiar people.

We were told of this already. We are simply now seeing it made manifest on a scale we haven't seen or been aware of before. It is The Shift. And it's happening.

But it's NOT the end of the story. Not now. Not later.

Not here on earth. And not anywhere else.

FIGHT.

CHOOSE LOVE.

DON'T LET THE PERFECT BE THE ENEMY OF THE GOOD

Have you ever viewed, through the lens of an electron microscope, the surface of what appears to your naked eyes to be a perfectly smooth object, such as a piece of glass or metal? If you do have the opportunity to ever see it, that alone will learn ya something about the true nature of the world. That nothing in life on this plane of existence is perfect, even when it may appear to be. It never will be perfect, simply because we, and everything in this world, are flawed.

We must always strive for our best, even when we don't feel as though we are up to it. Even when we doubt the veracity of its benefits. Even when we have all but given up on ourselves and on life.

Because the pursuit of perfection is its own reward, so to speak. But we must also learn to accept that imperfection is God's stopgap for keeping US honest. It helps us to understand that we don't have all the answers, or the means by which to act on such knowledge. At least not on our own. The existence of imperfection helps us to sustain our continued faith in Him—and for nurturing the pursuit of growth within ourselves.

I remind you that Lucifer was perfectly made. He had the perfect gig, second in command to the perfect boss. And yet, he still messed up because of his arrogance in, and his dependence upon, that very same perfection.

Eighteen

BLACK LIKE ME (AND SWEETPEA 'N NEM)

Growing up in the 60s and 70s while Black in America—child-hooding in the Hood, as it were—was a unique yet shared experience within the Black American Diaspora. To a fault, every Black neighborhood came stocked with at LEAST one of each of these: the Smooth, cool, and popular Brother everybody liked. The Fine Sista who always seemed unattainable and aloof. The Head Gangbanger who everyone respected and gave wide berth to, but who helped maintain a tenuous order to the block. The neighborhood comedian who made EVERYBODY laugh—even the Head Gangbanger. The uber-talented musician or band who always drew a huge crowd when they performed impromptu free concerts in the playground. The Sports Jock who could play any and every sport so well, you KNEW he was going to become a superstar and escape from The Hood.

And then you had the neighborhood mentally handicapped person, or in the politically incorrect vernacular of the day, the "retarded" person; the one whom everybody was afraid of because they would walk down the street talking to themselves, randomly lashing out at people, or just standing and rocking back and forth like a landlocked human buoy; a living, breathing navigation mark of the state of the Black Experience of healthcare neglect and lack of overall wellbeing. But beyond that oh-so-blatantly obvious neighborhood mascot for Black brokenness—was the neighborhood alcoholic. There were typically quite a few of those—poverty and despair always made certain that this was the case. But there were always one or two who stood out, even amongst their unwilling "peers." And in my Robert Taylor Housing Project building, my subdivided neighborhood internment camp in the heart of Chicago's Black Belt—that standout was Mr. Randolph—you know—of the Fourteenth Floor Randolphs.

Mr. Randolph was the equivalent of other neighborhoods' "get off my lawn" guys. When he was not locked away in his apartment, he held a court of one on the porch area in front of his apartment door. Mr. Randolph came complete with a single rusty kitchen table chair, his heavy wooden cane, a small battery-operated transistor radio, and either a six pack of Miller High life, Schlitz Malt Liquor, or a large silver flask wrapped in well-worn brown leather and filled with an unknown but healthy dosage of alcoholic forgetfulness and liquid escapism.

But the secret was that there was more to Mr. Randolph than his Throne of Drunkenness, his self-ranting, and his angry threats to chase down and beat any child who dared mock him, or who simply needed to get past his self-proclaimed bridge ogre position to the other end of that long, long porch, of which the only other route to the other end was to take the stairwell at one end of the porch, go up or down one flight, walk then length of that porch, take the stairwell on the other end in the appropriate up or down direction, and emerge tired, yet triumphant at the opposite end of the fourteenth floor porch. And by the way, the elevators were located smack dab in the middle of the building—and right NEXT to the apartment of Mr. Randolph. But they would typically be of no help when attempting to navigate around his inebriated and misdirected wrath. Because they mostly never worked anyway. And even when they did, the time it took for you to wait on the elevator to reach the fourteenth floor—you may as well have just done the trek to the stairwells.

The secret was that Mr. Randolph lived with Momma Randolph. And Momma Randolph was not only an alcoholic of the first order, but she was also suffering from what we know today as dementia. Of course, we didn't know anything about that as kids. We simply knew that every now and then, Momma Randolph would emerge from the apartment to make an impromptu performance. Dressed in a soiled house dress, Momma Randolph would typically rave in a loud, slurred voice, and then suddenly mumble to herself. She would often squat, and then urinate, in the middle of the porch. And then she would laugh to herself and begin ranting again.

As unaware and uncaring children, this was all, of course, stupidly funny to us, and only another arrow to be added to our quivers of ignorance and cruelty with which to tease and humiliate Mr. Randolph. We knew nothing about the tragedies and ravages of diseases such as mental illness and alcoholism. We knew zero about the societal cruelty of disproportionate mental and physical health care access in the Black Community. We had NO CLUE that we lived in one of many purposefully-prepared Petrie dishes of racial injustice and disparity; places that were built to corral and control the growing Black populace of Chicago stemming from the second coming of Great Migration from the South. We didn't know that we were being left there to either destroy ourselves or each other.

We, as little Black boys and girls, had no inkling of the true nature of many of our families' tenuous grips on sanity and survival. There was no education taught to us in our schools about the benefits of preventive health care; even many of our parents didn't know about that possible "get out of jail free" card. And even when our parents did know, they were either too impoverished or too fearful to take advantage of that ounce of prevention. We were locked out of access to medical innovations, technics, and cures. The Diaspora and the medical industry were NOT friends. We were still suffering the effects of decades of human experimentation brought upon us in the form of lies of benevolent inoculations from above. We were (are) the victims of organ harvesting and misinformed and uncaring doctors—who saw (see) us as being less than human, yet somehow possessing inhumanly higher tolerances to pain than those which their non-melanated bodies had.

And so we existed within our ignorance, passing that ignorance up and down and around to one another. We perpetuated the myths of Black manhood: that as a man, you were weak if you spoke to anyone, professional or personal, about the mental and emotional challenges faced daily by the Black Man . We passed on the myths of Black womanhood: that as a woman, you were being emotional or irrational if you told anyone that your doctor was not listening to your concerns and complaints about your health—and in fact, if said doctor was ignoring or adding to your pain, it was framed as just being in your imagination.

And so many, many times, Black people have suffered. We have never been given the information nor the means to prevent our ailments, illnesses, and terminal conditions. It all started with the conditions and conditioning of slavery—the unimaginable and unwarranted mental, physical, and emotional abuse. The lack of the ability to turn in any direction for help except for God and each other. In each of our individually broken states, we were often of little help offering consolation and encouragement for one another. And sometimes, a few of us would be part of the problem. We had to survive by eating the scraps of what the Colonizers did not want; we ate the "bad meat," and what good meat we did get, we had to preserve it with salt to the point that hypertension and diabetes has become part of our generational biological makeup.

Even today, many of us live in food deserts, leaving us with access geographically and financially, to only the food stuffs that are the unhealthiest for us. Many cannot afford the type of health care that promotes and encourages preventive medicine. And time and time again, the few physical and mental health resources that have ever been in our neighborhoods, schools, churches, and institutions get underfunded or downright taken away. Lack of knowledge and lack of access keeps many within the Black Diaspora in that perpetual loop of poor health—the one began those many centuries ago as a means of control.

And so we end up here—with every Black neighborhood having a resident Mr. and Mama Randolph. Every Black neighborhood having a dangerous psychotic or a violent alcoholic. Every Black neighborhood having self-medicating drug addicts, abusers, and gangbangers. We end up hosting corporate funded Dialysis Centers, but few high-quality hospitals, nursing homes, or mental health facilities. We fall prey to unscrupulous and predatory life insurance salespersons who sell us underfunded and overpriced insurance policies with loopholes which favor the insurers for days and leaves us with little or nothing to pass on to our heirs. And we don't often know what we don't know—until we need what we don't have. Because there is rarely anyone willing or able to tell us. No knowledge or wisdom passed down from generation to generation. Only inadequate coping mechanisms, vague cautionary tales, and pithy sayings that don't really help anyone—but they sure sound good when you say them.

We end up unprepared to take care of our elderly in the way they truly deserve to be taken care of. We end up uninformed about how to raise healthy children. And we end up battling our own often lifelong mental and physical health challenges that eventually inhibit our ability to effectively plan for the futures of either our elderly or our children. And then we, more often than not, end up passing that mess on down the road.

How then, do we end this cycle—this downward spiral into perpetual self-destruction? Let's not forget, there are forces both within AND without which benefit from the Black Diaspora staying right where a vast majority of it is: complacent, controlled, and content. How do we defeat apathy and lack of empathy when almost everything we see, hear, and experience daily attempts to point us to hopelessness and no way out? Let's be honest here; many of our most revered and vaunted community-based institutions—the churches, the schools, the local politicians—have failed us miserably. They have either become self-aware and self-important. To the point of existing for their own benefit, or they have allowed themselves to become irrelevant, unsupported, and underfunded.

I wish I had meaningful answers. Smarter people than I have tackled the matter and failed. Is it even possible in today's world to recreate a Black Wall Street? Is there enough social, moral, or political will to even try? It seems that even the potential power of social media to do good has been usurped to instead create division, disinterest, and disinformation to the point that its greatest success is as a distraction from the very same problems that could be solved by properly utilizing its power to reach the masses and inform, educate, and organize for the common good. The bad guys sure have learned how to use social media for ill; why can't we do better with it for the good?

Between social and political division, climate change, pandemics, war and rumors of war, and economic crisis and uncertainty—humanity is sailing straight into a perfect storm. It wouldn't be the first. But it certainly looks like the biggest one with the most at stake in modern history. And even with all that going on, I still believe in "one little acorn." As dire as my words may sound, I still believe that there is hope in repairing the socioeconomic miasma that exists within the Black Diaspora. I believe that the right little acorn can still be planted in just the right place to sprout a forest of positive change and reform. We've had a few great moments—the George Floyd movement and the appointment of the first Black female Supreme Court Justice. But there will always be a clear, present, and active danger and pushback against our progress by our aggressors. They aren't going to ever just sit back and watch us bloom. Hate and fear are like that.

But if we within the Diaspora don't do the actual work of planting those acorns consistently, instead of going from outrage-fueled movement to outrage-fueled movement, then we will never pull the nose of this crash-diving plane up. If we stop looking for Great Black Hopes and instead look to ourselves and to each other with love, respect, empathy, and admiration, instead of cultural cancelation and misappropriation—then we could greatly minimize the occurrences of raising so many lost children. We could truly begin to eliminate our own poverty and lack of access to quality health care, jobs, and education. We could rebuild Black Wall Streets all over the nation with the singular laser beam focus of reinvestment into us and the recirculation of our monies tenfold within our own communities—instead of depending on politicians and institutions that do not and have never had our best interests at heart. That includes those who "look" like us—"all skinfolk ain't kinfolk." And we could begin to make sure that there are fewer Mr. and Mamma Randolphs created who perpetually pass on our "generational curses" to our progeny and to our communities.

GOING MENTAL

All communities have their own discussions about maintaining mental health—although not as often as we need to in the Black Diaspora. But what we all fail to talk about as often as we should is not only the challenges of deciding to seek out help, but the obstacles of gaining access to those services. And this even before attempting to find the counselor who fits your specific needs.

They ain't all created equally.

Firstly, the extent of access and services depends on your insurance type. You can only get so much bang for your buck if you don't have insurance, have limited insurance (like HMOs), or even with great insurance—you have to wade through tons of uncaring and unqualified "counselors."

Then there's the "type" of counseling. I love God—but faith-based only counselors don't always cut it; I don't know about you, but simply throwing Scriptures or life experience stories at me is not an option. I need my counselor to not only be rooted in some type of faith, but to also have some clinical skillsets to help address the ENTIRE picture. That's why God created professionals.

Next up—CULTURAL SENSITIVITY AND RELATABILITY.

I am more than certain that there are many excellent counselors and therapists in the world of all stripes. However, the issues that plague the Black Diaspora stem from some unique places and spaces and are part of what I call an Active Crime Scene™, meaning that not only are our challenges ongoing, but many/most are baked into the society we have to exist within. There are micro and macro-aggressions abound each and every day for us, so we need someone who can fully and truly RELATE beyond the typical psychological and emotional challenges of life for the average person. ESPECIALLY in these times. All that doesn't mean that only a Black therapist can do us any good; it just means that that "other" therapist needs to be EXCEPTIONAL and in touch with the real world. Dare I say it—woke (😊)—in the way WE the Diaspora originated the term. NOT in the politicized messy weaponized way being bandied around these days.

And lastly, there's availability. Or the lack thereof.

These are trying times. Many—MANY people are broken. More so than before? I believe so. I believe that the pandemic lockdown brought a lot of mental and emotional faults lines that were already in most folks to the surface. And even before that, the sociopolitical and economic climate of the nation and the world was threatening to crack many people wide open. And for four horrific years—twelve, if you want to be technical—people were "given permission" to be their worst selves. The cover of truth, morality, respect, and accountability was ripped off like a scab. And many, many people took that open wound and ran with it.

And they continue to run with it. To the detriment of us all. But especially those of us who were already suffering the slings and arrows of a hateful and scornful society. And sadly, we even see more clearly revealed, the existence of the venom the disenfranchised level towards one another. Can you say Los Angeles Councilwoman Nury Martinez, or Gil Cedillo and Kevin de Leon? But that type of sentiment and behavior towards us has NEVER been a secret within the diaspora. It is just another layer of social-psychological issues needing to be dealt with daily by many of the disenfranchised; us turning on one another. And don't get me started on the mess within our own neighborhoods we have to contend with.

All that to say—the need for mental health services and counseling is at an all-time high. And the access and availability of that help is seemingly at an all-time low for those of us who need it the most. And the process of getting to that help can, in and of itself, cause some mental and emotional stress. I know there are resources out there to help ease that struggle. So if any of you know of a great counselor, service, or organization that helps folks navigate and find the help that, quite frankly, we all need—please post it HERE in this thread.

Outside of the obvious importance of physical health, our minds and emotional well-being are the MOST important things we need to protect at all costs. Let's help one another find quality and accessible help. I want to see us all be our best and live our best lives—in SPITE of the fact that is Rome burning around us.

Nineteen
CLOSING ARGUMENTS
WHO SENT YOU?

If you aren't paying attention to the truth of The Shift™ we are experiencing collectively—right now, in realness time—then you are not a good student of life. It's WAY beyond politics, or social justice, or global warming. It's a spiritual, existentially significant moment in our collective AND individual existence. It has repercussions far beyond SCOTUS, the WhitePower House, or anything else we are being led to focus on in a distracting way.

Folks, we are literally being asked to choose a side. And not a "racial" or political one, either. It's okay if you don't go in for that "spiritual higher power stuff"; it will continue to exist whether you believe it exists or not. Cause and effect are alive and kickin' it big time. And the Butterfly Effect is on the move. Call it Karma. God. The Universe. Whatever. There are major tectonic movements happening and being manifested in the ether. And we're being asked to choose the people who we will stand with through those movements, and those who we want by our sides; because we know that they are real, and true, and good.

No. They are not all saints. Well…probably none are. They are not perfect. They don't have all their shit together, ducks in a straight up row. They are not always outwardly powerful or strong; as a matter of fact, they are often more flawed and fragile, in many aspects of their beings, than you may ever know.

But their characters…

Whew…their characters, their minds, their hearts, and their spirits are undeniably WMD's to have in your arsenal against the entropy of life's constant millstone-like grind against our spirits. Our minds. Our flesh. Our souls.

The delineations are being made more and more clear-cut than they have ever been. Gradually…or maybe not so much, there will be no more mistaking friends with enemies, antagonists with pacifists, those who are for us or against us. It's all being laid out comprehensively. We just need to pay closer attention in order to see and FEEL it.

And then we need to act. We need to do less taking for granted and more active appreciation, drawing nearer to and holding on to those who are best suited for navigating and helping US navigate what is coming. We need to cherish those who have proven their connections to the Master Plans of our lives. Those who are more than a happenstance encounter, more than a coinkydink, an entanglement, or a casual involvement.

We need to recognize fellow warriors who are ON OUR SIDES for the impending war. Nope...not some childish "race" war that small-minded people are chomping at the proverbial bit to have come to fruition. That would only be a sad and unfortunate byproduct of the truly big picture.

Pay attention. Drop your petty. Gather your real and true people closer. And cherish them.

The funniest thing to me...and I think I speak for a few good people...is that what I desire from life is extraordinarily simple, especially when taken out of the context of today's human condition.

I desire Love that strives for unconditionality. Anything less is not really Love. Because God has defined what Love is, and His Love is unconditional. And His mandate for us is to, in all things, seek excellence and to strive to be Christ-like. Being humans, we won't ever fully achieve that status. But God looks at our hearts, not simply our actions or our "score." For us humans, unconditionality shouldn't count mistakes as tally marks to be weaponized against one another or to judge from a perspective of perceived strength when someone else may be weak but willing. We are all flawed. We all make mistakes. We foul things up and have good and bad moments...mornings...afternoons...evenings...days...weeks...months...years...

We are given purpose through our assignments. But we were also Blessed with the ability to improvise, to imagine. We are

Blessed with the gift of ingenuity and flexibility of mind and spirit. We have been given the means, over any other creature on this earth, to consciously alter our own course. And we were not meant to do it alone. It happens. But that was not the plan. Relationships are key to our survival.

Fellowship is a requirement God has for us...two or more gathered and all that. But to go beyond our blood—to love beyond family ties is one of the most sacred bonds we can form. Bonds can form out of an almost infinite variety of situations and circumstances. True friendship is a kinship that often becomes even greater and deeper than blood ties. And in many cultures, marriage is the penultimate expression of a true friendship and partnership between a man and a woman (I say this both because I'm writing from MY OWN personal truths, and not to exclude anyone else's) with the added bonus of physical and sexual attraction, similar goals, and faithful commitment. When we enter into covenant with God, we enter into a PARTNERSHIP. And of course, if you are a spiritual person, and specifically a follower of Christ in my instance, a relationship with God is at the top of the heap.

So y'all...please.

Love. Love God. Love one another. Live. Be excellent.

Because there is literally no time like the present.

Peace and hair grease.

Twenty
RHYMES AND REASONINGS

Sometimes what cannot be fully expressed in prose can only be expressed through the beauty and complexity of poetry.

~ October 12th, 1994 ~

TWO

May I play in your waters
So warm and deep
Can I stir up your passions
While you sleep

Shall I greet your awakening
With a gentle touch
Or a sensual caress
Would it be too much

If my fingers explored
The warmth of your Sex

While my lips greet your body
What then would come next

When I pull you yet closer
To whisper about Love
That what I can give you
Goes beyond and above

The warm gentle press
Of my Sex against yours
The slow wet sensation
As I glide thru your doors

The ripples of pleasure
That dance across your skin
Each time I pull away
And come in again

Slow, heavy rhythms
Both ancient and new
The fragrance of pleasure
Created by Two

Surrender and Seduction
Erotic and bold
Inviting and sharing
Spiritual and Old

Eyes I stare into
I drink long and deep
My attention they capture
My heart they will keep

Inside your temple
A Place to only be shared
In true love with someone
Who has shown that they cared

About more than the notion
Of having your Sex
About giving Love the same
Today and the next

A taste and a whisper
A touch and a moan
A thrust and a shiver
Don't answer the phone

A tongue on a nipple
A kiss, then a bite
A stroke down a naked back
A squeal of delight

Our slow rhythm quickens
Intense and so strong

We race towards sensations
We both knew would come

Your pleasure's my passion
Your passion's my desire
Your dreams my ambitions (oh)
My body's on fire

You pull me in deeper
And whisper "Now or never"
I say "Give in to me"
We give in together

❖ ❖ ❖

~ September 22nd, 2017 ~
<u>SHE MOVES ME</u>

She moves me

She moves me by her being.

She motivates me by her belief in me.

She supports me by her strength of character and belief in her own womanhood and all the

power that it embodies.

And all this in turn fuels me, strengthens me to continue to be what she wants and needs me to be for her.

It allows me to be me…to give her the love, strength, nurturing and support she deserves and receives from me.

And in and around and thru it all, God is the key; the glue; the thread; the chain…the tie that binds.

And that circle reinforces our "us."

❖ ❖ ❖

~ July 4th, 2019 ~
23 (Ode To Big Joe)

23

That's how long it's been

Since I saw your face
All up in this space
And we're so much poorer for it
And we've struggled to absorb it

23

That's the time denied
To your sibs when you died
Your mother, your brothers,
Your children, wife, others

Now you were no saint
'Cause we all got our taint
But you loved God no less
And He you, and I confess

That you stood in the gap
For your fam, that's a fact
That you gave all you had
To be good husband, good dad

23

Doesn't minimize the pain
Only dulls in the brain
All the thoughts that once seemed
Like a yesterday dream

23

We will never forget
No matter how high the numbers get
Between that then and this now
That your soul took a bow

To exit stage left with a nod
To go hang out with God
Tell Kirby 'nem I said "hey"
I know we'll see you again someday

That's how long it's been

23

❖ ❖ ❖

~ October 14th, 2018 ~

THEY DID NOT BECOME

They did not "become" after November 2016
They were already here

Their tribal compass, stronger than their moral one
Their hate, stronger than their common sense
They are the descendants of those who, on sunny Sunday afternoons when America was "great"
Left their church houses
Packed their picnics
Dressed in their children in play clothes
Greeted each other happily, beneath the big strong tree that has seen and been party to too much death

Waiting
Excited with kids in tow, smiles aglow
Waiting with bated breath, evil heft, and dark desire

Waiting
To see the noose pulled tight
To see the bruises and abuses heaped upon
The one who with sun kissed skin
Melanin-Blessed by God, created and given the breath of life in The Garden long ago
The Original Beloved, The First given dominion

But also

The one who they said winked, whistled, looked, walked by, looked in the eye, touched the precious porcelain of their female skin, went through the wrong door, drank from the wrong fountain, moved into their neighborhood, created their own wealth then created their own space where their dollars circulated in their neighborhood ten times before flying off into their pockets, innovated free lunch programs and armed themselves for protection against the encroaching blue line that ravaged their neighborhoods...
Got lost coming home with his Twizzlers
Sold loosies to make some money
Told them that he had a registered weapon in his car before reaching for I.D.
Took a knee
Lived in his apartment and was on his way to greatness

They were waiting
To hear horrific screams
The smell of burning brown flesh
The cheers of enraptured insanity
The joys and the coy remarks
The slurs and the laughter

Waiting to take the Polaroid family photo
With the spoils of the day in the background

The group photos, where they brandished smiles that would make The Joker run and hide

They waited
And then they ate their picnics and patted one another on the back
All the while sitting on blankets in the grass
Beneath the tree of death
And the soil soaked with the blood of centuries
Of tribalism and tradition and evil
Proud not only of the good ole southern food in their baskets
But also, of the Strange Fruit that hung from the trees behind them

All in a day's work

They did not "become" after November 2016
They were already here

❖ ❖ ❖

~ November 9th, 2018 ~

THE FEAR

It occurs to me

That what motivates the extreme "right" and the willfully blind and ignorant followers of "The 45" is less of a desire to be right...but more of a fear. Not Fear of God. Not Fear of man. Not fear of law

But a Fear of Change. A Fear of being wrong

Wrong about the bloody and brutal foundations of this nation

Wrong about the sins of their forefathers

Wrong about the history of the willful genocide of the Indigenous population

Wrong about the enslavement of a proud and powerful Diaspora.

Wrong about the empowerment of the "elite" at the expense of the common man and woman.

Wrong about the corruption and pimping of a nation by industry and corporations who crowned themselves "people" in the eyes of the law.

Wrong about the willingness of a government system to embrace profits over protections.

Wrong about the desecration of the natural resources of one of the most beautiful and varied landscapes in the world... these "United" States.

Wrong about the willful denial of the beginning of the end for life on this planet because of climate change.

Wrong about the Three-Fifthsing, lynching, segregation, terrorizing, internment, experimentation on, redlining, gerrymandering, suppression, relocation, the simultaneous cultural thievery and bias...and the flat out murdering of...

...the Melanated...
...the Beautiful
...the Colorful
...the Innovators.

Wrong about the state-sponsored harassment, suppression and executions of the innocent who are traffic stopped while driving...

Studying...
Sleeping...
Barbecuing...
Selling loosies...
Minding their business and answering their own front door to their own apartment...

Trying to return home TO their own condo...

Selling water while "childing"...

Wearing a Puerto Rico T-shirt while being Puerto Rican...

Trying to caravan to a better life...

Protecting their Sacred lands from uncaring and destructive corporations...

Wrong about their "moral majority higher ground" and actually being followers of Christ.

Wrong about embracing an apparent and well-documented lying, cheating, narcissistic, womanizing, inept, foul mouthed, verbally challenged, racist, corrupt, divisive, non-principled Oval Office sitter...

Because he reflects their basest thoughts, desires, beliefs, actions...evil...

And they look straight into that mirror.

And they smile at the image they see

Because it is an image that they are afraid to look at beyond the surface. Beyond a quick glance

They don't look deeper...

At the huge pores. The blemishes. The pock marks. The scars. The open sores. The rotten teeth

The missing patches of hair. The bloodshot eyes. The true image of themselves...and of America.

They only see the Emperor's New Clothes.

And they want to try those same clothes on themselves.

But they are truly afraid of what they will look like in them.

So, they settle for watching from afar.

In fear of change.
In fear of different.
In fear of doing the right thing.
In fear of building together instead of tearing down apart.
In fear of inclusion.
In fear of true equality.
In fear of truth.
In fear of...

The light being shone on their own souls.

And they will see that there is no sign of God abiding inside of them.

Only the Prince of this world.

Smiling back.

❖ ❖ ❖

~ June 11th, 2019 ~

WHO'S GOT THE BACK OF A GOOD BLACK MAN?

Ain't no such thing as no Superman
But who's got the back of a good Black Man?

Micro macro aggressions
Come for us from outside

Macro micro rejections
Come at us from the inside

So much so,

That some take it out on each other
Others take it in like a brother...becoming

Walking time bombs whose bodies give in
Whose manhood becomes their true sin
Whose minds sometimes don't comprehend

Redefined and realigned by the Other
With extreme prejudice eliminated, or simply smothered
(I can't breathe)

The protector and lead requires love that will feed

And hear
And forgive
And mend
And defend

The hands that are sometimes bound
The cracks that are often found
The ego that gets torn down
The indictments of his skin that is Brown
Ain't no such thing as no Superman
But who's got the back of a good Black Man?

Failure is not an option
Yet we fail all the time

Success is by adaption or adoption
So much so,

That some become that which they are not born to be
Others become reborn, but still fail to see He

Who charges us to be the head without charging us a fee?
Bought and paid for by His Son so that we can be free

To work
To strive
To cover
To protect
To grow
To learn
To be imperfect

Even under His perfect peace

Yes,

Our own worst enemies we can be
But sometimes...sometimes
It is she

Because Eve did it, but she didn't do it alone

We had a direct line, and we blew it right or wrong

'Cause the covenant was forever
And He Blessed their mess together
Until death did they part was the Original Plan
Made and ordained by God, not by man

So, as we stumble and fall
As we falter and fail
Both ourselves and each other
Sister...take your finger off the scale

'Cause ain't no such thing as no Superman
But who's got the back of a good Black Man?

❖ ❖ ❖

~ September 11th, 2019 ~
WORN OUT SOUL

Like a pair of new shoes
You liked the look, so you tried me on
And you walked all over me

But then you got bored with the style
So, you threw me away
After you had worn out my soul

❖ ❖ ❖

~ December 24th, 2019 ~
IF ON SOME DAYS...

If on some days,

...You wake up ready to take on the world...
...And other days you wonder why the world even tolerates you

...You wake up with grand ideas and plans for positive change...
...And other days you feel like your dreams are worthless and unachievable

...You wake up grateful to God for every wonderful thing you have been Blessed with...
...And other days you don't understand why everything is working against you

...You wake up feeling loved and accepted...
...And other days you feel the crush of loneliness and isolation

IF...on some days you wake up cherishing your life...
...And on others you see no purpose in preserving it

Know.

That.

We want you to stay. We need you to stay. Right here.

Know...that you are loved. That you are cherished. That family and friends would suffer great heartache from your absence.

That you have a place in this world. That your thoughts, ideas, and dreams not only have value, but that they are achievable.

Know that there is help. That there is a warm heart. And a kind ear. And an encouraging voice. Waiting to love you. To listen to you. To speak words of affirmation and positivity into your life.

Know that God doesn't make mistakes. That He has a purpose and a passion for you. That He knows your struggles, your sorrow, your pain. And that your challenges are ready to be overcome…by you…with His help…and with the help of those who have been placed in your life…

…who truly and genuinely love and care about you. And will not abandon you. Or ignore you. Or demean and dismiss your struggles.

And when you overcome your obstacles,
God's Glory will be manifest in your life,
And your victory in your purpose will be an amazing inspiration and testimony,
To all those who know and love you.

You ARE loved.

❖ ❖ ❖

~ May 8th, 2020 ~

TO ALL THE SO-CALLED LIBERALS WITHOUT LIBERATED MINDS

If you don't see Color,
Then you don't see ME
I see your hue
Because your hue is you

It tells me a story
Of your original tribe
It speaks to your journey
It reveals part of your vibe

It's not what defines you
But it marks all your kin
Your struggles, your triumphs
It's your Surname in skin

Your Reddish tint, or
Your Olive Skin, or
Your Lemon fresh complexion, or
Your minimal melanin

Your Ebony shade
Your Chocolate tint
Your Vanilla tone
Your Bronze-hued glint

I don't have White friends
Or Yellow, Pink, or Red
I have friends gift-wrapped in colors
From the infinite palette in God's head

❖ ❖ ❖

~ May 29th, 2020 ~

WEARY

My soul is weary.
My spirit is vexed.
My mind is troubled.
My heart breaks next.

Too many desire to stay ignorant.
Too many refuse to be wise.
Too many are rebels without a cause
Robots in disguise

❖ ❖ ❖

~ June 5th, 2020 ~
57

57.

57 law enforcement officers.

57 law enforcement officers quit.

57 law enforcement officers quit in support.

57 law enforcement officers quit in support of 2.

57 law enforcement officers quit in support of 2 officers.

57 law enforcement officers quit in support of 2 officers being disciplined.

57 law enforcement officers quit in support of 2 officers being disciplined for pushing.

57 law enforcement officers quit in support of 2 officers being disciplined for pushing a 75.

57 law enforcement officers quit in support of 2 officers being disciplined for pushing a 75-year-old peaceful elder protestor.

57 law enforcement officers quit in support of 2 officers being disciplined for pushing a 75-year-old peaceful elder protestor forcefully to the ground where he hit his head on the concrete.

And began to bleed.

Bleed from the ear.

And all 57.

One tried to help.

But all 57. Plus 2.

All 57 plus 2 stepped right over the bleeding, peaceful elder.

Who was seemingly only returning a helmet.

To the law enforcement officer.

Who pushed him to the ground.

Where he hit his head.

On the concrete.

And bled.

In front of all those good cops.

❖ ❖ ❖

~ June 19th, 2020 ~

WHILE BLACK

Being.
Breathing.
Barbecuing.
Kneeling for justice.
Standing for justice.
Peacefully protesting.
Sitting in your own backyard.
Sitting in your car at the mall.
Standing in your own front yard.
Going to a swim party at a pool.
Calling police while being attacked.
Calling police while being harassed.
Entering your own apartment complex.
Delivery packages in a company vehicle.
Waiting peacefully on friends in Starbucks.
Killing your captor and rapist in self-defense.
Being an innocent child playing with a toy gun.
Visiting your parents' house to check on things.
Being an innocent child selling water on a hot day.
Sleeping in the common area while at your school.
Asking someone to leash their dog in a park where it says to "leash your dog."

Being a well-respected, celebrated, and award-winning professor and historian entering your own home in a "nice" neighborhood.

❖ ❖ ❖

~ October 25th, 2020 ~

ALL IN

The goal.
True. Black. Love.
The ultimate partnership.
The greatest friendship.
The most beautiful relationship.
Unconditional.
Unquantifiable.
Is not based on roles but is built upon goals.
Is not lost in the midst of a storm.
It is patient.
It is kind.
It does not envy.
It does not boast.
It is not proud.
It is not rude; it is not self-seeking.
It is not easily angered.
It keeps no record of wrongs.
It does not delight in evil but rejoices in truth.
It is not for the faint of heart, mind, or spirit.
Often filled with struggle, but always strong.
Flawed but forgiving.
Unbothered and unstoppable.
It will truly and unabashedly fight for its own survival, by any

means necessary.

Imperfect, but always made perfect through covenant with God.

Individual, and indivisible.

True. Black. Love.

It's All In.

❖ ❖ ❖

~ May 5th, 2021 ~

THE BESPOKE LOVER

I've had many off the rack lovers
And I've tried to make each of them fit
Time and time I've tried each lover on me
But it seems that their fit wasn't it

So, I took them to competent tailors
To help alter and shape them to taste
While I diligently worked on self also
To trim down my own spiritual waist (waste)

I'd try sometimes to mend and to stitch up
All the rips, and the tears, and the snags
Fix imperfections and inconsistencies
To keep riches from turning to rags

And I've tried to have most of them altered
To reweave, and refit or resize
But I never seemed able to come up
With a suit made to suit my own eyes

Suit the eyes of my soul and my spirit
Suit the inner vision held in my mind
Suit the view my heart longs to see in her
The right lover, formed by the Divine

So, I now want a Bespoke Lover
Made to fit me, fit just as I am
One who takes all my flaws and then covers them
As we cover one another, our flaws be damned

Now I long for a Bespoke Lover
Hand stitched, monogrammed, made-to-order
By the Master Tailor, the only One able
To reweave and bespoke ME just for HER

❖ ❖ ❖

Twenty-One

MY WRITE FOOT
PITHY ASS LITTLE SAYINGS AND PASSING THOUGHTS

~ March 19th, 2019 ~

If you must define me...if you must measure my worth...then measure me by my whole being and not simply by my one aspect of my character.

Measure me by my sincerity and determination of effort, and not by my failures.

~ April 10th, 2019 ~

We have become conditioned to accepting our own demise with passive disinterest. If you don't value my here and now, don't bother shedding tears for my forever after.

~ August 15th, 2019 ~

When all is said and done, when the layers of "things" are peeled away, I simply want to live a spiritual, loving, musical, honest, meaningful, fun, and happy life and to share that life with spiritual, loving, music filled, honest, meaningful, fun, and happy people.

~ October 7th, 2019 ~

If everyone leans to one side of an ideological boat, then that boat will capsize and sink.

~ October 9th, 2019 ~

Judging others solely by what you consider to be your strengths... is your weakness.

~ October 25th, 2019 ~

The fruits of my lamentations stem from the seeds of my despair.

I don't know who needs to hear this besides me, but your God-given gift/talent is your blessing.

Whether that gift drives your career or you. Whether that gift becomes your testimony or your praise. Whether that gift has saved your sanity, your finances, or your life. Whether that gift inspires others or not.

~ May 21st, 2020 ~

The heart and mind should always work together when it comes to love.

The heart tells the mind to take a chance on love; it bypasses the illogical nature of love and informs the mind about what true love looks like.

The mind consoles the heart when it gets broken. It calms the spirit, reminds the heart that it did everything it could do to make things work out, and it helps the heart to understand that this too shall pass.

~ July 18th, 2020 ~

A person cannot "get over" what is still happening to them. A people cannot "move past" what is still being perpetrated against them. A nation cannot "come together" standing upon the rotten foundation which still supports it.

~ July 26th, 2020 ~

The top to the unflushed toilet seat of America is being lifted up for everyone to look inside.

~ August 15th, 2020 ~

I don't carry baggage from old relationships.
But I do take great notes.

~ August 20th, 2020 ~
A half-empty glass can always be refilled.

~ August 27th, 2020 ~
Fear is the sustenance of evil.

~ September 2nd, 2020 ~
Strategy must guide ideology, and ideology must inspire strategy in order to conceive and achieve real change.

~ September 16th, 2020 ~
We deny ourselves fulfillment in the blind pursuit of perfection.

~ September 18th, 2020 ~
The "founding fathers" didn't create America because they were tired of tyranny; they created America because they had next on being tyrants.

~ September 18th, 2020 ~
Just so you know...
When someone says to you, "Now, I'm not blaming you..."
They are LITERALLY real-time, low key
Blaming you.

~ *September 20th, 2020* ~

When you lean too far to the Right or to the Left of the Big Picture, you cannot possibly see the picture in its entirety, because your perspective will be skewed by the "angle" from which you are viewing the picture.

~ *October 22nd, 2020* ~

Now, remember, all you Black and Brown thousandaires, millionaires, and billionaires who suddenly don't know your ancestors anymore: at the end of the day...or the ring of the closing bell on Wall Street...or the dusk of this 2020 fiscal year...under THIS "administration":

The GREEN that you PREEN won't insulate you from their hate of the HUE that you GREW.

~ *November 3rd, 2020* ~

Wouldn't it be nice if being your BEST self was enough to keep people who proclaim love for you from abandoning you during your WORST times?

~ *November 5th, 2020* ~

Never stay in a space where you're not wanted or appreciated; let that space simply be a bathroom break and not a destination.

~ *December 10th, 2020* ~
Allowing vulnerability is the greatest strength.

~ *December 10th, 2020* ~
Sometimes, even when the move doesn't seem to have any relevance or make ANY sense at all...something drops HEAVY into my spirit, and I try my best to bypass ME and to be obedient to that still, small voice each and every time.

~ *December 10th, 2020* ~
Whenever you feel as though you're lost or have taken a wrong turn on the long and winding road that life can be...don't be afraid to pull over in a "safe place" ...and ask for directions.

~ *December 21st, 2020* ~
You cannot plant a new tree if you are standing in the hole where the seed needs to grow.

~ *January 14th, 2021* ~
The space that I'm in is the place where I begin.

~ *January 18th, 2021* ~
Are you living in your purpose? Or are you repurposing your living?

~ *February 1st, 2021* ~

The true characters of your closest friends and most devoted lovers are revealed when you are at your lowest lows.

~ *February 1st, 2021* ~

Black Woman: you have infinite value. Unlimited potential. You deserve to be cherished and protected. You are beautiful. You are phenomenal. You are loved. You are BOTH Black History and the Provenance of our Destiny.

~ *February 3rd, 2021* ~

Desire is simply need that comes with a choice.

~ *February 5th, 2021* ~

True Love is FEARLESS.

~ *February 16th, 2021* ~

Stay aware. Stay alert. Stay prayed up. Stay the course. Stay in sync and in truth with those you love and those who truly love you. Stay in forward motion.
Stay. In. Your. Purpose.

~ *February 26th, 2021* ~

Even when u feel as though there is nothing u can do about it, always know & acknowledge exactly what space u are in.

Knowledge & ACknowledgment are always the first steps towards doing something about where you are.

~ March 3rd, 2021 ~

It is a very sobering moment when you come to the realization that a person who you thought was a long-term active participant in your life was actually only a temporary spectator.

~ March 5th, 2021 ~

Some folks are too busy looking at and coveting that new roof on the neighbor's house to see and appreciate how strong the foundation on their own old house is.

~ March 5th, 2021 ~

Learn to value, appreciate, and love the people in your life with "good bones."

Some may require a little remodeling. Some may even require a gut rehab if they…and you…are willing to put in the work. But finding people with a solid foundation is a rarity. You'd better hold onto and cherish them while you can.
#DontLetYourPridePunkYou.

~ March 14th, 2021 ~

If your "moral high ground" puts your head in the clouds and you can't breathe, then you've gone too far up that hill, and you've overshot your intended destination.

~ March 17th, 2021 ~

Ladies: don't settle for choosing baser things to define your empowerment; empowerment is making moves in confidence and humility, being unbothered and unstoppable. Empowerment is strength, wisdom, and courage; it is not in self-exploitation.

~ March 18th, 2021 ~

Life is simple AND complex at the same time. It is multifaceted and multilayered. It is its own dichotomy. Be sure to take the time to peel back some of those layers and take a peek. You may actually learn something you don't already know.

~ March 18th, 2021 ~

Beware The "Woke-ing Dead."
They're everywhere.

~ March 31st, 2021 ~

Some people spend so much time in relationships "testing" or trying to change the other person that they never get around to actually loving them.

~ April 5th, 2021 ~

God. Love. Life. Faith. Peace. Joy. Grace. Mercy. Family. Friendship. Food. Music. Laughter.

In that order.

~ April 13th, 2021 ~

Life: it's the one thing that none of us comes out of alive. So, let's at least try to live our lives to the greatest extent that we can, all the while bringing LIFE to others along the way.

Be a Blessing and not a Blight.

Live. Laugh. Love. Life.

~ April 12th, 2021 ~

You "said what you said." But did you really SAY ANYTHING?

~ April 14th, 2021 ~

Some people have only seen Marriage: The Movie, sometimes more than once. So they think they know what the story is really about. They only know the "Hollywood" version. And even then, not even the "Director's Cut."

But many didn't read the actual book first to know the real story:

That marriage is a COVENANT...a promise between two people and GOD; and not a CONTRACT with loopholes that is made to be broken.

So, before you commit to marriage, GO READ THE BOOK.

~ April 16th, 2021 ~

Spotlight Own Yo' Soul.

If your identity is so wrapped up in something/someone/a title other than your actual character and who you ARE as a person and you are easily offended by a differing opinion on that same something/someone/title...then you may need to do some reevaluation of what being "self-defined" and "self-aware" truly means.

~ April 16th, 2021 ~

If you post in all caps all THEE time...especially when you get called out on something you said...tell me:
Why are you "yelling"?

Because being louder doesn't make your wrong "righter."

~ May 5th, 2021 ~

There is a difference between trying to "change" someone and helping to "grow" someone. One demands a different person to take your place. The other is an investment into helping you to become your best self. One is done out of selfishness. The other is done out of love. One does not recognize the value of who you already are. The other values who God made you to be.

Learn to recognize that difference.

THE LIVIN' END

Printed in the USA
CPSIA information can be obtained
at www.ICGtesting.com
CBHW021535140724
11413CB00010B/106

9 781666 404302